# Clara Istlerová
# A Life Among Letters

INVENTORY PRESS

Clara Istlerová

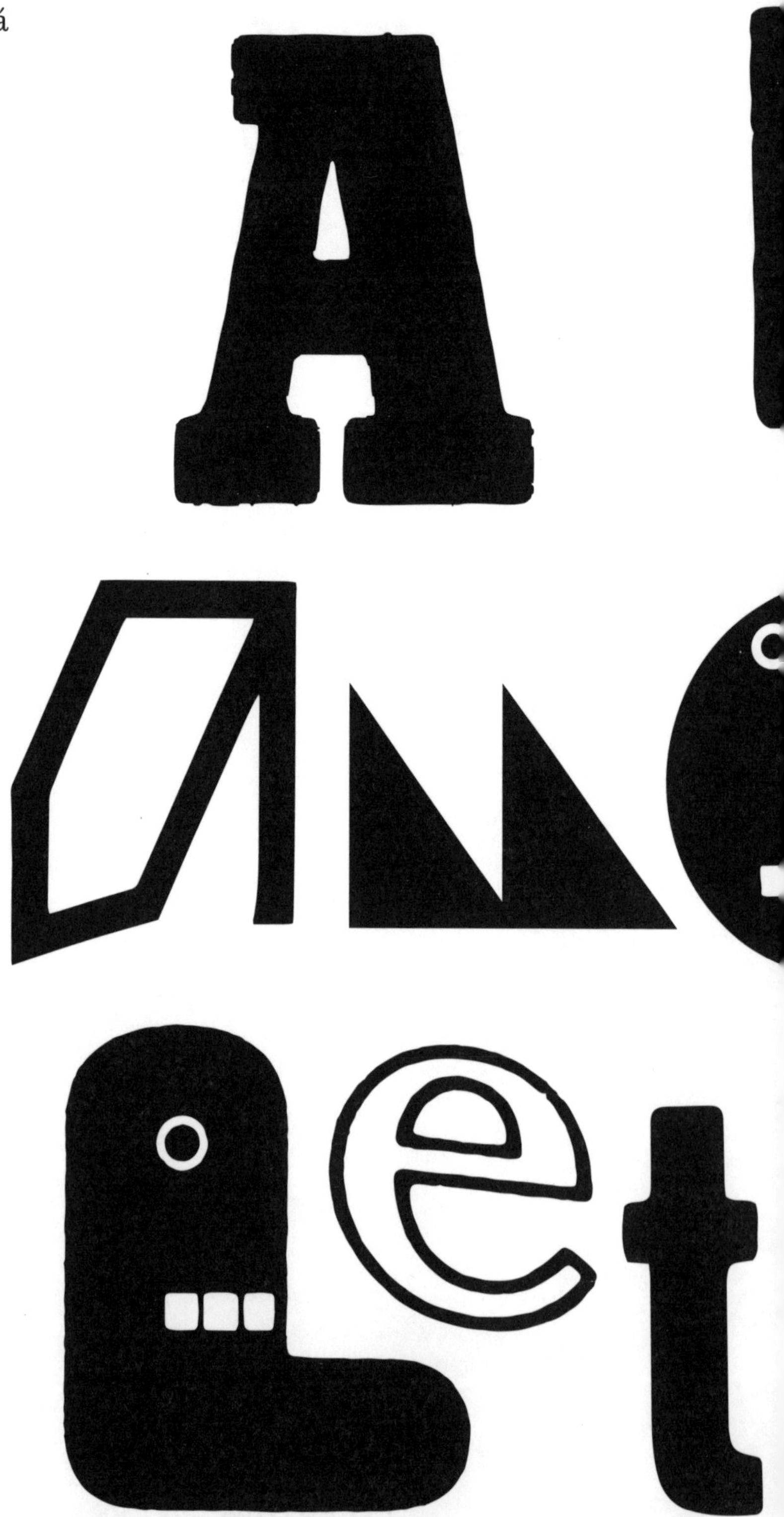

Edited by Anežka Minaříková

# Foreword
## Anežka Minaříková

"Our lives are at once ordinary and mythical. We live and die, age beautifully or full of wrinkles. We wake in the morning, buy yellow cheese, and hope we have enough money to pay for it. At the same instant we have these magnificent hearts that pump through all the sorrow and all winters we are alive on the earth. We are important and our lives are important, magnificent really, and their details are worthy to be recorded."

—Natalie Goldberg, *Writing Down the Bones*

*Clara Istlerová: A Life Among Letters* tells the story of an exceptional typographer, illustrator, and graphic designer who created some of the most impressive and intriguing works in Czech typography. Balancing her personal and professional lives while navigating a male-dominated industry, her journey unfolds against the backdrop of massive historical upheaval: the bombing of Prague during World War II, the Prague Spring and the events of May 1968, and the Velvet Revolution of 1989. But at its heart, this is also a story of love—for books, for letters, for dogs, and for the people in her life—a story I had the honor of listening to and now sharing with you.

Bringing this publication to life took years. I spent many afternoons sitting at Clara's wooden living room table, sharing delicious cookies and countless cups of Nescafé. But before any of this could happen, I first had to establish contact. While studying at Academy of Arts, Architecture & Design (UMPRUM) in Prague and preparing my bachelor's thesis on Clara and her work, I began searching for her phone number. Many advised against it: *Don't expect much. Clara doesn't seek publicity. She might not want a book like this to be published.* Their words only strengthened my resolve, and I eventually found her email address. To my surprise, she suggested a meeting—but only after 2 p.m., she's not a morning person. I remember how nervous I was as I rode the tram through Ořechovka, toward Petřiny, where she lives. I held a bouquet in one hand

and printed questions in the other, my mind racing: *What if we don't click? What if she rejects me?* It felt like a first date. All my worries melted away when Clara greeted me with a warm smile and invited me in. From that moment, our conversations flowed naturally and time flew by.

Two years later, those conversations have taken shape in the form of this book. It reveals overlooked aspects of a designer's experience, exploring the personal and professional influences that shaped Clara's body of work. It offers a candid narrative drawn from our conversations, diving into intimate topics often left out of traditional monographs. The inclusion of personal ephemera—photos of friends and family alongside her book covers, posters, and catalogues—challenges conventional assessments of artists and perhaps encourages young designers to embrace vulnerability and personal storytelling in their work.

At the core of the book is the interview between Clara and me, but it also includes a chapter, "On Books," in which Clara describes the stages of book production, often unknown to designers accustomed to working with computers. A text by theorist Jan Rous, a leading Czech historian of graphic design, places her typographic work into historical context, ranking Istlerová among the important pupils of František Muzika, as well as the heirs of the Czech typographic avant-garde, influenced by Oldřich Hlavsa's approach to typography. Additionally, contemporary Czech graphic designer Zuzana Lednická contributes an afterword. In her reflection, Lednická observes that if there is any difference between male and female creative work, it lies in how women approach it—with a natural multitasking that blends family, personal creativity, and countless smaller tasks.

This book is small and intimate—not your typical monograph—but a focused opportunity to introduce Clara Istlerová to a wider audience. Having played many roles in bringing this project to life, I am deeply grateful for the experience. After countless hours of talking, listening, and learning, I am proud to call Clara my friend.

In conclusion, I would like to extend my heartfelt thanks to everyone who helped make this publication possible—especially Jaroslav Tvrdoň for his magic with words, Filip Beránek for his meticulous photography work in reproducing vast amounts of material, and Zuzana Lednická and Jan Rous for their meaningful contributions to this book. My thanks also go to Inventory Press, Karel Hvížďala, the National Film Archive, Prague, the Postal Museum, Prague, the Otto Pick Library of International Relations, the editorial team at *Přítomnost*, Lukáš Broul, Památník Národního Písemnictví, my alma mater, the Academy of Arts, Architecture, and Design, Prague, the Graham Foundation for their support, and the Ministry of Culture of the Czech Republic.

But above all, my deepest gratitude goes to Clara Istlerová for trusting me with her story, and to my husband, Marek Nedelka, for everything.

# The Who, How, and What of Clara Istlerová

## Jan Rous

11

"Type fills our lives like little else. From waking in the morning to laying down in the evening, an endless chain of written messages crawls along before the urban citizen in the form of newspapers, books, street signs, warnings, movie subtitles ..."

—Josef Kaplický

Who, how, and what is Clara Istlerová? Her own answer is blunt and clear: "I am a typographer." This is also how she is usually described in the colophon of the books she has been involved with. While she is the "author" of the typography—meaning she chooses the typeface, which creates the basic structure of the book and its layout—she, in fact, works with the all the elements of a book, including the selection and arrangement of illustrations. This comprises Istlerová's concept of the whole, which is explicitly artistic and which characterizes her entire oeuvre: books, posters, exhibition catalogues, and magazines, including the extraordinary-for-its-time *Přítomnost*.[1]

Even though she studied in the studio of František Muzika[2] who, together with Josef Kaplický, Karel Svolinský, and Antonín Strnadel, represented a certain link to modernism and interwar art, it was not primarily Muzika who foreshadowed Istlerová's path, just as it was not the case for her peers Aleš Krejča or Jan Solpera. She ended her studies in 1969, still in the reverberation of that period's remarkable, if not entirely free, atmosphere. But even before this, the art world opened up to Clara Istlerová in the studio of her father Josef Istler, a surrealist painter and graphic artist, and a younger member of the generation that never abandoned the principle of super-reality. For many years, however, the work of his generation was exemplified by the great personalities of the surrealist line of postwar Czech art: Václav Tikal, Mikuláš Medek, Jan Kotík, Libor Fára, Vratislav Effenberger and, until his death in 1951, Karel Teige. This was also characteristic of post-1948 Czech modern art, including during the years of normalization after occupa-

    The Who, How, and What of Clara Istlerová

tion by Warsaw Pact armies in August 1968.[3] The conditions for
art and art-making remained essentially unchanged, once again
debating in studios or cafés. And while the elder generation was
united by Karel Teige and Vratislav Effenberger, after 1968 it
was Jindřich Chalupecký[4] who coalesced the movement.

The journey through her father's studio, his artistic friendships,
and those friends' libraries became a journey of Istlerová's own
artistic talents and intellectual quests, which both culminated
and concluded in Muzika's studio (although the interview in
this book reveals that at the time she was more concerned with
herself, "men, and dogs," or with traveling around the world).
Nevertheless, Clara Istlerová did not leave school untouched
by Muzika. More than her studio work, what she took away
was Muzika's personality and his impact during the interwar
period. There was no denying his accomplishments as a member of Devětsil,[5] no avoiding his typography, his illustration
work, his theatrical sets, but also his postwar turn away from
his own avant-garde past toward the classical form of the book,
as Jan Tschichold had done. In Muzika's case, this was exemplified by the writings of Vladislav Vančura, the book series
*World Reading* with its ingenious color differentiation between
each nation's literature, and finally the writings of Franz Kafka
from the 1960s. The familiarity of Muzika's design work with
the book and his knowledge and popularity of the work of rep-
resentatives of the avant-garde, the Russians, Bauhaus, Kurt
Schwitters, and Teige thus created another area for the movement of Istlerová's artistic thought.

It is interesting that it was at this time, still benefiting from
the creative freedom of the late 1960s, that a specific feature
of Czech book culture began to assert itself: the need to create the book as a beautiful artifact. Beauty here is more than
a function, as formulated by Ladislav Sutnar, for example, and
embodied by the book production of Družstevní práce,[6] but it
is also something other than Teige's conception of the book as
a graphic, purely artistic project, one that should always bear
the marks of its time. It is an expression of an idea formulated

by F. X. Šalda in the title of an essay he wrote for *Typografia* in the early twentieth century: "The Book As a Work of Art."[7] It was this essay that Clara Istlerová also prepared for the 1967 edition of student work *Edice speciálky F. Muziky* (F. Muzika Special Edition). "I was never really lacking free expression, because you have to put a lot of yourself into typography," says Clara Istlerová at the beginning of the interview. She sees typography, along with calligraphy and graphic art, as part of free creation. Her calligraphic and artistic approach to type is also evident from her first large-scale editorial work: the Czech poetry series *Československý spisovatel*.

Alongside the individual volumes of poetry an essential feature of her work emerges: the ability to think within the broader whole of the series, whose individual volumes, while unique in form and reflective of the nature of each text, also belong to the clearly articulated framework of the whole. When we look at Vyšehrad publishing house's Reflexe series, its structure and respect for the reader is fascinating. However, the series and its character are carried not only by the distinctive typography, the stylized typeface of the cover, binding, title, and frontispiece, but also by the artwork, which included the author's own handwriting and period illustrations, chosen to be as broad a statement as possible about the time, its style, and its expression. Working with type as a medium, so to speak, also points to the typographic thinking of the time and the influence Oldřich Hlavsa had on my work. However, it was not only his editions and the books that he edited, such as *Klub přátel poesie*, the Bohemia series, or *Plamen* magazine, but also his book *Typografická písma latinková* (Typographic Latin Typefaces) from 1957, which was the first extensive look at and explanation of modern and contemporary typography from around the world.

The books of the Reflexe series[8] were a revelation in their content and form in their time—Pascal, Eckhart and European mysticism, Erasmus, Boethius, Bohuslav Balbín ... and they were written with great creative sensitivity and intelligence.

     The Who, How, and What of Clara Istlerová

What is also remarkable about the Reflexe series, however, is that the volumes are printed only along the expressive scale between black and white and their values. This approach is characteristic of Clara Istlerová and is not only due to her respect for the authentic form of the document. In the 1980s, she began to work with Jan Malý, a photographer of extraordinary sensitivity, whose work in black-and-white was highly motivating for Istlerová. Malý was, among other things, an excellent photographer of modern Czech architecture, especially cubist architecture, and his photographs have been used to illustrate several key monographs on the history of architecture—for some of which Clara Istlerová also served as art editor. As she also mentions, the specific sensitivity to the non-color palette between black and white might not have come into being without her collaboration with Jan Malý. She did, however, expand her expressive register—her William Blake in the Klub přátel poesie series, *Napíšu básně kytkám na listy* (1981) (I will write poems on the leaves of flowers) is black and white, but most of her exhibition catalogues, albeit with color covers, are also on the scale between black and white, such as *Devětsil* (1986), *Skupina Ra* (1988), *Aventinská mansarda* (1990) or *Česká móda 1918–1939* (1996). Her conception of Nadi Plíškové's alphabetical poetry book *Plíšková podle abecedy* is also based on "noncolor." At the same time, however, the volume represents some of her most free work with typography: lines shift direction, recalling a time when typography was a playful art, as in Kurt Schwitters's work.

Of course, this is not about any preoccupation with the black-and-white scale, but something essential about respect for the original form of everything that is worked with, because even the key publications of the interwar period were black-and-white: Nezval's *Abeceda*, the anthology *Život II*, the magazine *ReD*, the *fronta* anthology. Photography and typography of that time spoke the language of black and white. Clara Istlerová works with this type of material, which is a testament to its time, in an unusually sensitive way. For her, typography is not an exhibition of her own ingenuity and expression, treating the material in her own image. Nevertheless, her works are clearly recognizable and one can see in them specific and distinctive solutions that are all her own. The previously mentioned editions and Reflexe draw attention to her ability to build a series of books in an edition as a series of individualities. The volumes of the Střed series of books, published by Prostor, composed of retro elements from the nineteenth century, are similar evidence of this ability. Here, Istlerová sensitively combines the neutral decorative surface of the paper, created by bookbinders of a bygone era, with paint, brushes, and combs, with the title label in a variety of typefaces. Their variation is built entirely on the old handmade paper methods and the use of the label. The new, already publisher's version of the edition, has turned the colored neutral ground with the label into various decorative screens.

However, the exhibition catalogues also benefit from typographic reasoning and respect for the nature of the document. Their pictorial content are reconstructions of a time that Istlerová elaborates on using her spirit while moving within a field she knows so well. In the case of the catalogue of surrealist work by the members of the Ra group, almost confidentially. Her catalogues of large exhibitions are unparalleled; they may be simple, but their informative value is commanding.

*Přítomnost* magazine also belongs to those works that demand respect for its ingenuity, accuracy, and reliability. In the first years of freedom after 1989, it was not only unique, but also exceptional in look. To give each issue a specific form, to equip each column with a distinctive treatment, and to incorporate the artistic flourishes of Karel Nepraš,[9] all during a time that did not yet enjoy the efficiencies of a computer, required not only patience and technical skill, but also the ability to imbue the work with your opinion. The editorial board, of which I was a member, admired Istlerová's work and appreciated her utter reliability.

I have space here to consider only the most important examples, but they represent the essence of Istlerová's work. Istlerová

     The Who, How, and What of Clara Istlerová

approaches journalism, which demands a much wider use of visual documentation, in a diverse and dynamic way. She also utilizes color and book cover design as a form of advertising, following the approach of Karel Teige.

In 1974, Istlerová became a member of Typo&, a generation-spanning association of typographers and graphic editors, which included Milan Jaroš, Pavel Hrach, Rostislav Vaněk, the slightly older Jan Solpera, Zdeněk Ziegler, and founders of the field, Jiří Rathouský and Oldřich Hlavsa. Community and friendship bridged the misery of the time with debates over work. The field of typography was not among those protected by the state, which enabled those who were to defend their existence and gain a small space for their own creativity. It was also made possible by the fact that typography is considered an ideologically neutral area. That is, until the moment when the content and its artistic demonstration defy the ideology. In retrospect, typography and its application is one of the most significant messages of its time.

## NOTES

1   *Přítomnost* is a Czech political and cultural magazine, founded in 1924 as a weekly publication by Jaroslav Stránský, with support from Tomáš Garrigue Masaryk. Its first editor-in-chief, Ferdinand Peroutka, established the magazine as a respected platform for democratic and intellectual discourse, featuring writers such as Karel Čapek and Milena Jesenská. Although it was shut down and repurposed under Nazi control during World War II, *Přítomnost* was revived after 1989. Today, it operates primarily as an online publication, continuing its tradition of critical commentary on Czech society and politics.

2   František Muzika (1900–1974) was a Czech painter, graphic artist, stage designer, and professor. From 1945 to 1970, he taught at Prague's Academy of Arts, Architecture, and Design, specializing in book and poster design. Initially a member of the avant-garde group Devětsil, he later joined the Mánes Association of Fine Artists and served as the art director at the Aventinum publishing house and editor for *Musaion*. Muzika designed over 100 stage sets, including forty-three for the National Theatre, Prague. He is the author of the important theoretical work, *Krásné písmo ve vývoji latinky* (1958), which also appeared in German as *Die schöne Schrift* in 1965.

3   On August 20–21, 1968, Czechoslovakia was invaded by the Soviet Union and most Warsaw Pact members to suppress the reforms of the Prague Spring, a period of political liberalization under Alexander Dubček that had begun earlier that year.

This invasion marked a pivotal moment in the country's history, as it ended hopes for "socialism with a human face" and brought about years of repression. The event is remembered for its profound impact on Czechoslovak culture, shaping the country's intellectual and creative circles, which sought ways to preserve their heritage and identity under harsh restrictions.

4   Devětsil was founded on October 5, 1920, in Prague as the Umělecký svaz Devětsil (Devětsil Artistic Union) by a group of socialist-oriented artists and writers, including Jaroslav Seifert, Karel Teige, and Vladislav Vančura. The group later became the Svaz moderní kultury Devětsil (Union of Modern Culture Devětsil) in 1925. Devětsil's focus was on proletarian art, magic realism, and Poetism—a uniquely Czech movement developed by Nezval and Teige that aimed to make art an accessible and everyday experience. With branches in Prague and Brno, Devětsil organized exhibitions, avant-garde events, and published magazines like *ReD*, *Disk*, and *Pásmo*. The group sought to dismantle elitist artistic traditions, advocating for collaboration and accessible art for the masses. Membership fees helped finance events, such as lectures and recitals. As membership gradually declined, Devětsil officially dissolved in 1930.

5   Jindřich Chalupecký (1910–1990) was a Czech art historian, critic, and curator, best known for his efforts in promoting Czech modern and avant-garde art. He played a pivotal role in shaping postwar Czech art discourse and established the Jindřich Chalupecký Award in 1990, which honors outstanding young Czech artists. His writings and curatorial work fostered connections between Czech artists and international art movements, helping to preserve and develop Czech cultural identity during times of political repression.

6   Družstevní práce (dp), founded in 1922, was a cultural institution in the First Republic, dedicated to integrating art into everyday life through mass culture. It published nearly eight hundred titles and launched the Krásná jizba branch to promote home culture. The progressive visual style of dp was crafted by designer Ladislav Sutnar (1897–1976), known for his innovative graphic design and typographic work, in collaboration with Josef Sudek (1896–1976), a renowned photographer celebrated for his atmospheric imagery. Their combined efforts significantly influenced twentieth-century Czech art and design.

7   František X. (F. X.) Šalda (1867–1937) was a Czech literary critic, writer, and intellectual, known for his influential role in Czech literature and art criticism in the early twentieth century. In his 1905 essay "Kniha jako umělecké dílo" (The Book as a Work of Art), published in *Typografia*, a periodical dedicated to printing and graphic design, Šalda argued that a book should be appreciated not only for its text but as a crafted visual object reflecting the creator's artistic vision.

8   The Reflexe series, from Vyšehrad publishing focuses on philosophy, history, and humanities. Known for its intellectual depth, the series includes works by prominent thinkers and scholars, aiming to engage readers with critical and reflective perspectives on cultural, philosophical, and ethical issues.

9   Karel Nepraš (1932–2002) was a Czech sculptor, illustrator, graphic artist, and university professor. Recognized as one of the most distinctive Czech artists of the 1960s, Nepraš was known for his innovative use of new materials and techniques, infused with playful, subversive irony and dark humor. His work is associated with the Czech Grotesque, a movement overlapping with New Figuration, which provided a subtle critique of the communist regime. Nepraš faced restrictions under normalization, and was unable to exhibit his work publicly, but was later appointed as a professor at the Academy of Fine Arts in Prague after 1989.

# Interview

## Clara Istlerová
## Anežka Minaříková

AM: You were born in 1944.

CI: Yes, in the sign of Sagittarius, at the end of the year. Shortly afterward, in February 1945, was the last American air raid on Prague, which they allegedly mistook for Pilsen, where the Škoda factory, which produced weapons, was located. At that time, we lived in a street near the Emmaus Monastery, which was hit during the bombing, and in one of the buildings that was totally destroyed, my parents and grandparents lost everything. That building completely disappeared. Fortunately, at the time of the bombing, my mother was with me on Charles Square for a walk, my grandmother was shopping, my grandfather was at work, and my father was in his studio nearby. We lost everything, and Dad, unfortunately lost his first oil paintings.

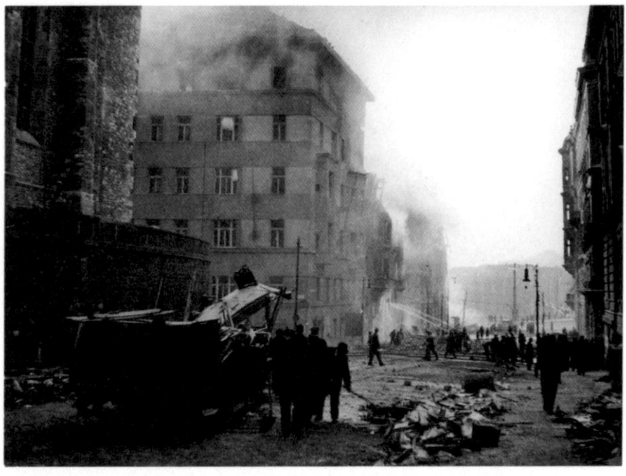
Reslova Street in Prague, 1945

And you remember that?

I only know it from stories, of course. I was only three months old. But this event made the whole family strongly aware that material possessions mean nothing, because at any time you can lose everything in half an hour. They understood that there was no point in getting too attached to possessions, to money. I'm not saying that this was just because of the bombing, but

                    Interview

certainly my parents' attitude toward material things was very much influenced by it. They had to start over from scratch.

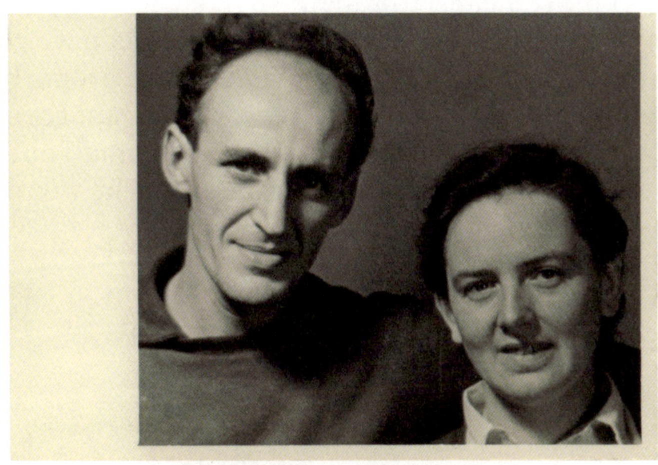

Josef and Gerda Istler, 1950s

Where did you move after that?

The war was ending, so the authorities assigned us a replacement apartment in Karlín, on Křižíkova Street. It had belonged to some Germans, and was big enough for two generations to live in, and later three. My grandparents eventually died, but I lived there with my parents and my own children until I was forty. It wasn't until 1984 that I moved to Dejvice, to Kafkova Street.

Why did you live with your parents for so long?

My first husband, Jiří Šuhájek, got an apartment in Karlovy Vary, where he was employed at the time as an independent artist at Moser's glassworks. It was a company apartment with a shared toilet in the hallway, no bathroom, just rudimentary conditions. It had been a dormitory, in Dvory, a suburb of Karlovy Vary, originally intended for workers from the nearby glassworks. My daughter, who was born in 1974, contracted severe pneumonia there, and the doctor said that because of her predisposition for asthma, staying in an environment with

constant haze and rain wasn't recommended. At that time
Karlovy Vary didn't have very good air quality—for example,
there was an undesulfurized incinerator in Vřesová nearby.
That's why I moved back to Karlin to live with my parents.
I only returned to Karlovy Vary for a while, when we got
another apartment. But I couldn't work there properly, and
taking the bus to Prague meant losing more than three hours.
And you can't travel like that too often with small children.
It was a pain for me. So, in the autumn, when the weather got
worse, I packed my bags and left for Prague.

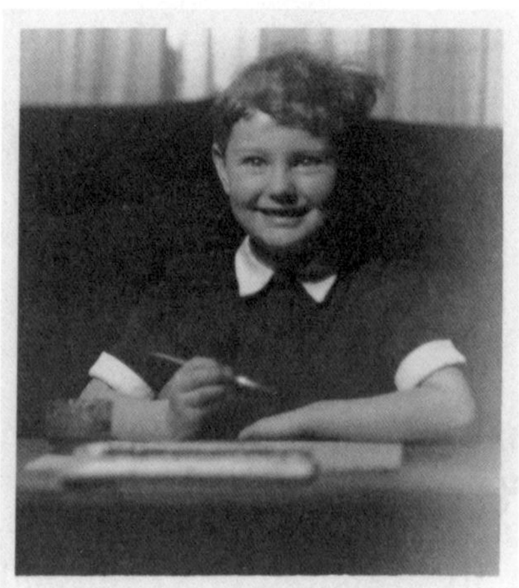

Clara Istlerová, 1950

Your father was the painter Josef Istler. How did that
influence you?

A lot, but I felt that working on art independently didn't
satisfy me as much as working on a book, where you first have
to identify with the content and then look for a form that
suits it—the journey is the goal in this case. So, the reasons
for my turn to book design are simple. I grew up in a cultured
family environment and was led from a young age to love literature. I've always been drawn to the form of the book—its
natural combination of utility and beauty. I was fascinated
by the contrast between the pure white paper and the black



Interview

text, the relationship between light and shadow. This was just
a step toward understanding the principles of book typography. Those features of typography were gradually confirmed
for me both in the work of the constructivists of the 1930s
and particularly in the work of the Bauhaus, their followers
and, in our country, Karel Teige[1] and Ladislav Sutnar. And
I think that later I wasn't the only one who was influenced by
Oldřich Hlavsa,[2] who made type a dominant feature—the character. While studying at the Secondary Industrial School of
Graphics, I underwent a thorough preparation, including not
only calligraphy, through which I acquired an almost intimate
relationship with type, but also printing techniques, including
prepress. This knowledge later helped me many times in communicating with printers when I had to justify and defend my ideas.

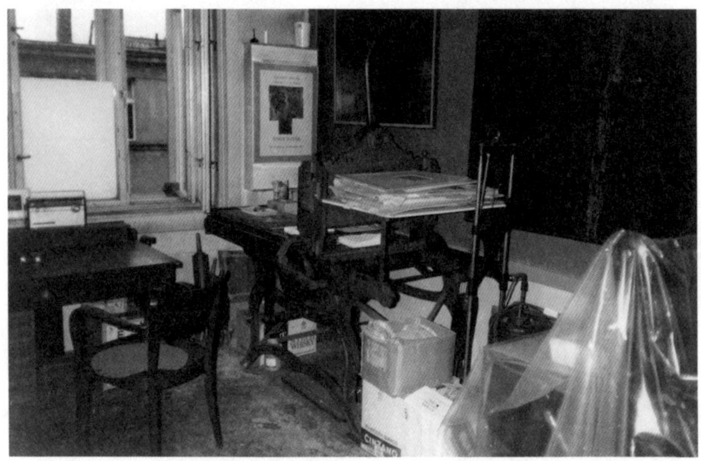

Josef Istler's studio in the Karlín apartment

Did your father discourage you from artistic activity,
as often happens with artist parents?

No, no, no. And even if he had, you absorb it without anyone
having to tell you anything. There were paintings hanging
everywhere at home and my father had a studio and a graphic
workshop in one room where he worked for days on end. It
wasn't until the 1970s that he found a painting studio in

Šárecká Street in Dejvice at the Stretti family villa[3] and later
in Žižkov in Ostromečská Street, which was his last stop before
he died. But actually, when I was in primary and secondary
school and university, he was always in our apartment in Karlín,
painting or making prints. From the time I was twelve years
old, I was grinding lithographic stones and helping him. I got to
know the craft from the very bottom, and in doing so, he also
prepared me well for high school.

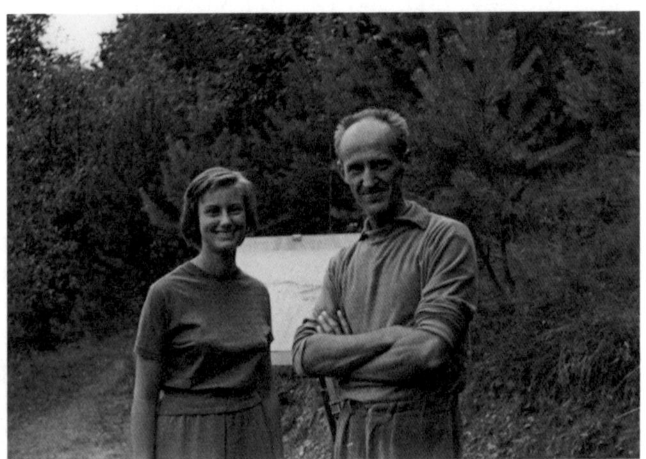
Clara and Josef Istler, summer vacation, 1958

You worked as your father's assistant from a young age?

And I really enjoyed it. My father was self-taught, he knew
I wouldn't learn what I couldn't teach myself. He wasn't a huge
believer in schools. He tried to pass on to me as much as he
knew. I got my first camera when I was about eleven. We took
pictures together and then developed and enlarged them, all at
home in the bathroom, to my mother's displeasure, of course.
The bathtub was completely yellowed with chemicals. Thanks
to my dad, I went to graphic design school so well-prepared that
during my first year I was able to do work on my own schedule.
But getting in wasn't easy because I didn't have the right class
background; I was eventually admitted on appeal.

                    Interview

The school didn't like that your father was a painter?

I simply wasn't of working-class origin. It was 1958, and admission to school was dependent on a preliminary class-background check of applicants by a cadre of the street committee.[4] I was eventually invited to take the talent tests at Hellichova[5] and I passed with flying colors, which was an argument for the school authorities to admit me. Interestingly, the school principal, Alois Tomasy, turned out to be someone who always supported my goals in work and, later, teaching. Of course, 1968[6] played a role in this, when he, a former hardened communist, lost his illusions. In the '70s, on the other hand, he made it possible for many professors to teach at Hellichova who wouldn't have found work elsewhere at that time.

And how did the previous regime interfere with your father's work?

My father wasn't allowed to exhibit, but he remained independent in his work. In the 1950s he earned money by preparing, designing, and producing panels for exhibitions. They used to bring huge exhibition panels to our apartment, which he worked on late into the night. First he prepared scaled-down designs of compositions, then he painted large color surfaces based on them, glued photos, and wrote texts with a brush, as sign painters did then, because there was no phototypesetting or digital printing. The whole thing involved a great deal of manual, not to say physical, skill and stamina.

Your father was engaged in graphic design the entire time in general, wasn't he?

In addition to exhibition panels, he also designed book covers, mostly using his monotypes. But not only that. For [record label] Supraphon, for example, he updated the drawing of the lion in its logo. It was linear, very stylized, very nice.

And what ignited your love of type?

I really enjoyed calligraphy. When you do calligraphy, you get
a kind of symbiosis between the letters. You can't compare it at
all to when we create designs on the computer now and choose
any font we want. A hand-drawn font allows you to know the
shape of each letter from the ground up, in detail. This kind of
preparation is essential, if only because you don't have a problem when you're working with spacing. The old printer type-
setters who experienced stock hand-typesetting were totally
connected to this. They not only knew how to space all caps
well, but they also had the necessary knowledge of Czech spell-
ing, and thus of written Czech. Now, when someone is making
a hasty design on the computer, they don't even check if the
V and the A will fit well next to each other. Just like L and M
in capitalized form. You'll find mistakes in magazine headers,
too. They have weird gaps in them, and graphic designers don't
see that the letters need to be manually retracted or often the
whole title or typesetting needs to be adapted to it.

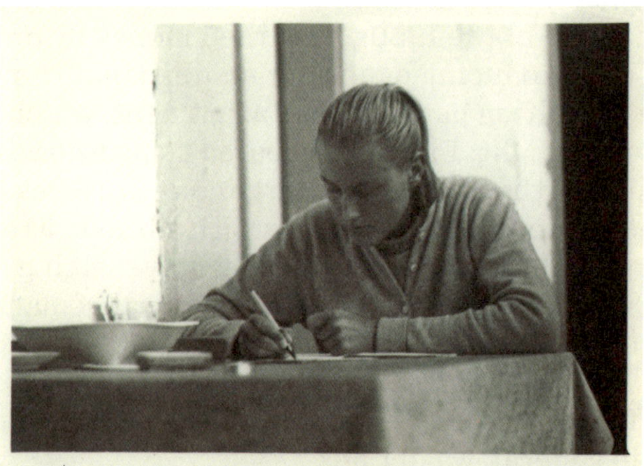

Clara Istlerová practicing calligraphy, 1960s

Could it be said, then, that in calligraphy
there's a harmony between the lettering and the body?

Yes, you write in a certain rhythm with the body. In fact, you
try to make the letters form a perfectly uniform flow through-

out the written lines. But Czech is aesthetically tricky in that
respect. Look at hymnals or at handwritten manuscripts in
Latin—there are beautiful lines where you have u, i, e. Whereas
in Czech you have y, v, ž, ř, or Hus's conjugations—something
terribly fragmented visually. Whenever I was writing a Czech
text, I always had the Latin lines in mind, which flowed beautifully without being distracted by anything.

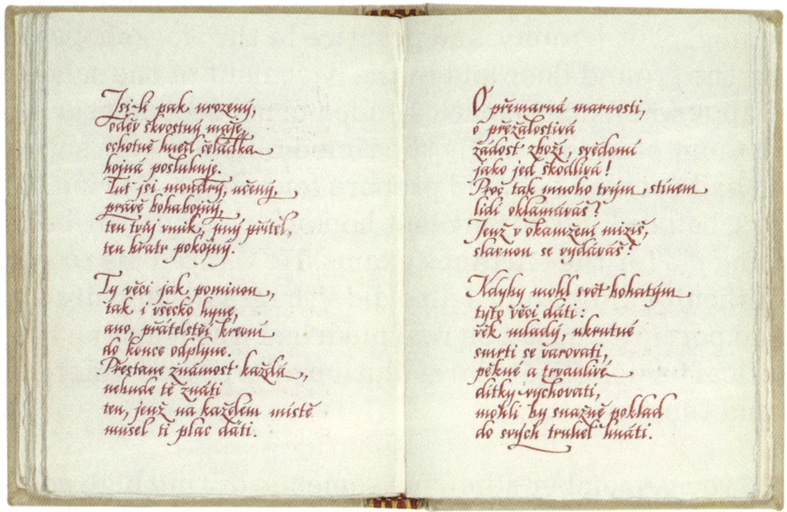

*žalostné a plačtivé rozmlouvání jedné ztracené duše s tělem svým*
(A lost soul's sad and tearful conversation with his body), 1963

I think all this established a deep relationship with letters
in me. In fact, I was never really lacking free expression,
because you have to put a lot of yourself into typography
anyway. You have to feel when it's good or not good, whether
the letter wants more right, left, up, down, what to do with it
compositionally and color-wise. I think creation as such is part
of it. It's not something mechanical. Human beings are very
much marked by how they evolved, that is, by what preceded
computer processing. In high school, we typeset by hand from
letter sets, separated them, traced them, and corrected them.
You learned everything, including proofreading marks. The
Secondary Industrial School of Graphics was, and I think
still is, excellent. Two basic subjects were taught there—

Clara Istlerová & Anežka Minaříková                    27

photography and printing. We book designers were a small group. They only ever took four or five people in a year, so we were put in the photography class. That's where we took the basic subjects. The vocational classes and workshops were always given to the first and second year, and then the third- and fourth-year graphic editors together in one class. Kind of like the old days: small classes where kids of different ages sat together and were given appropriate assignments. Apart from art, we had theory of printing and reproduction techniques, retouching, photography, and practice in the workshops which were on the ground floor and in the basement of the school. I was happy when mathematics ended in my second year. I was given a C out of kindness. By the time I finished high school, my dad had decided I should prepare for college. During the holidays, before I left for my last hops-harvesting job, he was preparing me for the entrance exams. He wanted me to submit more difficult calligraphy. I also did lithographs and drew still lifes and portraits based on real models. I was learning the theoretical basics about the evolution of type and different fonts and their creators.

Do you remember admiring someone during high school?

Of course, I've always been attracted to the 1920s and 1930s. Cubism, Futurism, the Russian avant-garde, Bauhaus. All of it. In our country, Teige, Sutnar, and in the '70s, of course, Hlavsa, who was very prominent.

Did you have any extracurricular activities?

While I was learning lithography, drypoint, and etching with my dad, my parents arranged for me to learn German and English. From the age of eleven I took private lessons regularly, first German and after a year they added English. Two language classes twice a week. I was taught by a married couple, one in German, the other in English. I only had to change rooms.

You've had some luck in your life.

Yes, but I didn't appreciate it until much later. I often went to concerts at the Rudolfinum. At one of them, my father met the flutist Václav Žilka, who at that time led the chamber ensemble České noneto. I remember exactly that it was at a concert of the famous French flutist Jean-Pierre Rampal. It could have been sometime in 1956. Carried away by the beautiful music and the performances of the musicians, Dad said, "You will learn to play the flute."

As if it wasn't enough.

Right! So that I wouldn't get bored!. He bought a transverse flute and I began lessons with Mr. Žilka once a week, at his apartment in Bohnice. It also meant practicing scales and études every day. Žilka was a kind but strict teacher. By the time I learned to finger and breathe properly, I stopped enjoying it.

How long did you stick with playing the transverse flute?

Three years. But as soon as I entered the graphics school, I announced that I couldn't manage it. Classes started at 7:30 in the morning and ended after 6 p.m., three days a week. It took over an hour to get to Újezd by the old tram from Karlín and then a walk to Hellichova Street.

And was your mom at home at that time?

She was a housewife before she started teaching drawing at the Svoboda Polygraphic School in Smíchov in the late 1960s. She graduated from the French Gymnasium in Prague-Dejvice and then went to the Academy of Arts, Architecture and Design, which closed in 1939. Right after that she met my father and they got married. During the 1950s, they worked together for the UVU (Union of Visual Artists) and the ÚLUV (Institute of Folk Art Production), which was located on Národní třída and later moved, under the banner of ÚBOK (Institute of Housing and Clothing Culture), to Příkopy. They created designs for woven and printed fabrics, used textiles, engraved glass, painted porcelain, and ceramics. At home, she took up drawing and watercolors of flowers. Her favorite were dried, oddly twisted plants or vegetables—that was her world. And she took care of us. Dad worked at home and required hot lunches. Mom was a homemaker. It was actually great that my grandparents still lived with us for a long time, two or three generations living together, it enriches a person.

School was a piece of cake for you. Did your mom help you with homework?

No way! I wasn't very studious, but I didn't study with my mom anyway. Chemistry, physics, and math were always horrible for me. Eleven years in an academic high school would not have been fun for me. That's why in the eighth grade I did the entrance exams for the Secondary Industrial School of Graphics in Hellichova Street.

And who taught you in high school?

Our department was headed by Professor Vladimír Ringes. He was a landscape painter. A terribly nice man who had no great creative ambitions. It was great that he didn't direct us, didn't influence us too much. He led the class in such a calm way. He just set the assignment according to the syllabus he had for the year for each grade. We progressed from simple calligraphy, first with a dip pen, later with a French pen, to drawing letters, to designing ads and posters, which we carried out in the typesetting room and the school print shop in the workshop classes. I slowly moved away from the classical concepts that were taught and started to experiment. But it never bothered him. He never said: "Not like that, Istlerová, it's going to be done my way!" He let me try everything out.

So, you freely improvised?

I loved letters so much that I played with them. I didn't want to stick to typographic composition just on the axis. I tried to

                    Interview

feel the surface with the type so that there was a charge, a tension between the type and the surface, so that it was never too balanced, because then it lost its effect. You notice either the surface or the typeface to arrive at a certain balance in the effect. But, of course, old prints from the seventeenth century still have enormous charm, even though they follow the composition and are mostly written or set on a central axis.

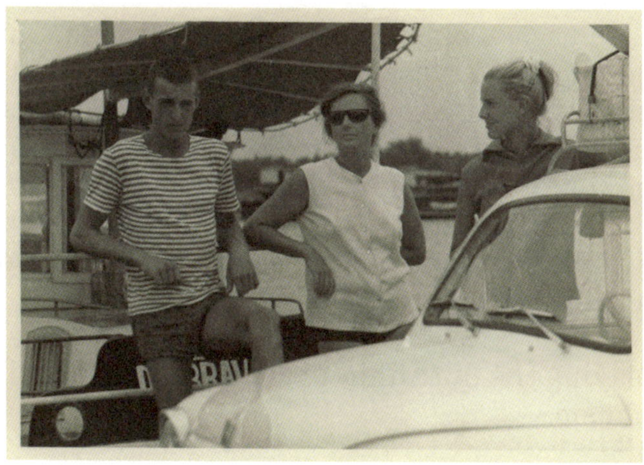

Tomáš, Gerda, and Clara Istler in Bulgaria, 1960s

You probably came to that mainly through watching your father work, didn't you?

We absorb throughout childhood, adolescence, all our lives. Everything we see, experience, is stored somewhere, we process it, and without realizing it, it affects us in some way.

From my dad's studio, classical music or jazz sounded from the gramophone or later the tape recorder nonstop, all day long. Then, when my parents went to the pub or to dance in the evening, I would sit in the studio and play classical records on the old gramophone, 33s, hard and high, which couldn't have more than one or two movements of a Beethoven symphony on one side. When I was fourteen or fifteen, I bought season tickets to the so-called Musical Youth. These were concert cycles intended partly for normal audiences and partly for young people from the age of thirteen on. A season ticket cost fifty crowns, but for little money there was a lot of music. Every season, always from September to April, I attended at least two cycles, one orchestral and one chamber. In May, the Prague Spring Festival began.

Have you retained your love of classical music?

I still prefer classical music; that's stuck with me. But it's true that the older I get, the less I feel the need to put on the radio or a CD. I don't need it so much anymore. Music used to help me concentrate. Or I was sort of immersed in both music and work at the same time. I realize in retrospect that it was mostly when I had kids, when they were small and noisy. Over time, of course, this falls away and one concentrates on the work without needing any crutches.

But playing the flute didn't last, despite your relationship with music.

Well, it wasn't my groove. But what was important for me in the 1950s was that there were a lot of interesting people in our apartment that I could talk to. Meeting publicly in bars wasn't easy for people who didn't support the regime at that time. Both Jan Kotík and his father Pravoslav Kotík, whom my father taught lithography to, often came to our house. Then there was the painter Václav Tikal, a very gentle and quiet man, or the poet Vratislav Effenberger, to whom I later went to Smíchov to borrow books that I would never have had access to at that time. I've loved to read my whole life. I always got a stack of books for Christmas. That was the best present.

Do you remember your favorite book?

Since I was ten or twelve I read, besides Jules Verne, the classics: Balzac, Zola, Tolstoy, Maupassant, Rabelais, later Faulkner.

Lstivých a podvodných
lidí svět nestálý
obyčej má. Neb marné
cti lstivě podá-li
kterým, ty hned podvede
a život jich zmaří,
též místo zlata červy
a smradem obdaří.

Jenž hotové službami
sloužiti živému,
nechtí oči skloniti
v zemi pohřbenému.
Čemuž tělo srozuměvše
přehořce plakalo,
a poníženou řečí
mluviti počalo.

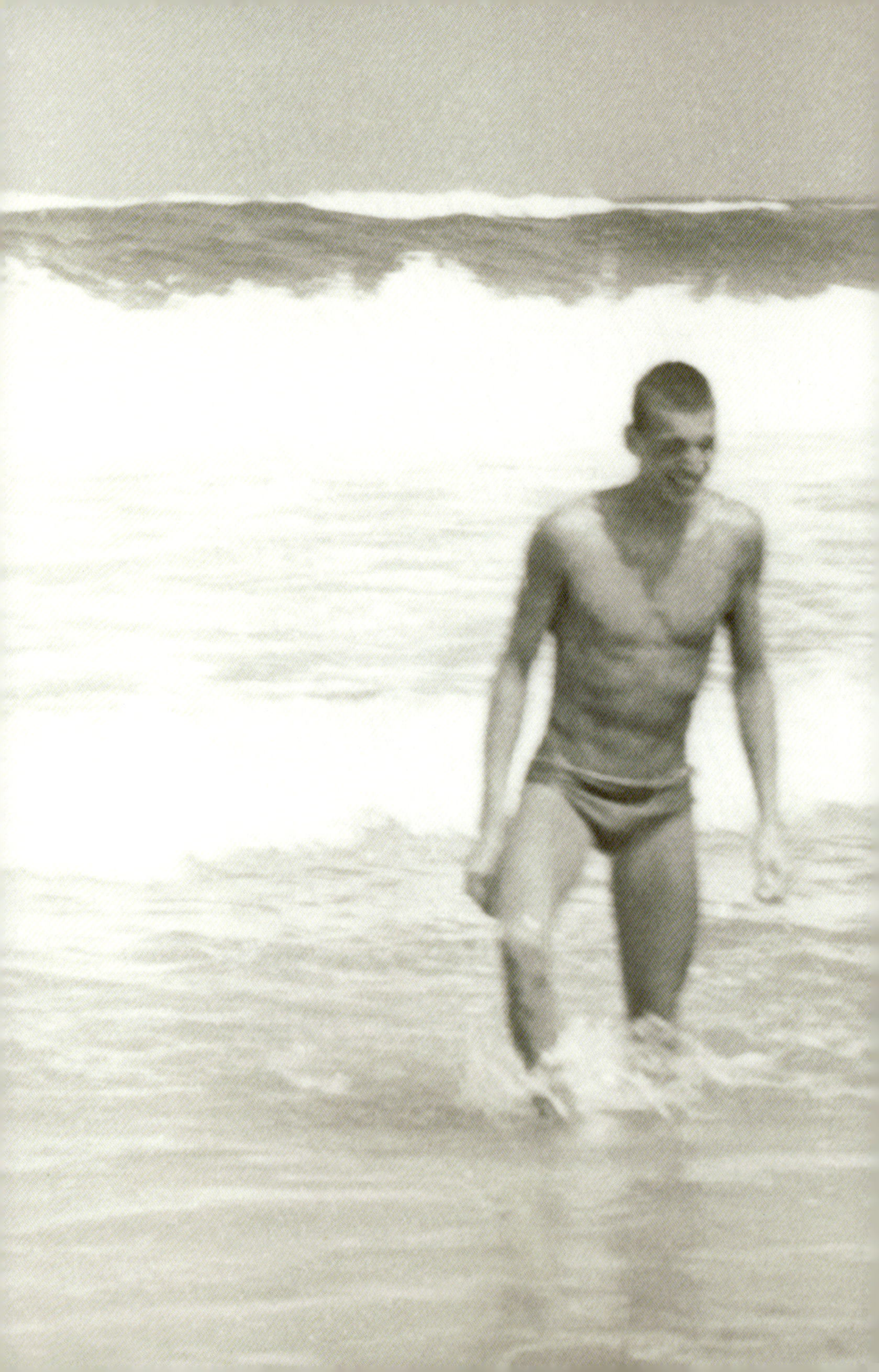

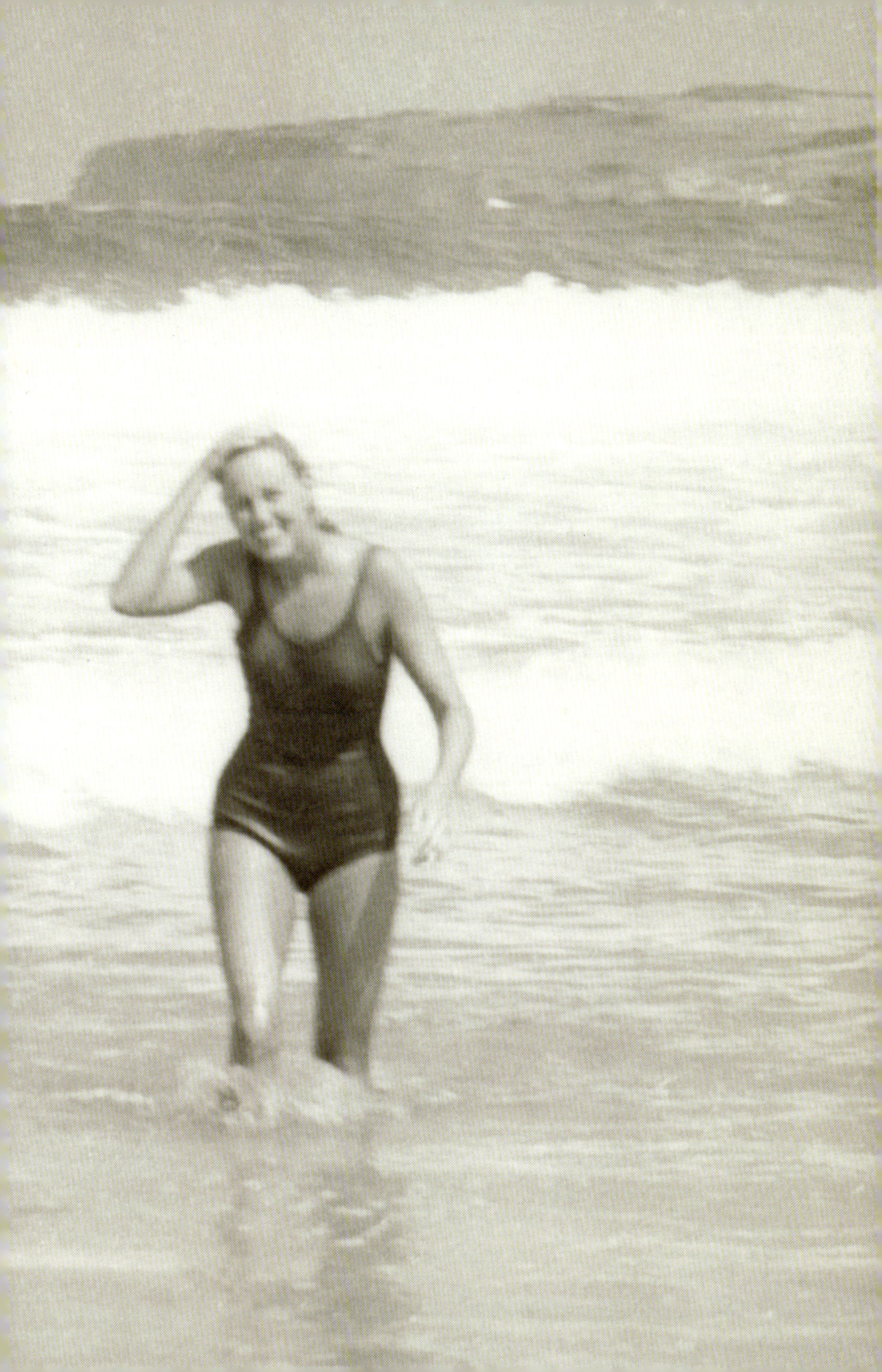

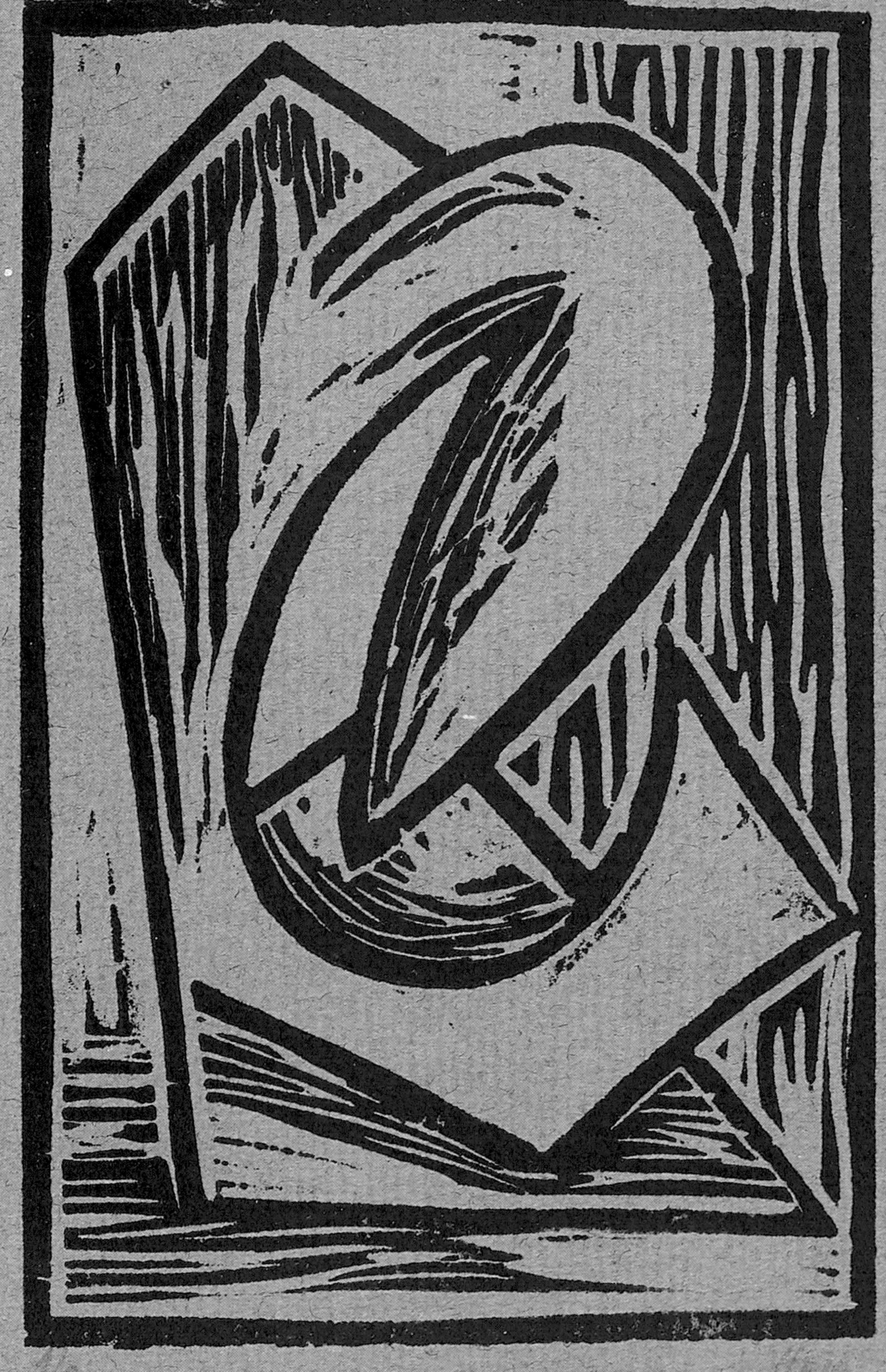

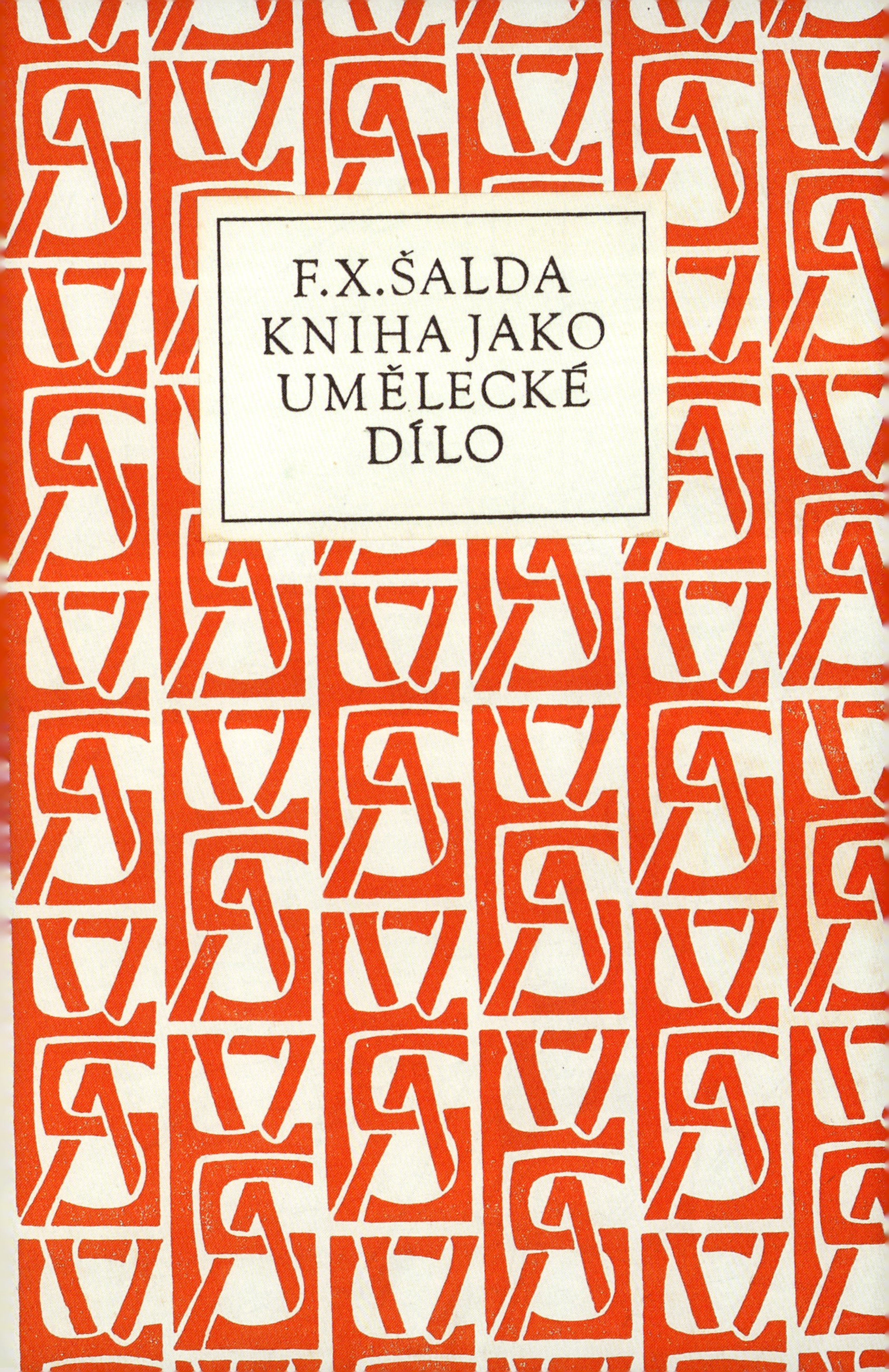
F. X. ŠALDA
KNIHA JAKO
UMĚLECKÉ
DÍLO

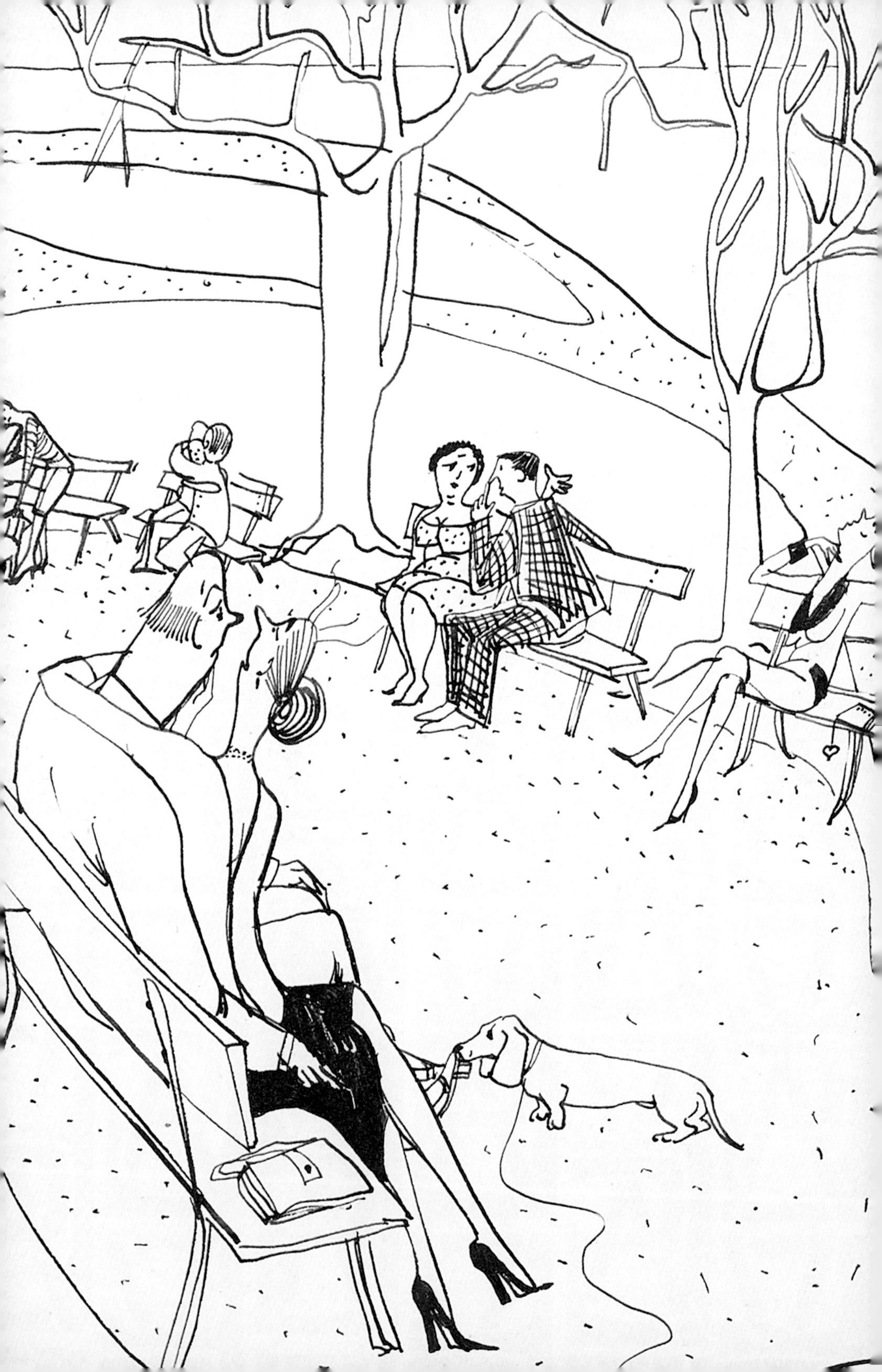

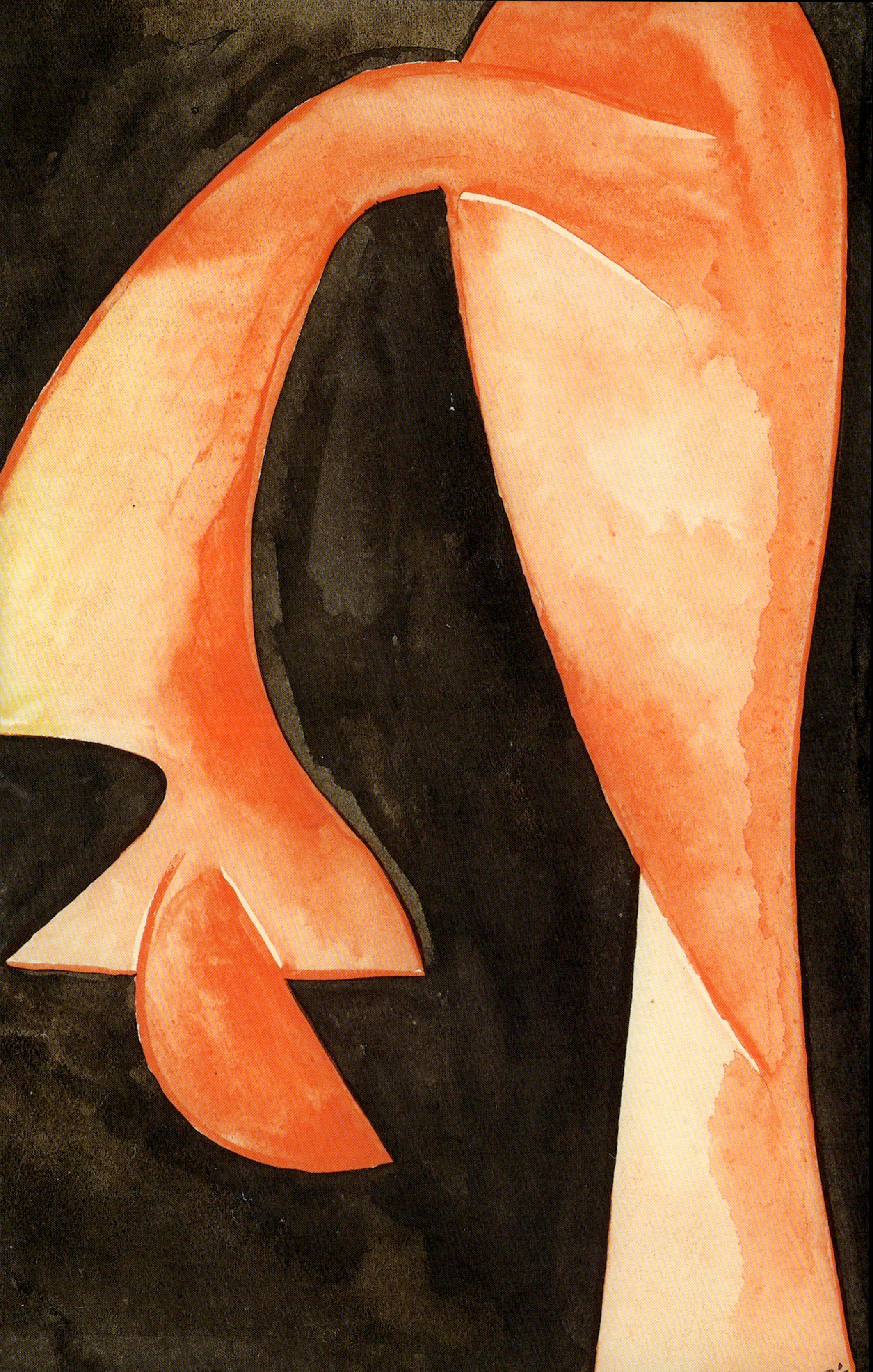

# GLEB GORBOVSKIJ

# INTELEKT VKUSU JELENI

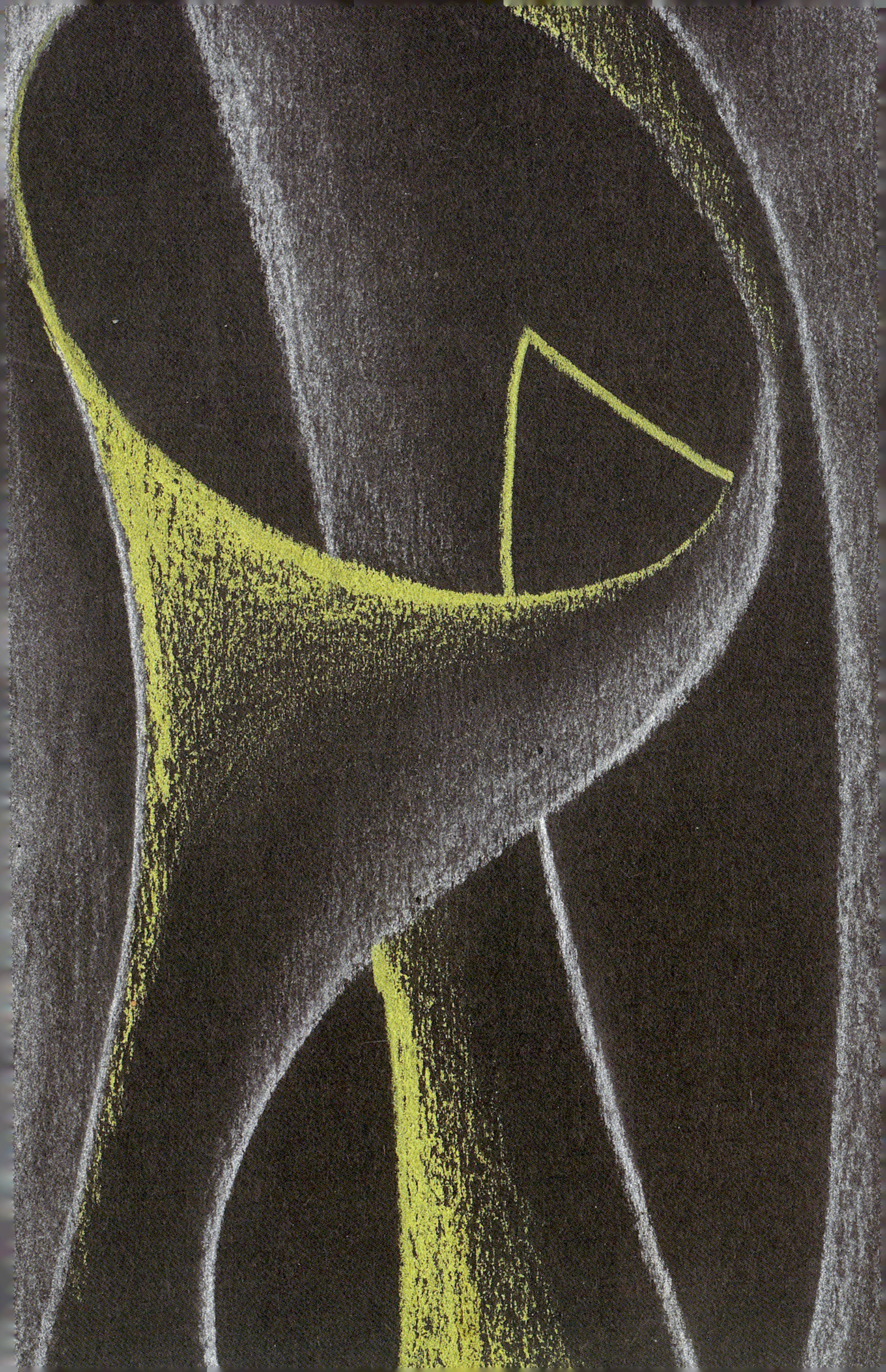

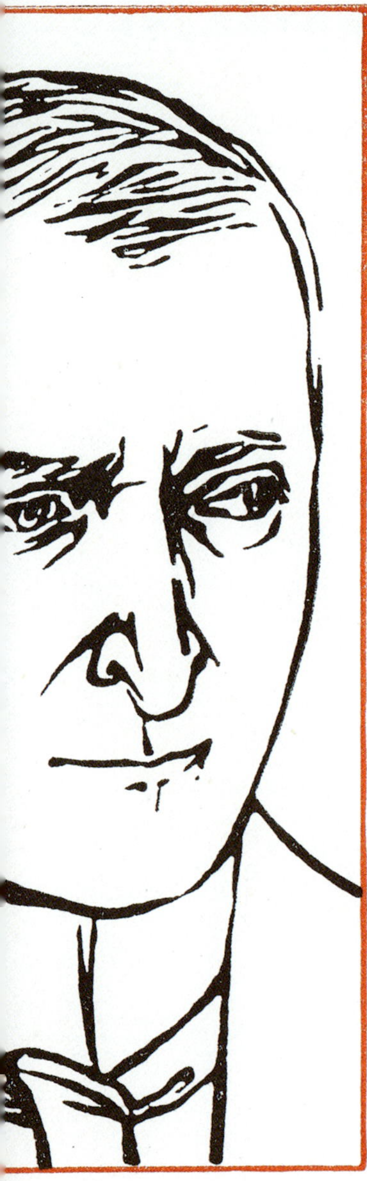

F.X.ŠA
KNIH
UMĚ
D

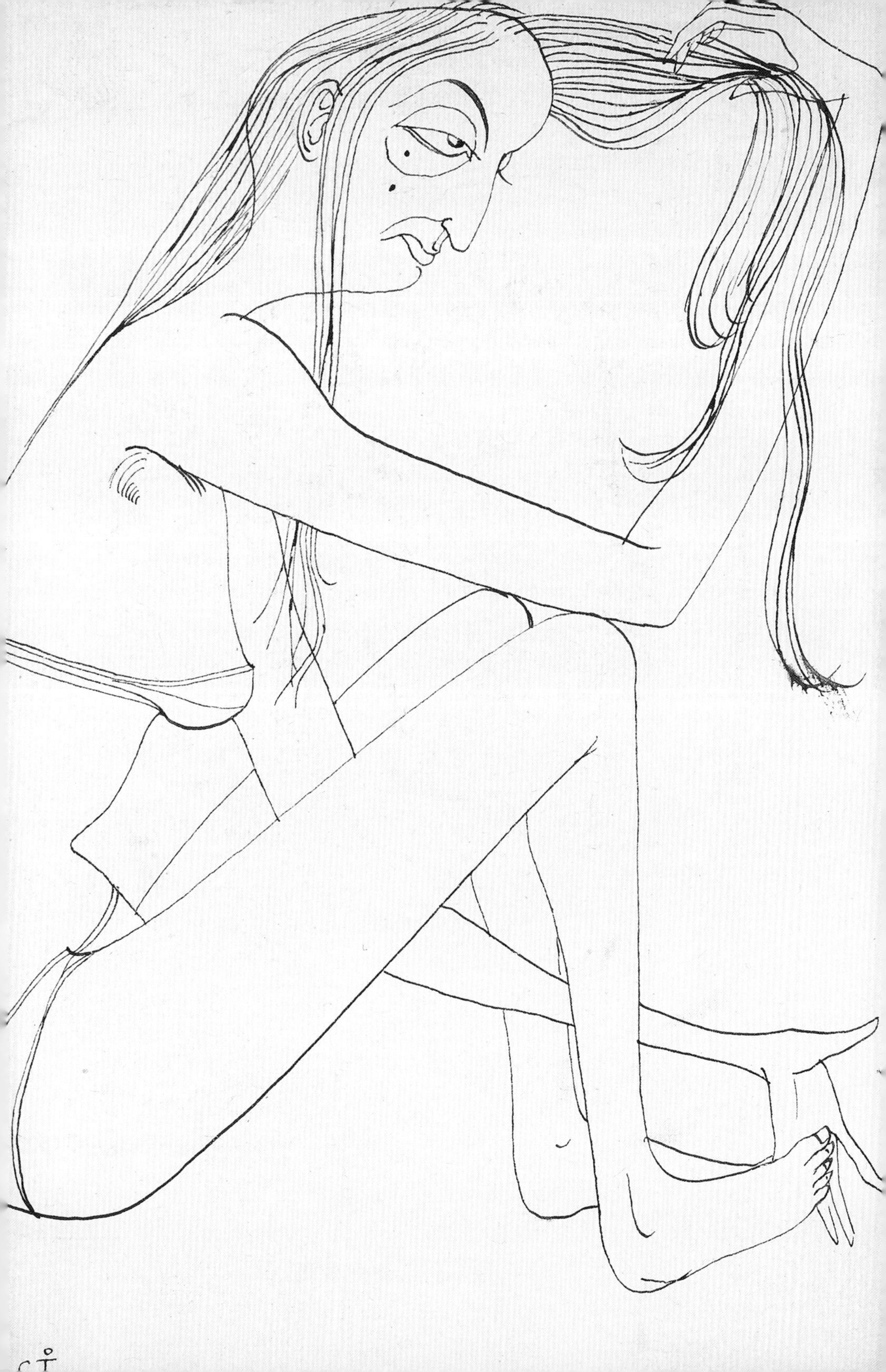

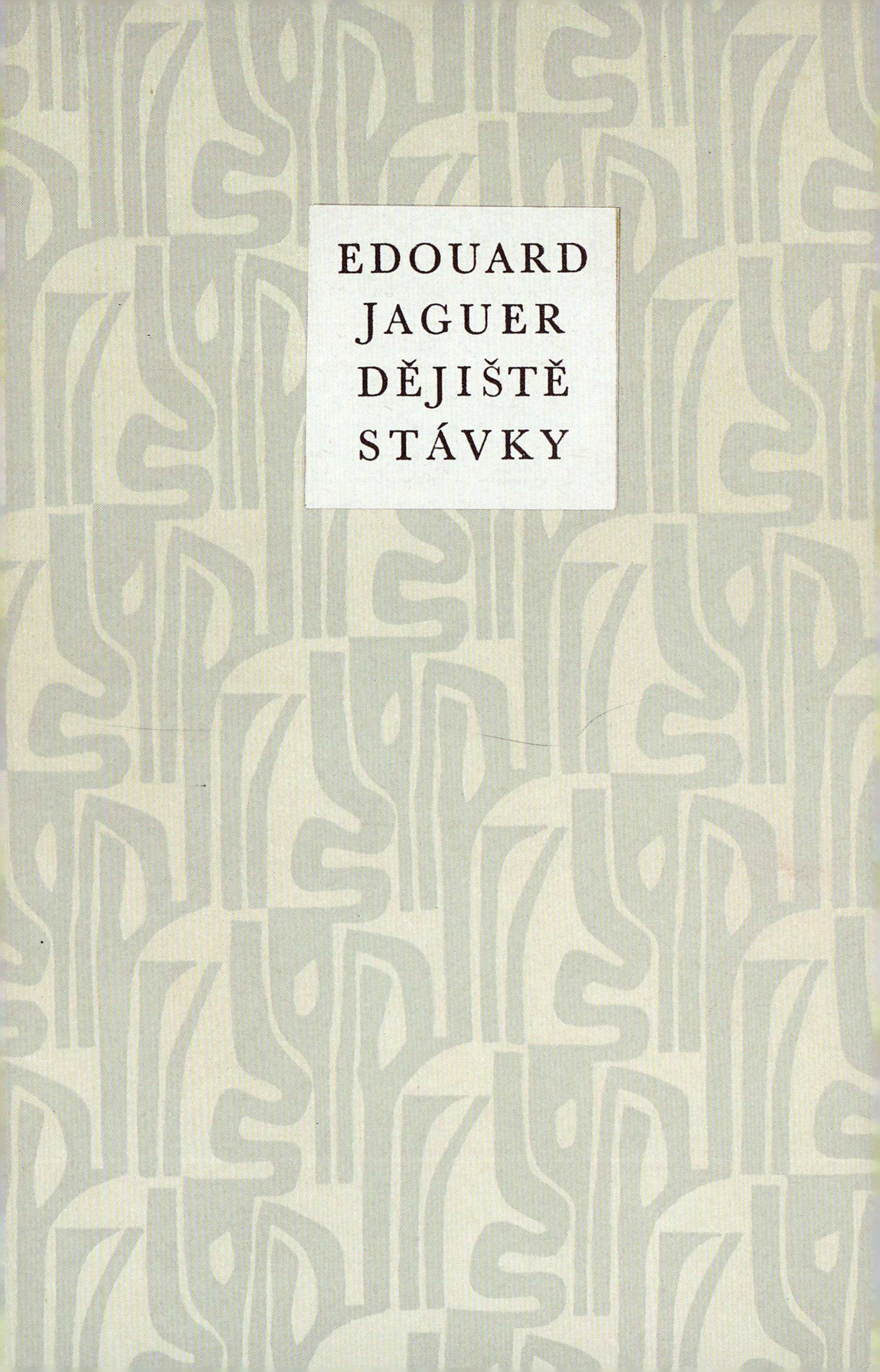


EDOUARD
JAGUER
DĚJIŠTĚ
STÁVKY

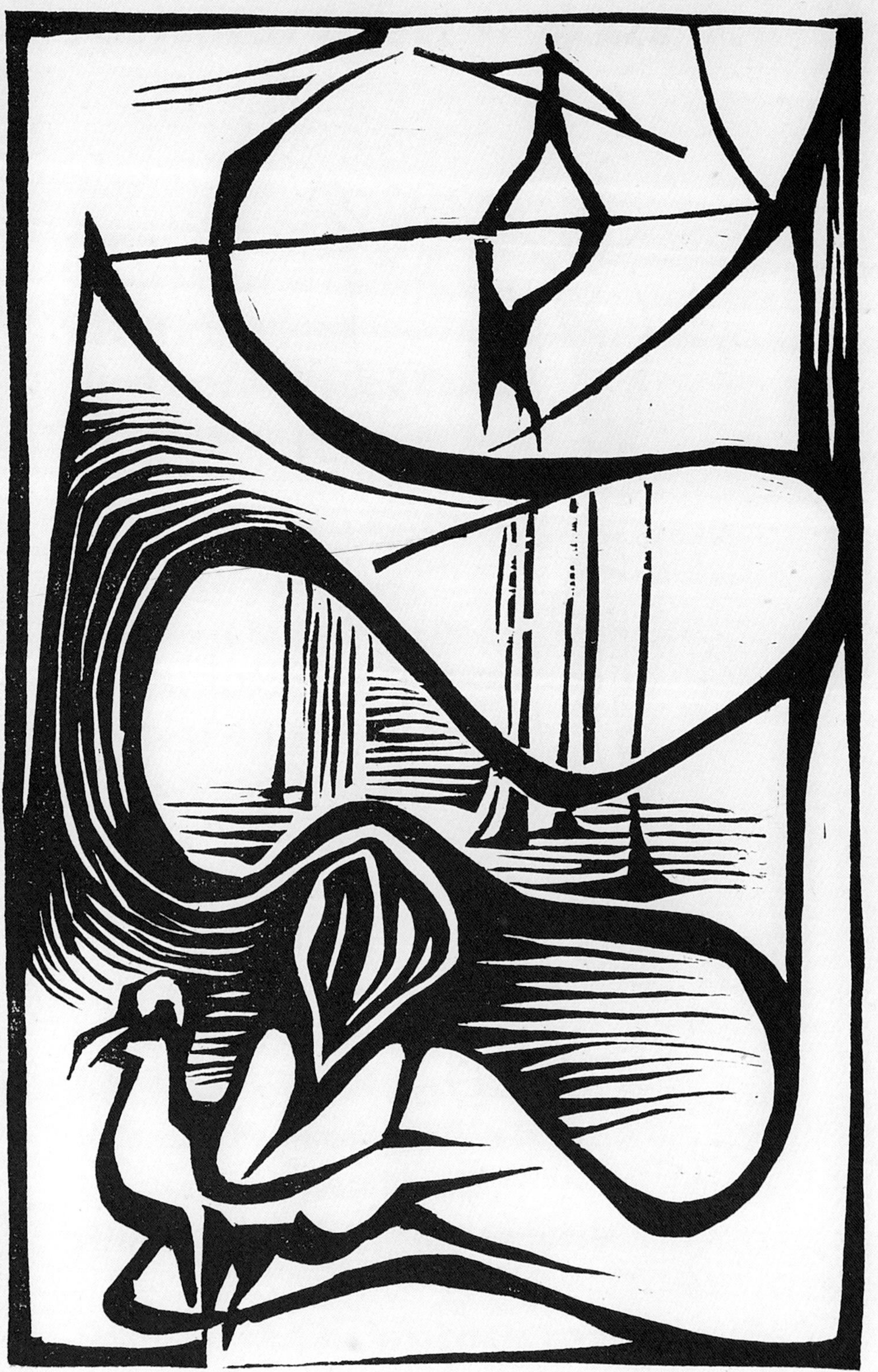

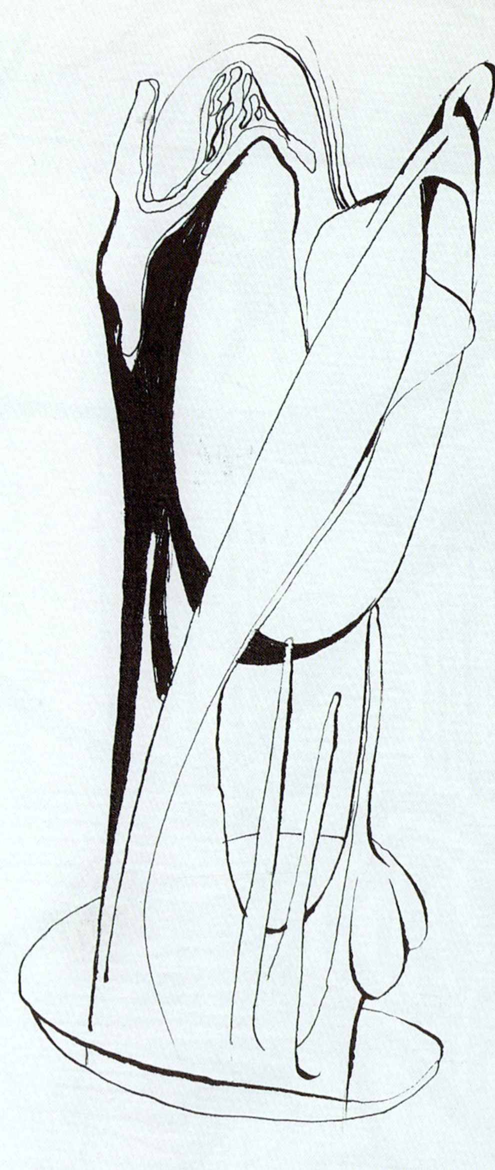

ČI PAČČIVÁ OTÁZKA 1966

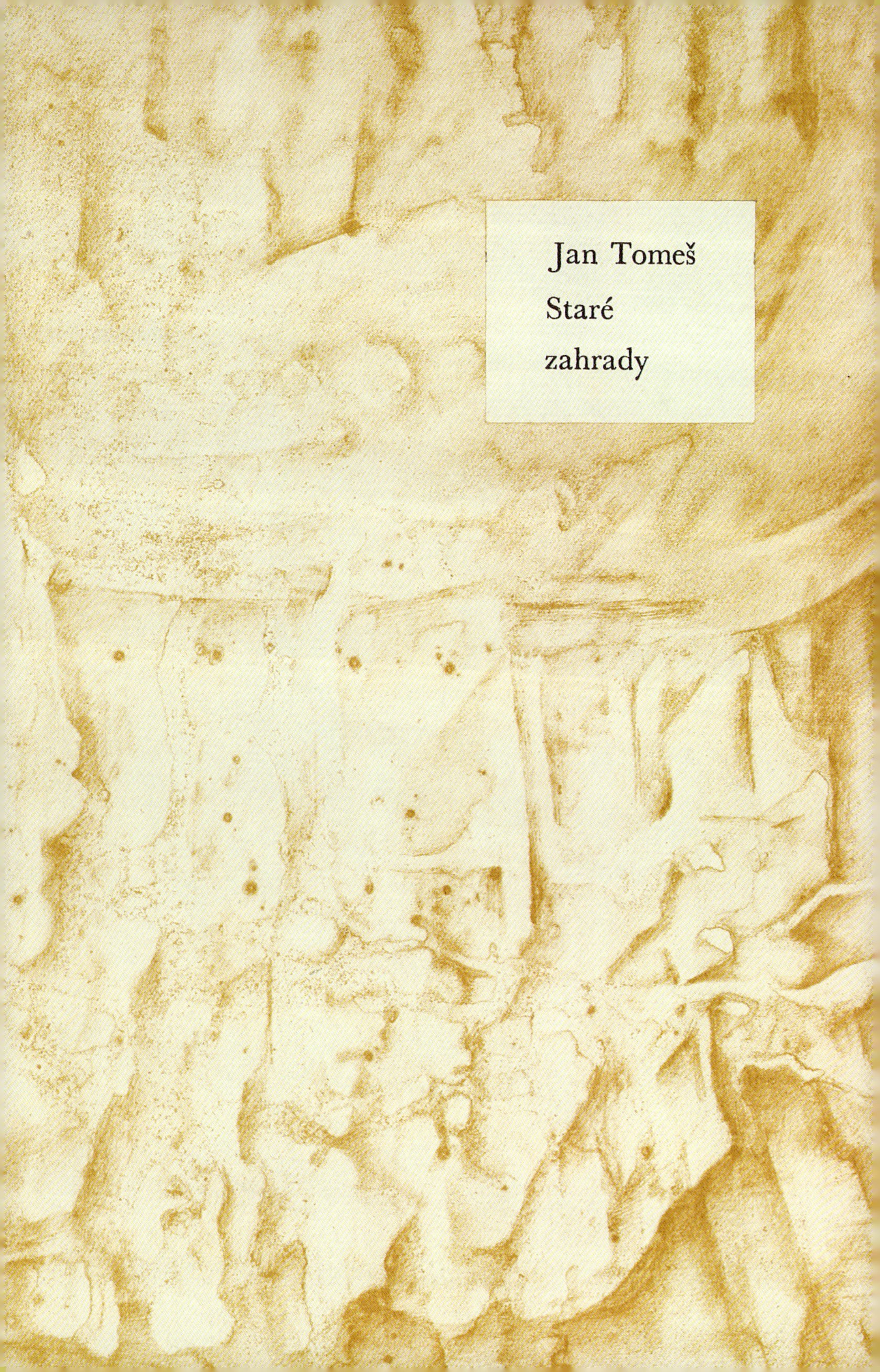

Jan  Tomeš
Staré
zahrady

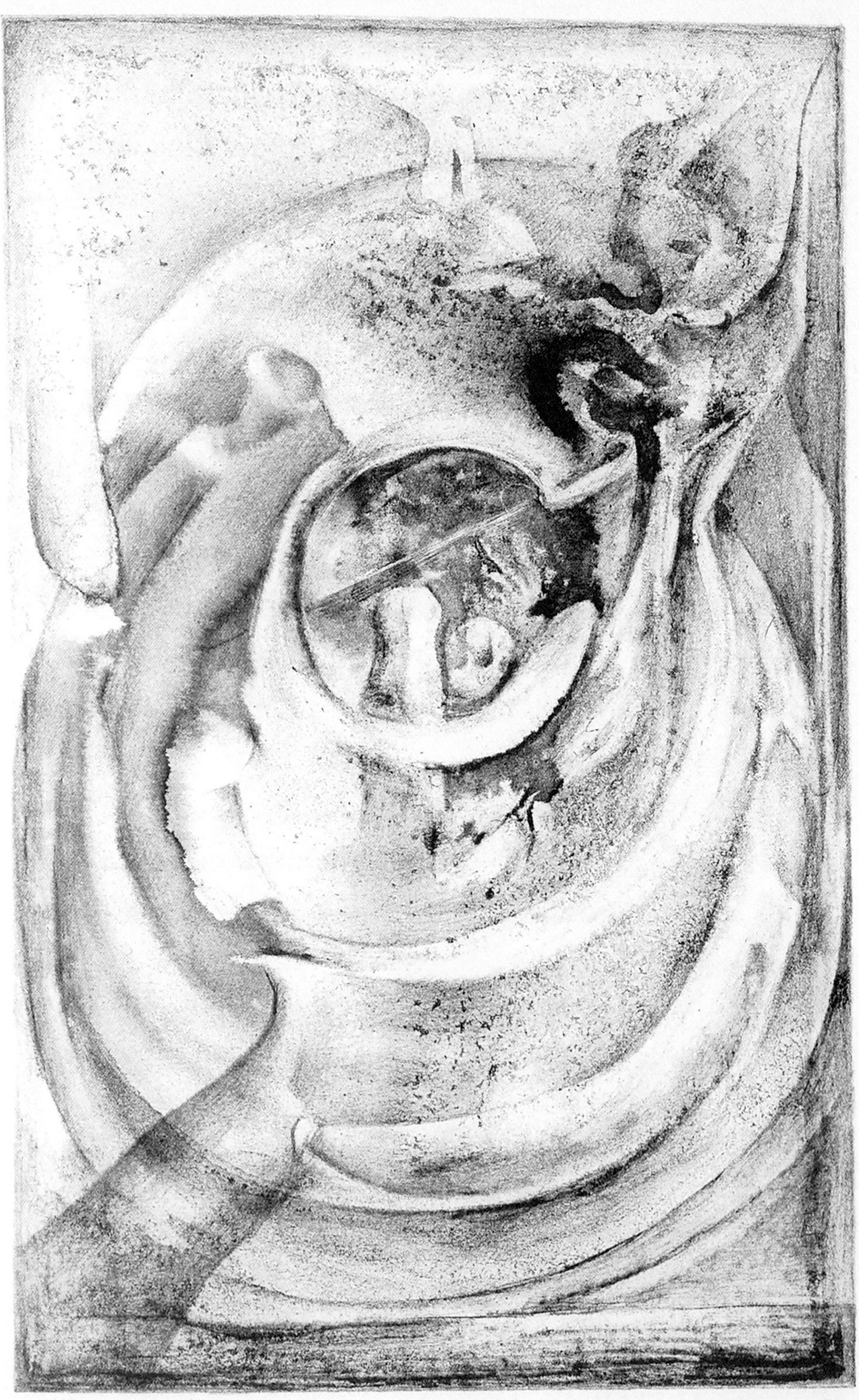

That's not easy reading.

No, on the contrary! I borrowed Nietzsche and stuff from Effenberger. Literature that I couldn't find in libraries. But, of course, in between there was Walter Scott and Jules Verne. In the transition between childhood, young adulthood, and adulthood, you can always find the literature you currently need for a kind of inner nourishment or orientation in the world. I know I loved Rabelais's *Gargantua and Pantagruel*, two fat tomes illustrated with original engravings. Also, because we were bombarded, my grandmother's classic library—by subscription from the European Literary Club—and books from [publishers] Vilímek or Borový during the First Republic, had disappeared. The library was rebuilt, mainly thanks to my mother. And Dad, he never actually read fiction as such. He bought mainly specialized literature. How to take photographs, how to paint, how to do lithography, and everything that concerned his work, painting and printing inks. He was perfect at that.

He was an all-round talent.

Well, he tried. And it's true that whatever he did, he wanted to do it properly. He studied it thoroughly. I guess it's because he was self-taught. He'd only had a short summer training with a Croatian landscape painter.

And he also wasn't burdened by school.

Yes, he wasn't deformed by anything. No one was ordering him from the inside, telling him what to do. But on the other hand, he said to me, quite firmly, "You have to do this school, and do it properly. We have to get you in there."

And what did your brother do?

My brother Tomáš was two years younger than me, but he's already passed away. Unfortunately, our parents had a negative effect on him. He was more inclined to manual work, he was

very fond of cars and wanted to be a car mechanic. But my dad
started taking him to pubs at a certain age, maybe sixteen,
seventeen. He taught him how to drink and made him a compan-
ion and a helper. Tomáš was very skilled manually and helped
dad make his various molds, he also worked with resin, casting
models. Dad didn't avoid sculpture either—he mainly made
reliefs. Tomáš graduated with a diploma in plastering and went
to study sculpture at the Academy of Fine Arts. He had an eye—
he made several excellent portraits, including of our father. The
bust that's here in the apartment is by him. If only he hadn't
drunk so much ... I think it ruined him, he was addicted to alco-
hol. He got sick, got tuberculosis, and I think he had cancer
when he died. He was only fifty-five. We didn't get on very well,
but he was a very nice man and unfortunately he went through
life hard and too quickly.

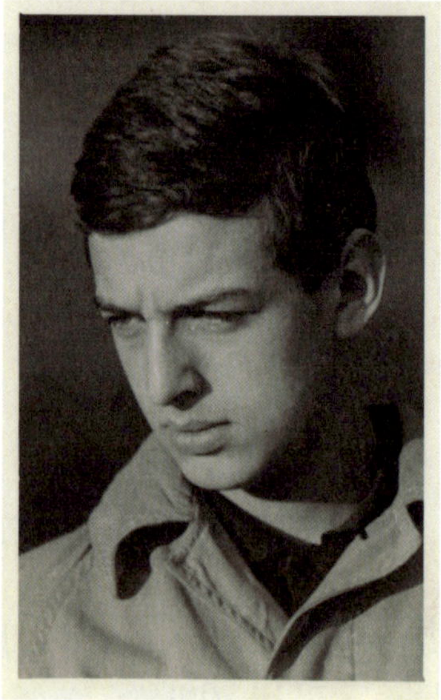

Tomáš Istler, 1960

But you got along when you were kids?

Yes. My childhood was also nice in that we all regularly left the
city for the summer holidays and went to the country for two

                    Interview

months. My parents, although they didn't have much money, always rented a small house, a cottage, or we stayed directly with the peasants. One summer we even stayed in the attic above the inn where the amateur theater used to be. We only went with my brother and my mother, my father stayed in Prague and painted or prepared panels for exhibitions. In the late '50s, ironically, it was very bad even because they allowed us to study, because there wasn't much money left. But once I had children myself, I kept up this summer holiday tradition. At the stroke of the thirtieth of June, all my work deadlines ended.

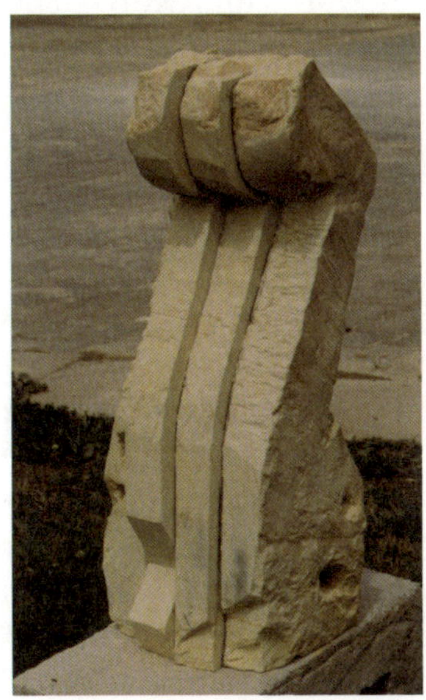

Tomáš Istler, *Stéla*, 1997

What did you do there for two months?

When my children were three and four years old, I managed to rent a farm in Sebečice through an ad, a small farmhouse. The owners lived in another village, about twenty kilometers away, where they had another farm they still worked. Although they had given their cows and horses to the cooperative, the fields were returned to them. They were real peasants. We used this so-called farm until 1996. The children grew up there among the villagers. It was beautiful. The pond, the woods—and the children got a proper social education in an environment where they had to make their own place among the local children. And they were out in the fresh air for two months. An outhouse, cold water. When the cold weather came, and some summers, unlike now, it rained a lot, the stove was heated and I cooked on it.

It wasn't just a change of scenery, but reality.

Yes. The kids rode bikes, swam, and learned to take care of themselves. When they were ten, twelve, they started going to the summer cinema in the evening with a bunch of local kids. They had fun. They remember it fondly now.

Just like when you went with your mom when you were a kid, only you didn't go to the same place.

My parents never knew in advance if they would have money the next year. And it was great that we were somewhere different every time and got to know a different environment every summer. And that's why I was happy when I rented the whole farm in 1978. The rent was very cheap, the only condition was that I couldn't change anything. I worked even then, but I didn't make much money with the children when they were small. The typography fees weren't very high back then either. But in the end, you pass on to your children what you've been given. That's why I keep a close eye on how my children are raising their own kids. But I don't want to give advice. I think one educates just by the way one lives, by the way one behaves.

And how do you remember university?

I dedicated myself to my studies at university, but only as much as was strictly necessary and only to what I enjoyed. To this day, I still think that by the time you're eighteen you're more or less complete, that high school was more important than college in my field. Unless, of course, you run into a real personality there. František Muzika was a great personality, but very closed and he tied his studio teaching too much to the classical concept of typography and illustration in the spirit of [Swiss typographer] Jan Tschichold. He ran the studio rigidly and, I would say, one-dimensionally. He devoted himself to his painting and discussed little with us. We grew a bit like weeds in there. The tasks he gave us, in their classical content, only encouraged a certain imitation of what he himself did. In consultations and evaluations, it always became clear that he preferred work very similar to his own artistic expression.

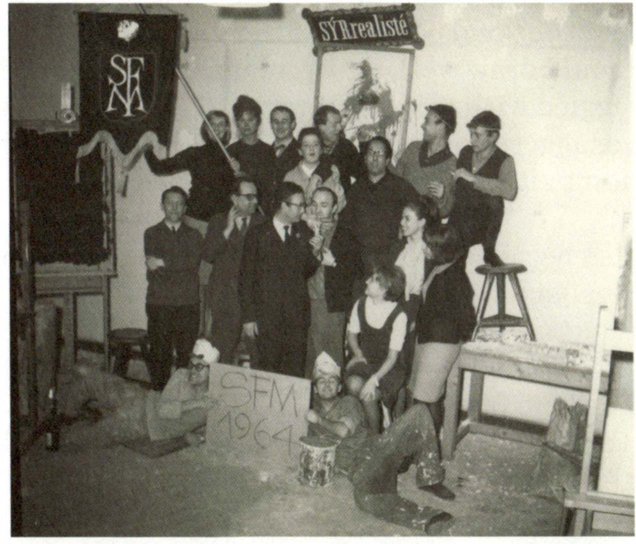


Clara Istlerová with classmates in the Studio of František Muzika at the Academy of Arts, Architecture and Design in Prague, 1964

That's a shame.

And a waste of time! For lack of creative impulses, I went to work in the school typesetting room at UMPRUM and tried my hand at typography. They had old forgotten letters. Or I'd go do ceramics. In the workshop there was a wheel, clay, glazes, and if you arranged it, you could create something and then have it fired.

What was the focus of František Muzika's studio
at that time?

On type, books, and posters. I enrolled in 1964 and it was actually a great disappointment and disillusionment for me. The
first foundation year didn't suit me very well because I struggled a bit with drawing from a live model and other assignments, like drawing en plein air or at the zoo. At the same
time, we worked in the sculpture studios twice a week. The
ongoing lectures were interesting. But then the studio classes
in the second year disappointed me even more. The first year
was most enjoyed by the students who had completed the art
*žižkárna*[7] and thus had completed the main artistic preparation. They could draw well, they had mastered figure drawing
while I struggled with it. I had always seen figure drawing as
more of an exaggeration, a shortcut, and the realism that was
required didn't sit well with me.

And also because in high school you studied primarily
book design.

At the graphics school I got a rather technical foundation, and
that distanced me from free creation. I've always drawn, but
according to my vision. In drawing, I transformed reality into
something else. Maybe I subconsciously pushed the teaching
away because I knew I had my own expression. And it seemed
completely pointless to me to learn to draw realistically. In the
later years, the lectures in art history and philosophy were
particularly interesting. Of course, we also had Marxism-
Leninism and Russian. I somehow got through that, too.

I understand that your high school and the tutelage of
your father were much more important to you developmentally. Did František Muzika's guidance not suit you
all through your studies?

It didn't suit me because the books that were produced there
had to be in A5 or A4 format. There was a classic typographic

design for the center, more or less the whole typesetting, including the format and the placement of the illustrations. That can't be fun when two or three years earlier I was much more advanced than that.

And did you ever talk to Muzika about the fact that you weren't satisfied with his way of running the studio?

I didn't. I didn't go to consultations as I should have, nor did I stay in the studio as often as another professor would probably require. Muzika didn't supervise us. I only went to the most important consultations, the ones that were mandatory and where proposals were submitted or approved. I did more work at home. Definitely because I could, unlike the students outside of Prague, but at the same time I devoted most of the morning to my dog, who I walked up the hill in Žižkov. I practically boycotted studio teaching.

And how did you spend holidays?

In 1967, at the end of my third year at UMRUM, Rostislav Vaněk and I, who also studied graphic arts, won a school prize. Rosťa studied with Svolinský. We both won the award for the best thesis—a study trip to France plus a travel permit and a kind of pass for any train in France. That brought us closer together. But I don't understand, or rather I don't remember, how we paid for our accommodation and food. But I do know that we slept in an hourly hotel about three times because it was the cheapest.

And was the official purpose of the trip?

It was supposed to be a study trip. And it turned out to be in the end ... Rosťa was always drawing something, he was so enthusiastic. He was afraid he'd miss something. He most liked to talk about things and he was really inspiring, it was great to debate with him. I think he's still the same today, he hasn't changed much. That's why he taught at UMPRUM until recently and was very popular. And, of course, it was better traveling as a pair. If you went alone, you wouldn't enjoy it as much or notice as much. We walked through cities, towns, castles, museums, galleries ...

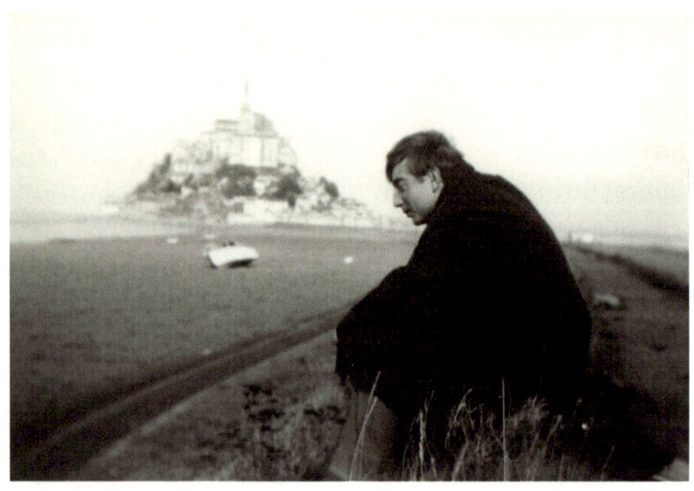

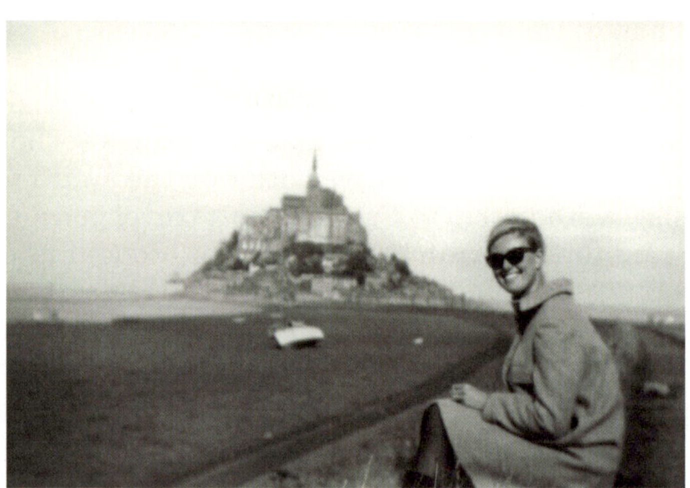

Rostislav Vaněk and Clara Istlerová
in front of Mont-Saint-Michel, France, 1967

How long was your trip?

A whole month. It was unusual but nice. We usually only had wine and a baguette for dinner.

     Interview

That's probably why I still remember it. I think I still have some photos from that trip. But it was because of that trip I later broke up with my first boyfriend, the bookbinder Antonín Vopálenský. We'd always go to his friend's cottage in the Jizera Mountains together in autumn before school started. There on the terrace, I'll never forget it, I once had the thought: "As soon as I go abroad, we'll break up, the relationship will end." I remember that moment very well. It was a strange feeling, I knew something was slowly closing and I had a similar feeling another time when my second long-term relationship ended. That time, I felt that as soon as I take one step into another world, the relationship won't be enough for me anymore. And it happened. For a while after that Vaněk and I dated, but I'm not sure it could be called dating. The topics of our conversations were mainly about art, graphics, pictures, letters, typography… endless conversations and then here and there something else.

Soon after that came 1968 and you were still studying. What was the impact of that year's events on your university?

After 1968, there was obviously a lot of movement in studio leadership and among professors. Adolf Hoffmeister left the studio of animation and puppet films. He got his pension in 1970 when his request to extend his contract was rejected. His assistant Miloslav Jágr took over leadership of the studio.

So, they basically forced Adolf Hoffmeister to leave.

Yes, he was one of the victims of that horrible period. He got sick soon after that and died of a heart attack in 1973. I think his studio and the animation extension eventually moved to a higher floor in UMPRUM at the end of the '70s. Then even František Muzika left and his place was taken by his assistant Milan Hegar and then by Jan Solpera. Hedvika Vlková ended in the studio of fashion design and was replaced by Zdena Bauerová, and in 1970, Antonín Kybal, the founder of the studio of textile and tapestry, left. Professors who didn't agree with the 1968 invasion were fired and replaced by conforming trusted party members.

So František Muzika didn't supervise your master's thesis?

I don't remember anymore which thesis I did with who. I really don't. That school left a very small mark on me. A waste of seven years. I devoted most of that time to my dogs. And men. And so on. I had time to do things another way. It's a shame things didn't work there the way they do today, exchanges with foreign institutions, I missed more access to the world. It was a very closed institution for a very long time. If we don't mention the 1930s, that is, when renowned artists taught there and managed to impart something to the students. These days the situation there is different—fortunately.

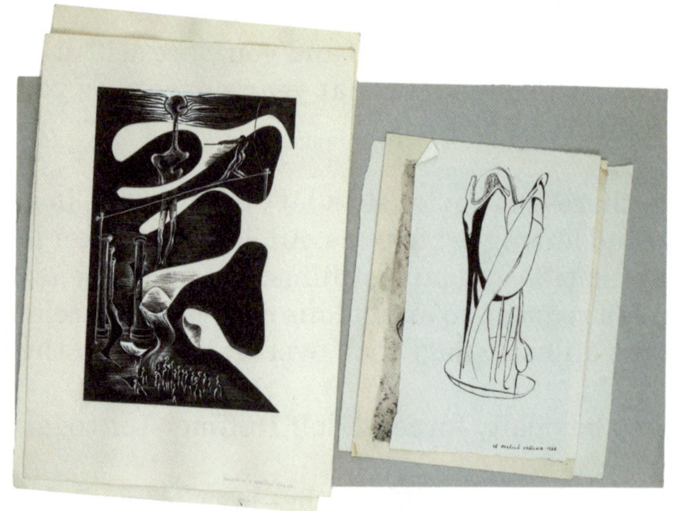

Sketches for Jan Tomeš, *Staré zahrady*, 1969,
František Muzika's Special Edition series (diploma thesis)

I found your diploma thesis. In it, you dealt with Jan Tomeš' book *Staré zahrady*. You accompanied his text with your characteristic lithographic illustrations. Why didn't you continue to illustrate?

                     Interview

That assignment was mandatory in the studio, I could only choose the author of the text and the illustration technique. In this case I chose offset as an experiment. I created the illustrations directly on the sensitive surface of the zinc-coated plate. The illustration's close connection to the text did not suit me very well, and that's why I didn't return to such projects.

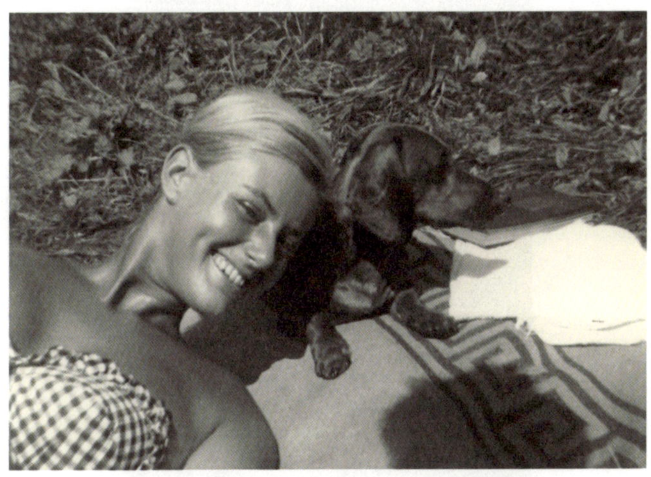
Istlerova in the Jizera Mountains
with the dachshund Sepl I, 1963

Tell me about the dogs that you've mentioned.

I had two dogs in a row. Dachshunds. It was the only type of dog my parents let me have. I didn't want a toy dog like a Pekinese, for example. I wasn't interested in those. I chose a dachshund, which is small but a hunting dog. I tried to train them both. They both had certificates from spring and autumn tests, badger and fox burrowing. I went through everything with them. Even to shows, so they were well-bred. They were dogs with papers and had to have external evaluation. We went by train to international dog shows in Brno. I also later participated in several graphic design biennials there. Same place—different purpose.

Instead of having studio consultations, you were going to dog shows?

Yes. And besides, the big international dog shows were always held at the end of June, and nothing was happening at school anymore then. Honestly, I enjoyed it more than school and it made more sense to me.

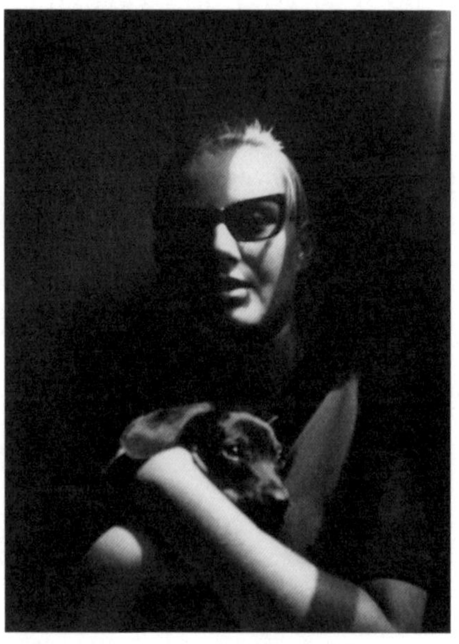

Istlerova in the Jizera Mountains
with the dachshund Sepl II, 1965

Going back to the fateful year of 1968—where were you in August of that year?

On August 12, 1968, me and Jiří Šuhájek, my classmate at UMPRUM and a student in the glass studio of Professor Stanislav Libenský, left for England. He convinced me that we would have a place to stay in London because his good friend Aury Shoa lived there. Aury really gave us a place to stay in the flat where he lived with his then-wife Myrna and two-year-old son Nahem, near the Westbourne Park tube station, at 69 Prince's Square. From this base, we took several trips to different corners of England and Scotland, traveled by hitchhiking or by bus, we lived in various bed-and-breakfasts available at the time, or with Aury's friends. On the evening of

                    Interview

August 20, we were approached on the street in Bristol by an elderly couple who wanted us to celebrate their anniversary with them and spend the night with them after dinner. Amazing, except that they woke us up at three in the morning to tell us that the Russians had invaded. Then there was a speedy return to London ... On the second day of the occupation, August 22, 1968, my parents and my dog left Prague for Switzerland to visit friends in Zurich. They wanted to wait and see how the situation at home developed. I flew to them from London in September. Their friends generously made available to us a house near Chexbres, in a beautiful landscape between Lake Geneva and the mountains. Mom flew from there to America because an exhibition of her drawings had been organized there. My dad and I went back to Prague at Christmas.

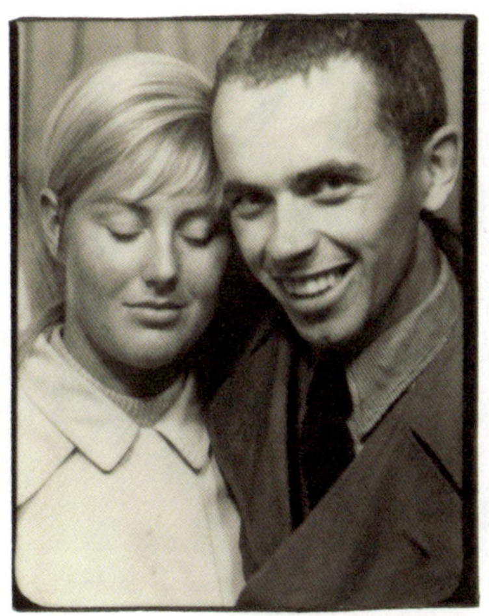

Clara Istlerová and Jiří Šuhájek,
August 13, 1968, in London

It was cold, there was snow everywhere. Ours was the only car headed in the direction of Czechoslovakia. I remember that we were sipping on a flask of some excellent cherry brandy on the way. When we drove across the border, the border guards just shook their heads in disbelief. Our car was packed to the ceiling. Dad was bringing paint and canvases home because he had made a little money in Switzerland by selling a few paintings. No one checked us at the border, no one asked us anything, they only looked at us in amazement.

Why did you come back?

Dad was unhappy in perfect Switzerland. He didn't have his pubs there, women ... Swiss society was too moderate for him; everything was calculated, predictable. He didn't like that. He couldn't paint well in such a calm place. He felt very uneasy. But Jiří Šuhájek stayed in London because he got the opportunity to study regularly at the Royal College of Art in the glass studio. I came back to Prague mainly to take care of the post-graduate program offered to me.

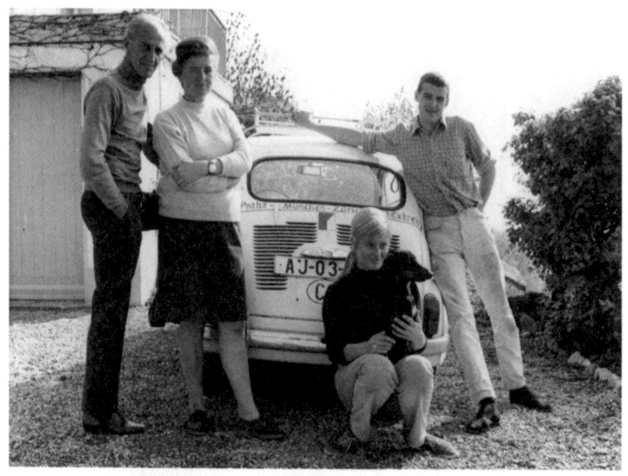
The Istler Family in Chexbres, Switzerland, 1968

And that's why you left again in 1969.

I graduated in 1969, and the school allowed me to take the last plane to America with my mother before our country's borders closed for good. I got a paper stating that I had graduated, which then allowed me to attend graduate school at the Central School of Arts and Design in London. The Prague school treated me very well for that time, but the overall situation wasn't good. Like the rest of society. People started behaving badly,

                    Interview

there was a stuffy atmosphere and it was a cruel time for many. My mom and I were in America for a full three months. Our hosts put us up in a former Kennedy summer home on a ranch they'd bought near Washington. They happened to see my mother's drawings—still lifes with flowers, drawn only in pencil á la the Dutch masters—at friends' houses in Switzerland, and as a result she was commissioned to decorate their kitchen with watercolors of vegetables. They told her there was no point in sending the pictures across the ocean, that it would be better to draw them on the spot in three months. They paid for our flights and our stay. We got some pocket money, which was absolutely wonderful to live on. In the cottage they assigned me a tiny corner above the former stables where I could draw and listen to music for days. It was three wonderful autumn months made more beautiful by an American named Gage Bailey. We met in a New York nightclub where my mother and I were invited for a drink. He heard there were two Czech girls there, so he came to see us. Probably also a bit under the influence of the mood that prevailed in the West after the invasion of "friendly" armies into Czechoslovakia. On the spot, he offered to marry me so that I could stay in America legally and travel freely. I reacted reluctantly to buy time. Later, when I was in London for my studies, he flew to see me and repeated his offer. He was an awfully nice man, probably too nice for me. I didn't appreciate it at the time.

And did you use your time in America to travel?

I was invited to go on trips from time to time. Like on a boat. What an experience! One guy, I think he was a journalist, had a big old two-masted sailboat that we took out to sea. But we got caught in a storm and I got seasick. I threw up, had diarrhea, and was totally exhausted. When I recovered, they took me to the glass-enclosed captain's cabin, where you could see beautifully how they (all experienced sailors) had to drive the bow of the boat perpendicular into the walls of the huge waves that were crashing in on us to keep us from capsizing. A wonderful experience. I wish you could experience that.

That would probably be too much adrenalin for me.

We had to stay on the high seas for three days. Anchor and wait for the sea to calm down because the waves would have smashed the boat on the rocks in the harbor.

And then from America you returned to London?

Yes. We found out that my grandmother was dying, and so my mom returned to Prague quickly. I packed my bags for London again. Most of the space was taken up by my gramophone records and graphic arts supplies. Otherwise, I took one pair of jeans, a gray sweater, a white shirt, a black turtleneck, underwear, and that was it. I don't think my wardrobe has changed much since then, except for the size.

And what was your life like in London?

There wasn't much money. I sold colorful crocheted vests at Portobello Market on weekends—the hippie era. There were also batik clothes and Indian dresses.

And did you also make them?

Yes, I crocheted them with Myrna, who I lived with. Her husband Aury Shoa's family owned textile shops where we used to go to sell. I was grateful for the little money I earned.

Did you like it in London at that time?

Hugely. It had only one flaw—they were Jewish and they went to their parents' house every Saturday for dinner and ritual bath. So, they made a warehouse out of their own bathroom. I did all my hygiene in the kitchen at the sink for washing dishes, or once a week in the public baths. That was the only unpleasant thing. And I didn't have any privacy either. I slept in a room that everyone had to walk through to get outside. Classic London houses with a couple of steps and windows that didn't open and



Interview

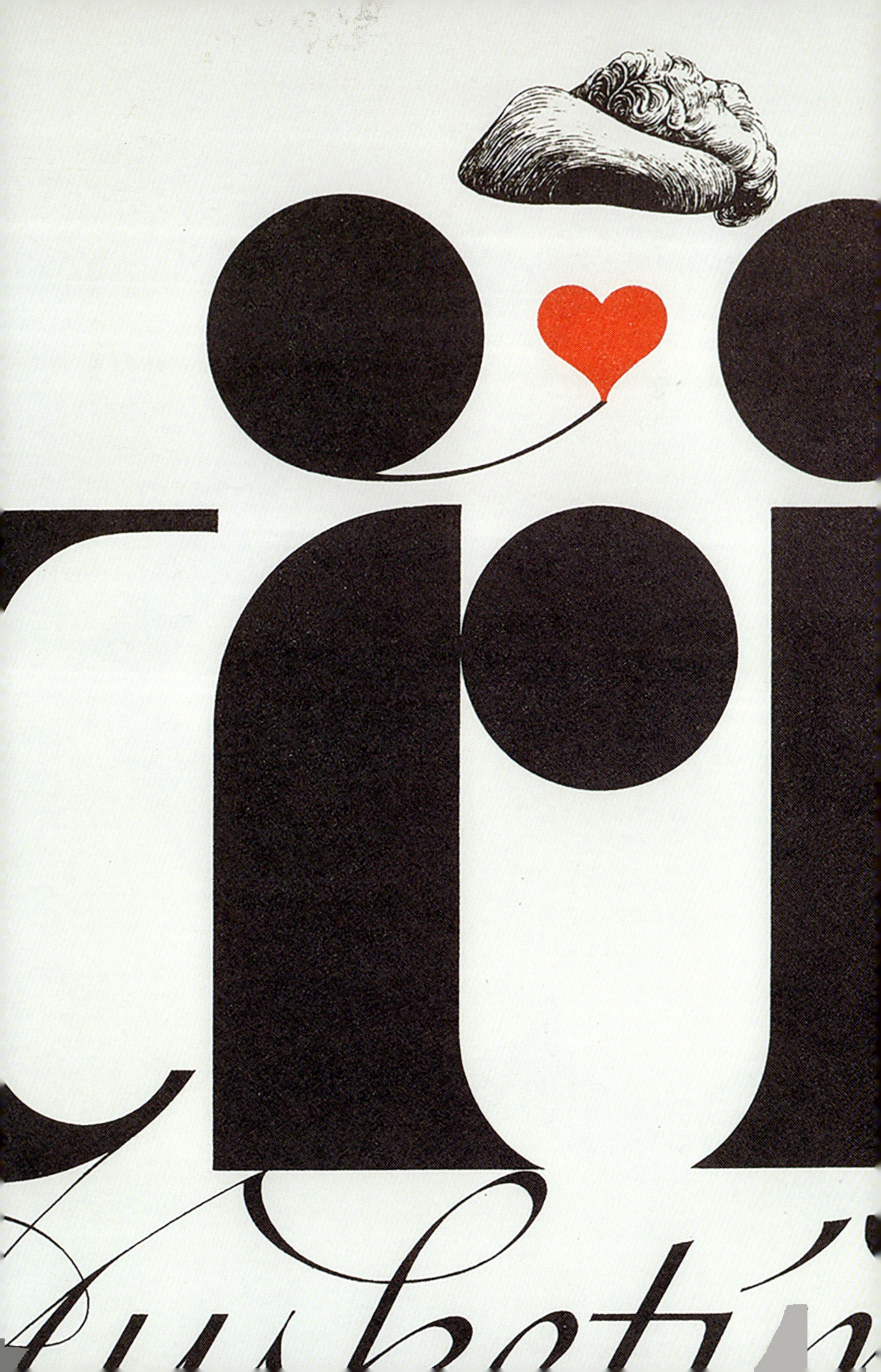

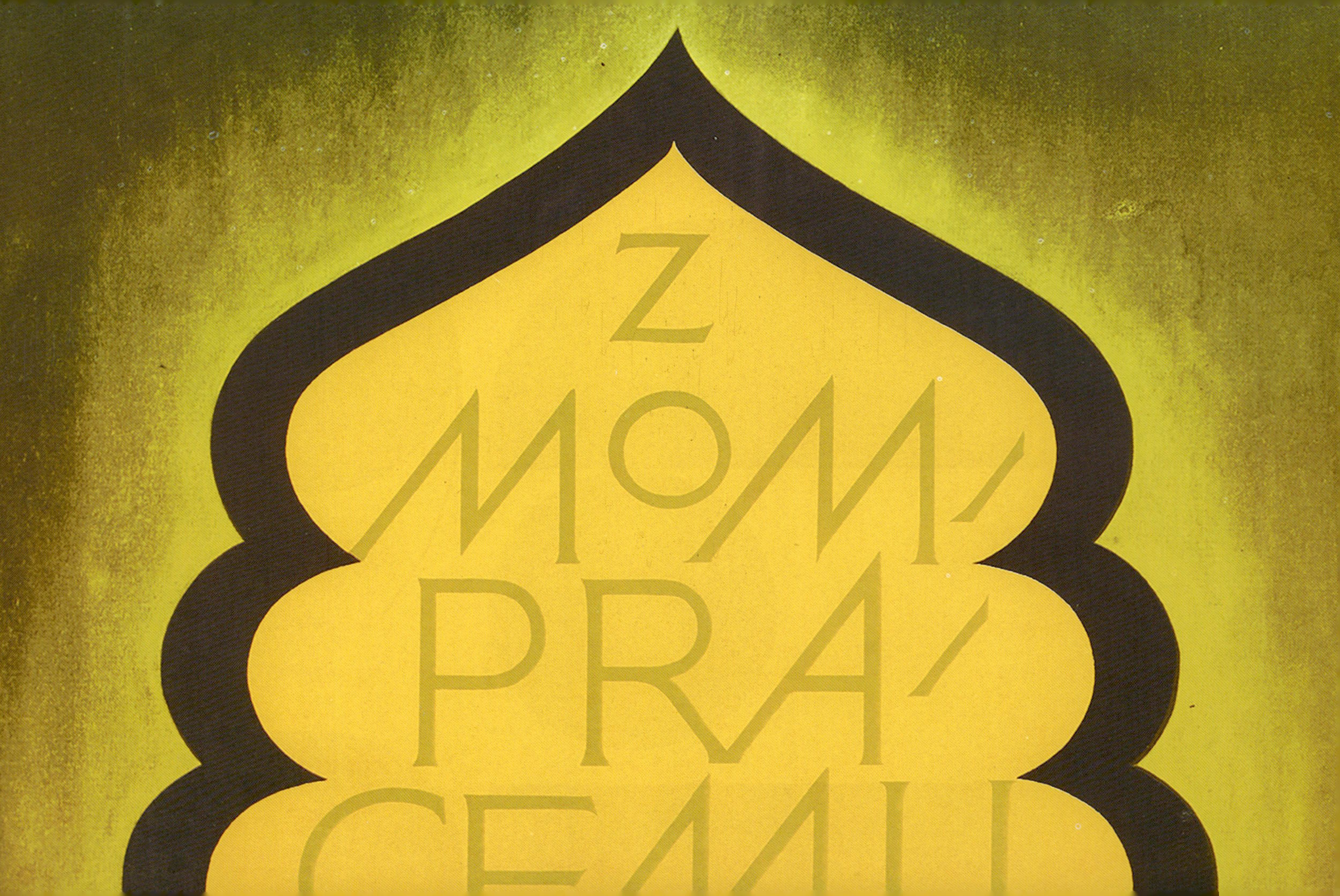

Z
MOM'
PRA'
CEMU

tygr

ITALSKÝ FILM
DOBRODRUŽNÝ
PŘÍBĚH MUŽŮ,
KTEŘÍ MSTILI
POROBENÍ
SVÉ ZEMĚ
REŽIE:
MARIO
SEQUI

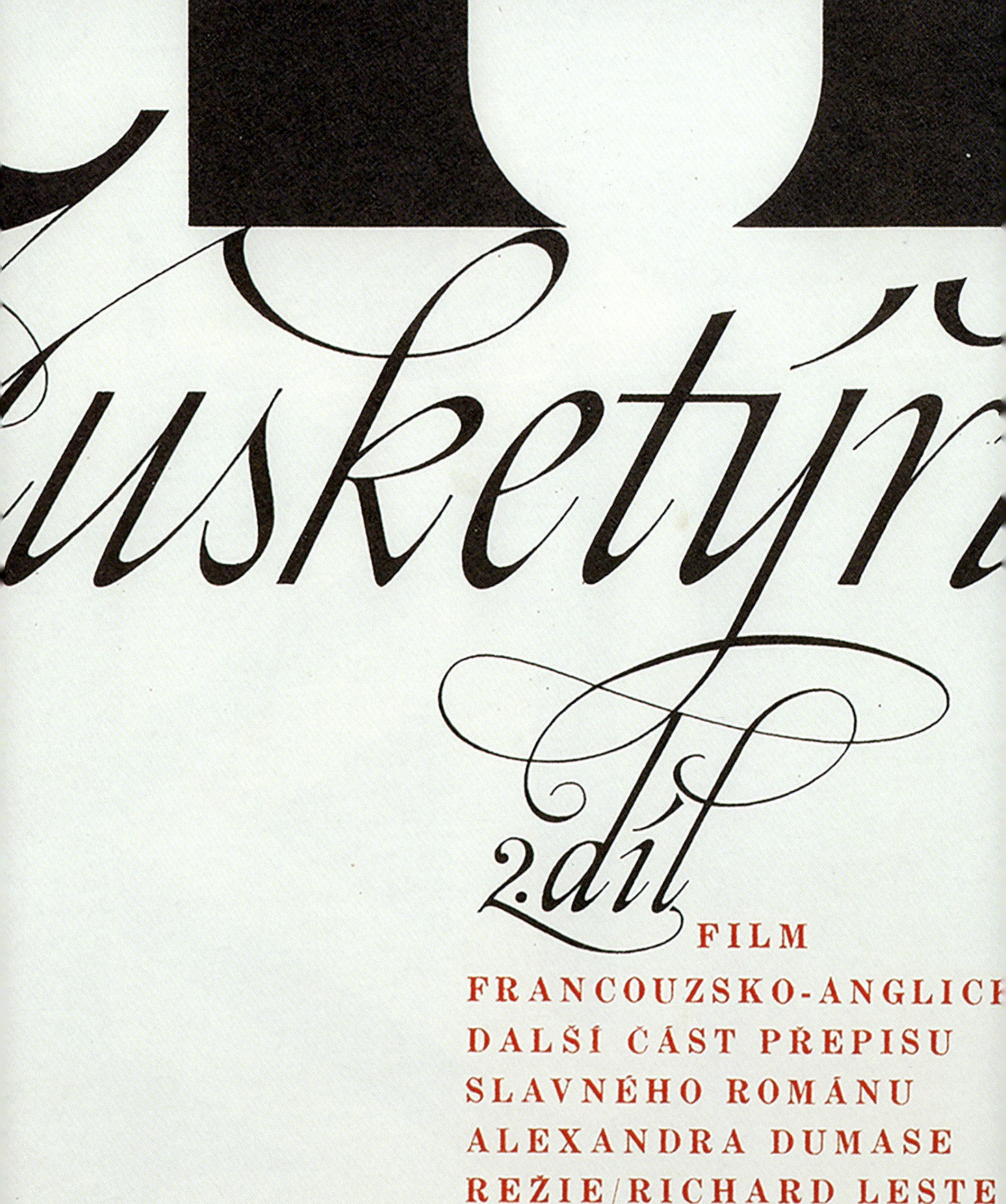
ušketýři
2.díl
FILM
FRANCOUZSKO-ANGLICK
DALŠÍ ČÁST PŘEPISU
SLAVNÉHO ROMÁNU
ALEXANDRA DUMASE
REŽIE/RICHARD LESTE

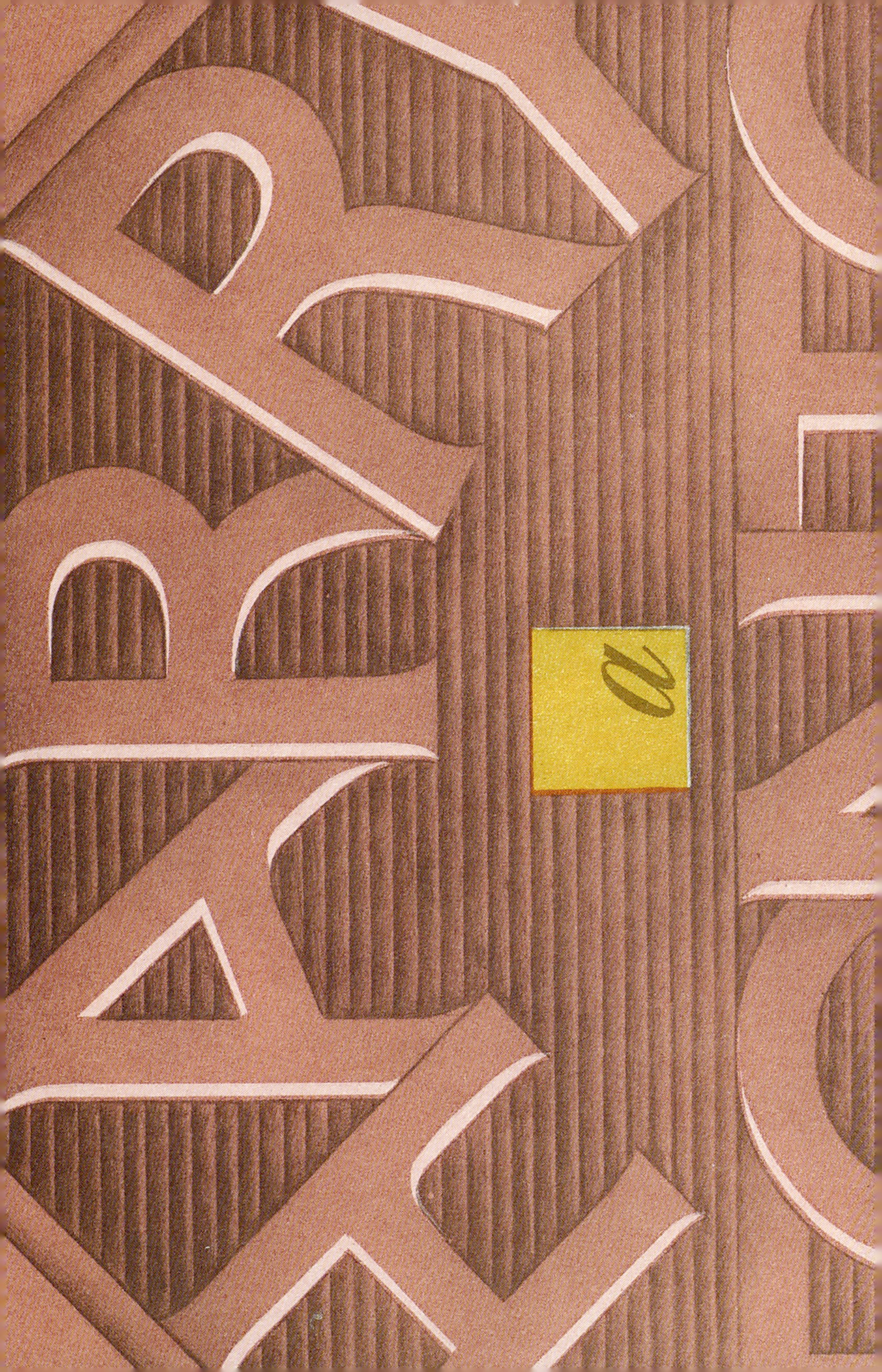

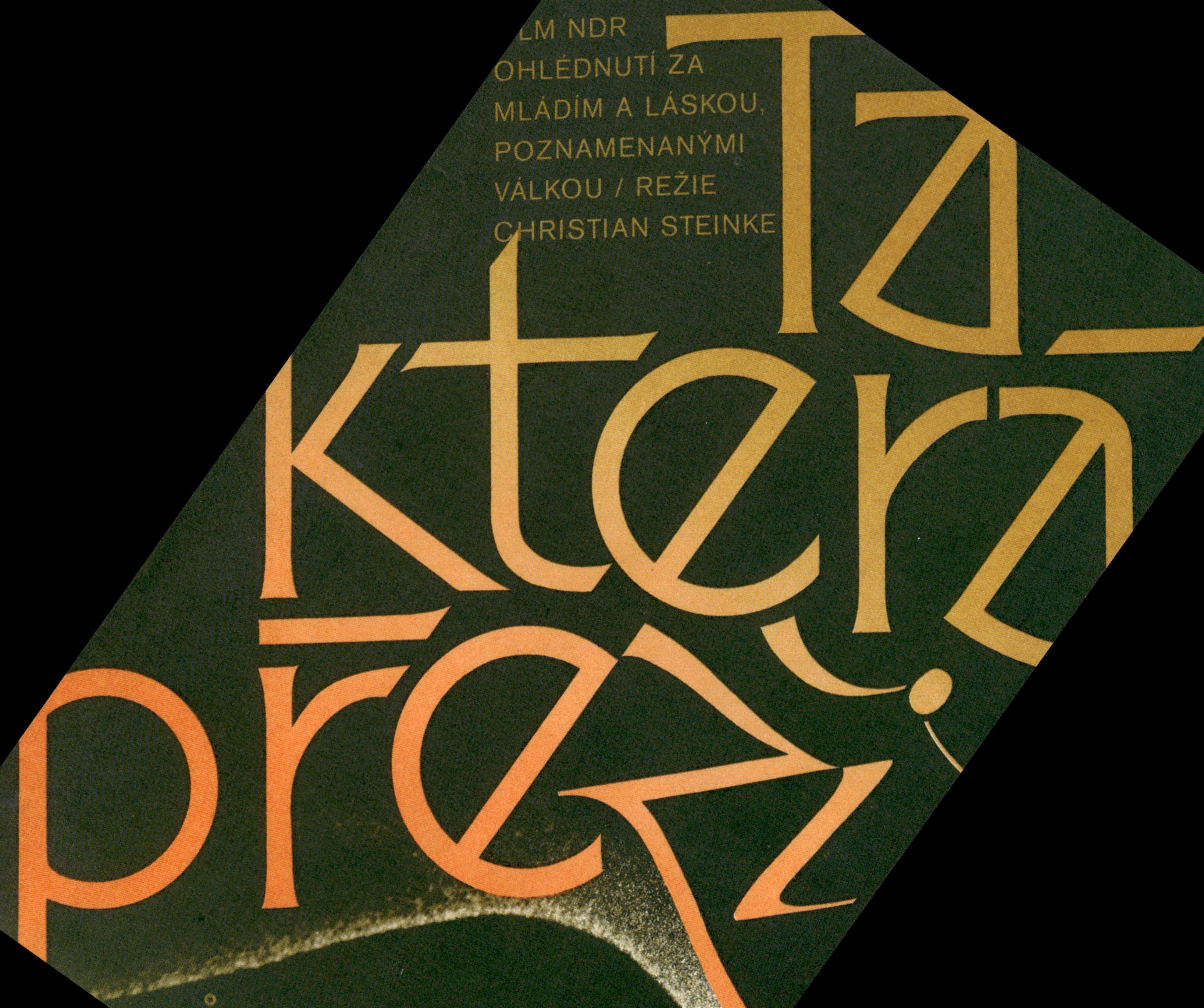
LM NDR
OHLÉDNUTÍ ZA
MLÁDÍM A LÁSKOU,
POZNAMENANÝMI
VÁLKOU / REŽIE
CHRISTIAN STEINKE
Ta-
která-
prez

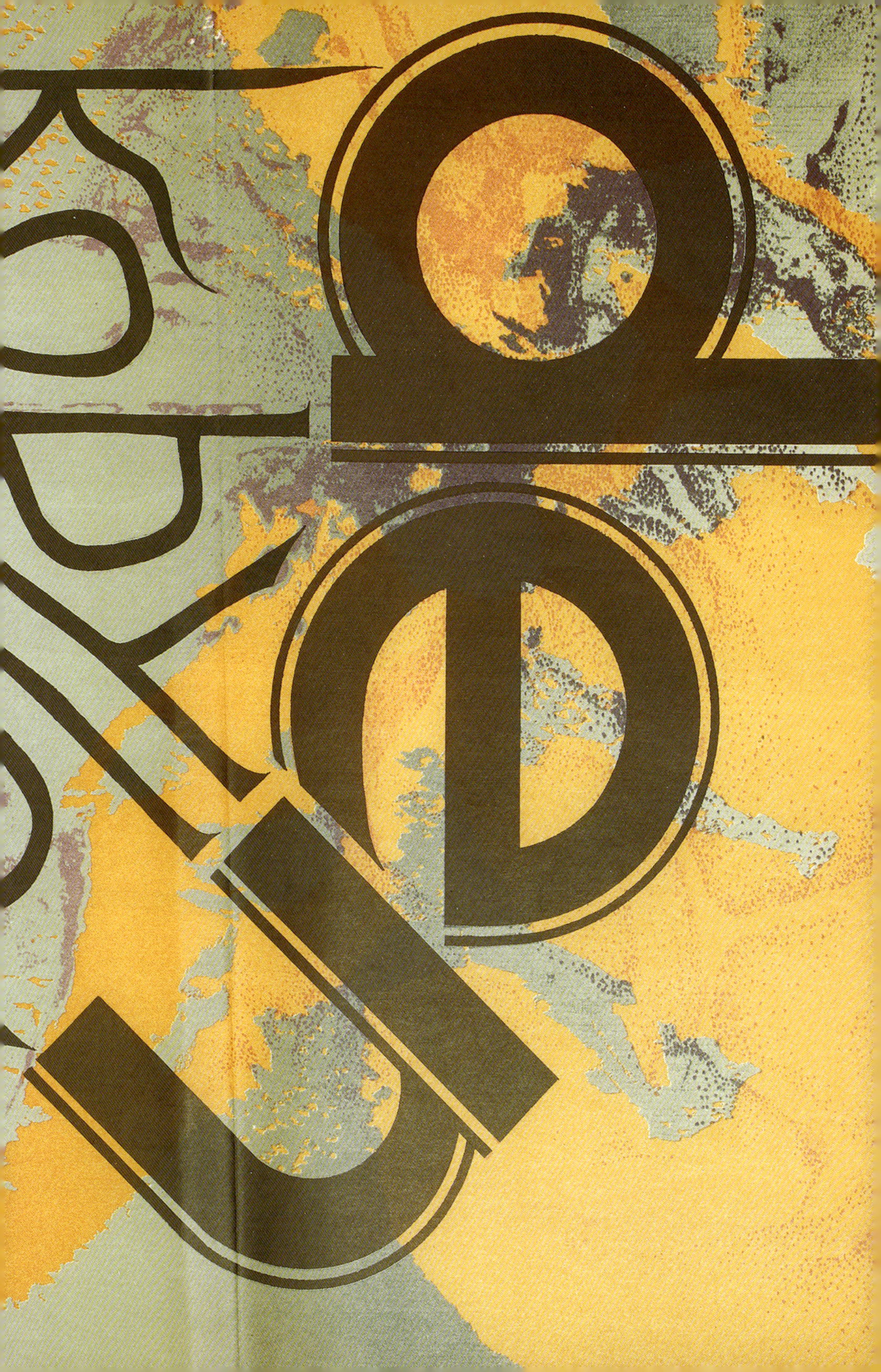

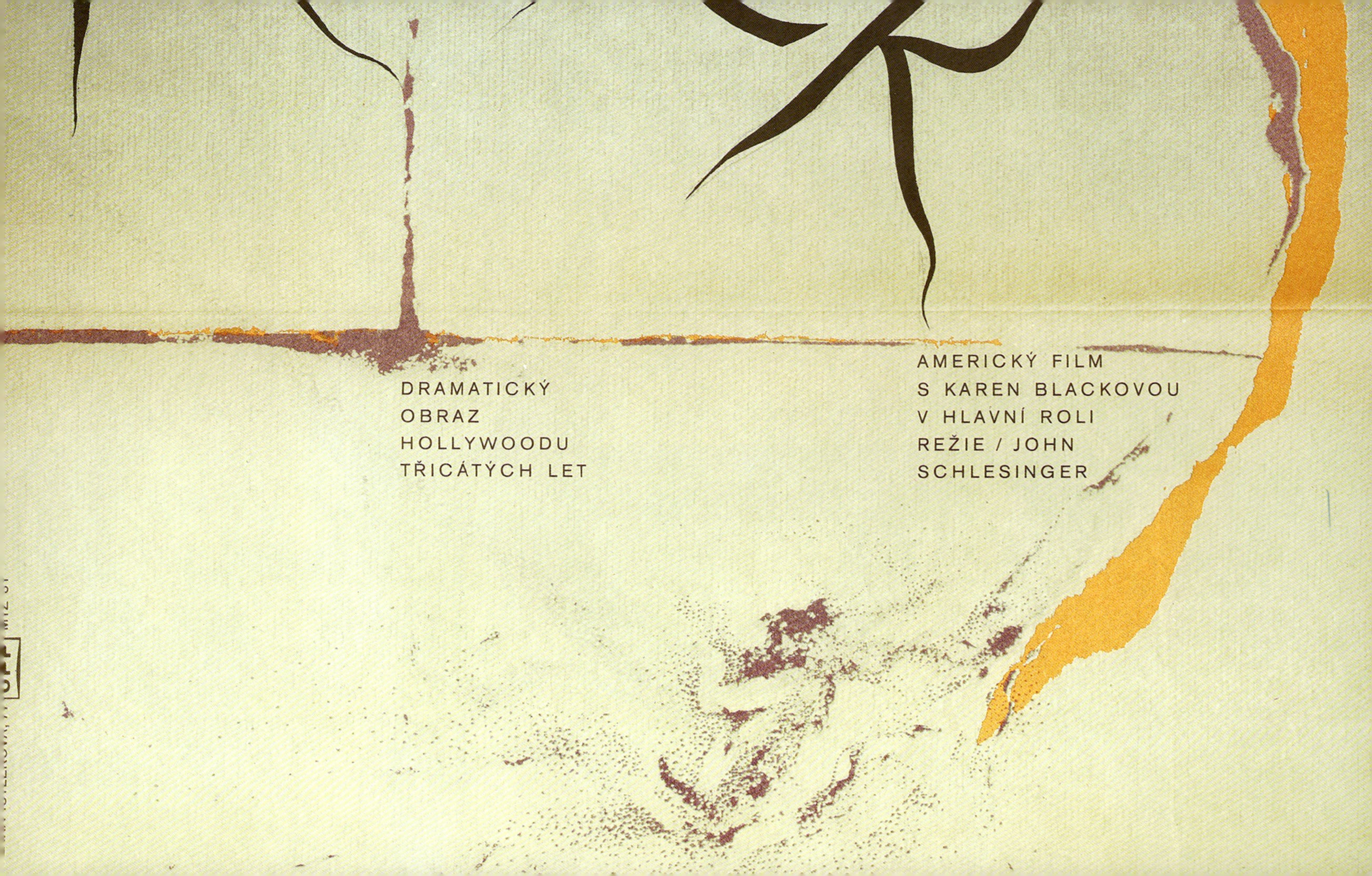

DRAMATICKÝ
OBRAZ
HOLLYWOODU
TŘICÁTÝCH LET

AMERICKÝ FILM
S KAREN BLACKOVOU
V HLAVNÍ ROLI
REŽIE / JOHN
SCHLESINGER

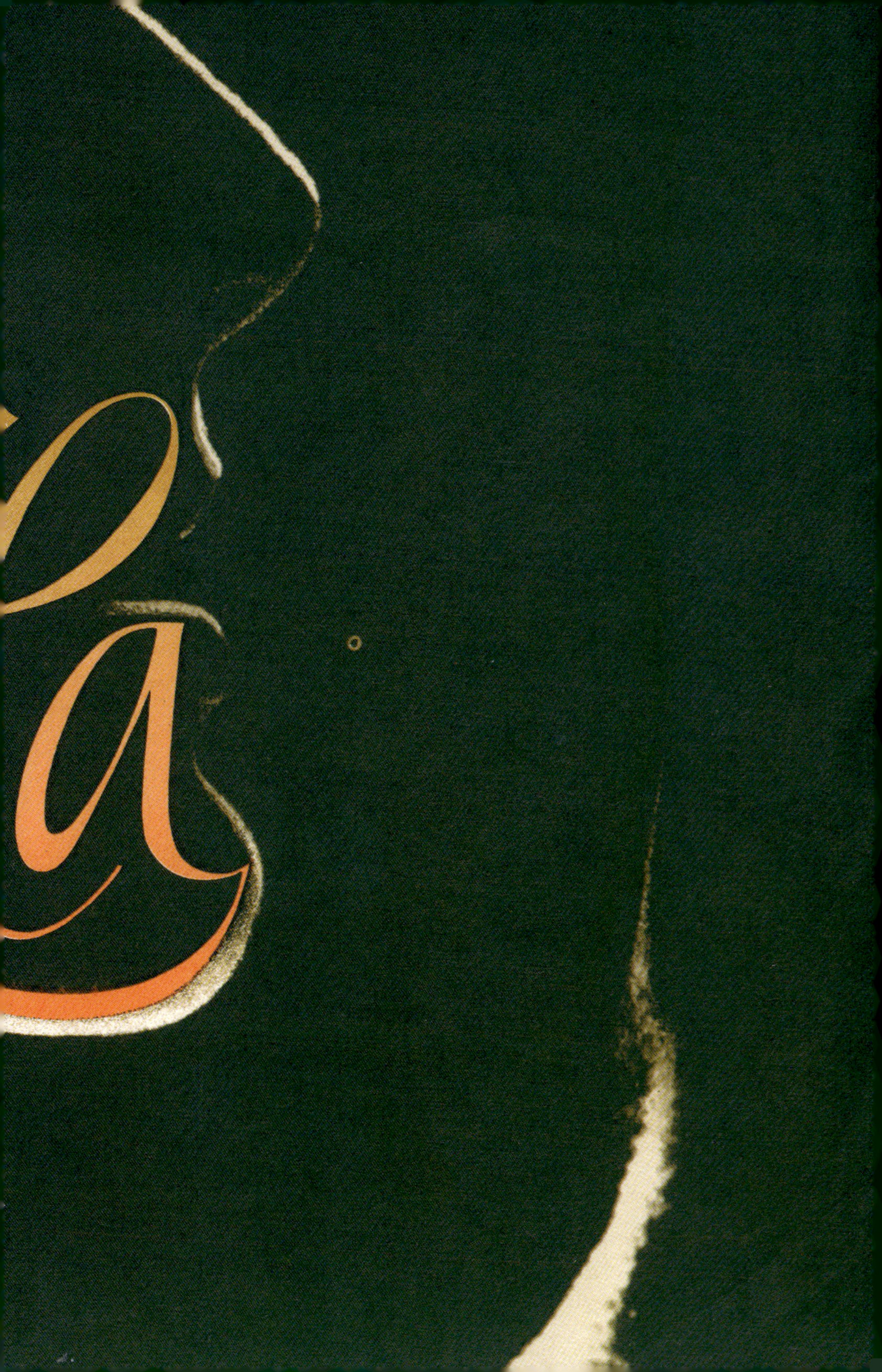

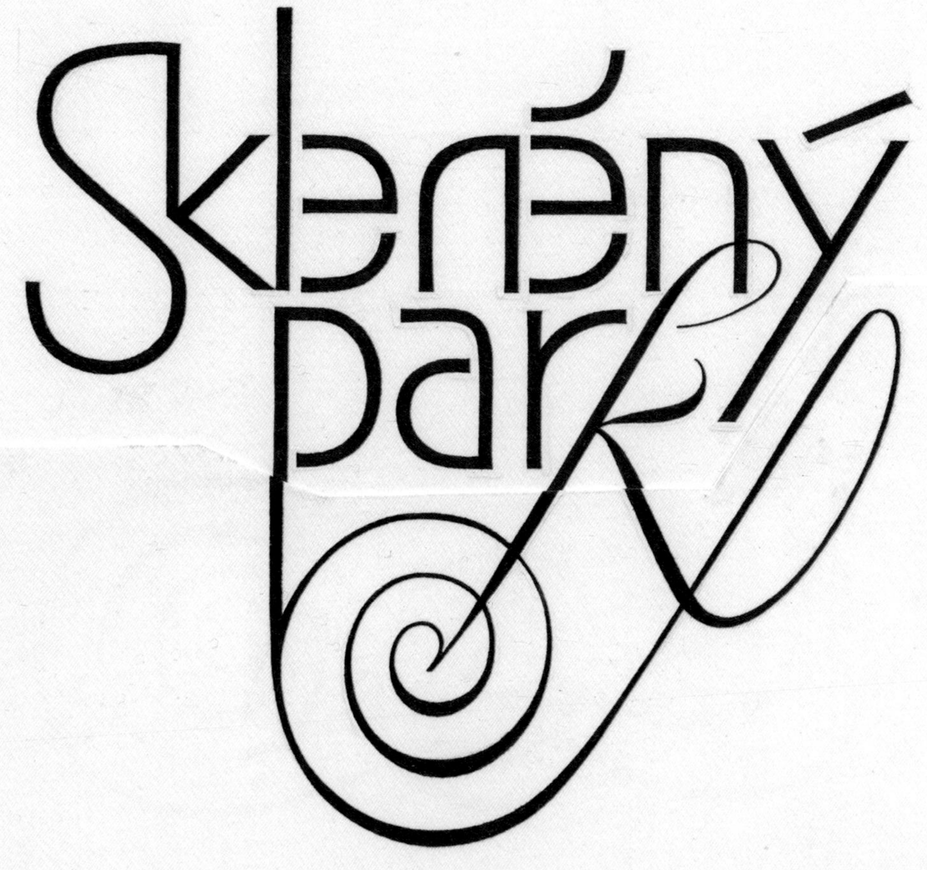


1)            1:1

2)        na šíři 35 mm

# Skleněný park

Oldřich Nouza

československý
spisovatel
Praha

ČESKÉ BÁSNĚ
ČESKOSLOVENSKÝ
SPISOVATEL
zelená
hetná

## CLARA ISTLE

(nar. 11. 12. 1

Studovala na
uměleckoprůmys
v ateliéru pro
a plakát prof.
solvovala v roc
je obálky a g
knižních edic
ství Čs. spisova
ké básně, výbě
Mladou frontu
Naše vojsko a
je filmové pla
(Památník nár
nictví, Pressfot
(Košické muzeu
ra Jilemnického
ské muzeum aj.
Samostatně vyst
ském muzeu v K
a v Ibize (197
nila se výstavy
ilustrace (1972)

Vodopád

A7-90603 = 2 lu

# oheň spěchá

IVAN SKÁLA

dalekostín
dalekosad
šíře 63 mm

were always drafty. I had a mattress on the floor that I had to roll up every morning and unroll again in the evening. It was just a little harder. The toilet was shared by several people and it was in the hallway. No luxury. But it's good to experience that because it makes you appreciate things you take for granted, and it's true that in more modest conditions you also have time to think about other things. Sometimes we would sit until two in the morning discussing philosophy and history.

V Praze, dne 6.1.1970

Ministerstvu školství a ministerstvu kultury

v Praze.

Vřele doporučuji, aby mé bývalé posluchačce Kláře Istlerové, která v letním semestru 1969 s vyznamenáním absolvovala studium na Vysoké škole uměleckoprůmyslové v Praze, bylo umožněno postgraduální studium na londýnské Central School of Art and Design, Department of Print-making.
Klára Istlerová byla od počátku svého studia na naší vysoké škole vzornou žačkou, vynikala zcela mimořádným nadáním, výtvarnou fantasií a kultivovaností a především bezpříkladnou pracovitostí.
Proto také ve všech disciplinách odborného i theoretického studia byla vždy nejlepší mezi nejlepšími, a bylo by tedy zajisté radno ji všestranně podpořit i v jejím dalším uměleckém vývoji. Domnívám se, že v jejím vlastním užším oboru, knižní grafice, by byly nocenitelným přínosem nové zkušenosti, které má příležitost získat v prostředí anglického knihtisku, svým záviděníhodným vysokým standardem pro českou polygrafickou tvorbu nepochybně příkladného. Byla by to pro ni tudíž navíc i skvělá kvalifikace pro její budoucí aspiranturu, s níž pro ni na naší vysoké škole napříště s určitostí počítáme.

S projevem dokonalé úcty

Prof. František Muzika
Vysoká škola uměleckoprůmyslová
v Praze.

František Muzika's recommendation letter from 1970, allowing Clara to study at the Central School of Arts and Design in London before Czechoslovakia's borders closed

## What was the focus of your postgraduate studies?

The focus of the school in London brought me back to freelance work for a while. But what was more important was the opportunity to live for some time in a culturally different environment. I was placed in the graphic design department, so I picked up where I left off with my dad. He taught me drypoint, woodcut, wood engraving, and lithography, and here I learned

aquatint and I printed. I was very interested in screen printing, and there was a well-equipped workshop. I learned that
technique there and printed some stuff that I actually brought
home with me. I never had the opportunity to return to it.
I then taught at a graphic design school in Prague for a while,
maybe because I felt the need to pass on the freedom of thinking of another world to the upcoming generation.

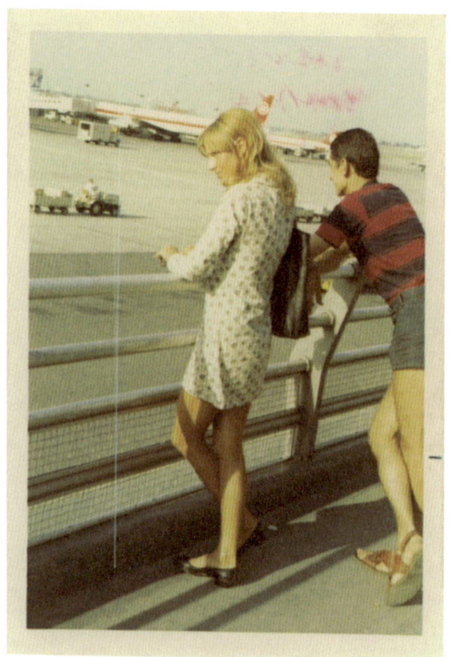

Clara Istlerová at the airport
Montreal, Canada, 1970

**Did you travel through England?**

Yes, but from London I was invited to Canada by an ex-boyfriend
of mine who emigrated after 1968. We dated for a while in Prague.
After breaking up with the bookbinder, I had a bit of a searching period. His name was Jiří Tichý, he was a chemistry graduate and got a great job in Montreal, where he taught at the
university. He wrote that he was doing great and asked me to
come. So, I spent a month in Montreal. Fortunately, he had



Interview

a dog. A beautiful blue-gray Kerry blue terrier. I walked him
every day on top of a park in Montreal. That month was a little
strange. There was only one interesting trip, which we took
with other Czech emigrants, to the Bear Lakes. We took a week-
long hike with tents and ventured into real wilderness.

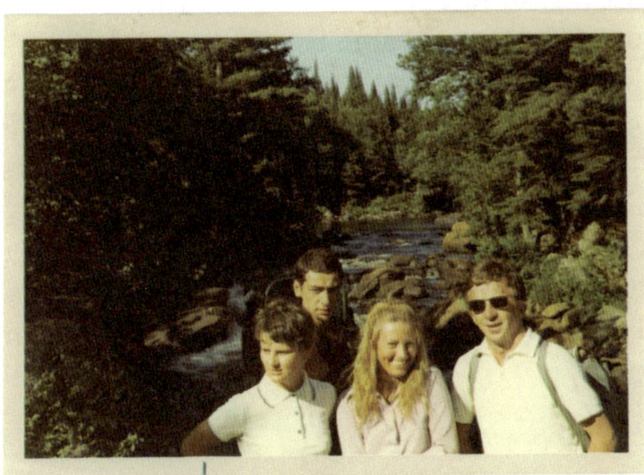

Clara Istlerová with friends
Park Mont Tremblant, Canada, 1970

Did you meet any bears?

One morning I went to the lake we were camping at to rinse off.
Suddenly, something moved on the other side. And it was a bear
in all its glory. I'm grateful I had the opportunity to experience
Canadian nature. It's amazing. Of course, our relationship went
to hell because he had this idea of a white-carpeted mansion,
and that wasn't for me.

You went straight back to Czechoslovakia from London?

Yes. In 1971, I returned to the Czech Republic and was immedi-
ately offered to teach at a graphic design school. A professor
in the department I had once myself attended was just finishing,
and I was offered the position. I started teaching, and at the
same time introduced a slightly different system of instruction
at the school. I tried to have students try designs and realizations

in collaboration with businesses, such as designs for wrapping paper or wallpaper, in addition to academic assignments. This kind of practice is now common at UMPRUM, but it was new then. And I was lucky to have talented students. I remember this period very fondly. Then, in 1972, I married Jiří Šuhájek. Actually, for the second time, because we had our first wedding in 1970 at a London registry office. But Czech authorities didn't recognize that marriage. So, Jirka said, "Let's get married in a little church!" We got married at St. Mary Magdalene in Česká Lípa. And at the end of the summer of 1973, when I was with the students on a hop harvest brigade, I started to feel strange. I was pregnant. So, at the end of January 1974, I slowly concluded my teaching because in March I went into labor and Marijánka was born. But I worked two years at the school. Then exactly a year later, on the same date, my son Matej was born.

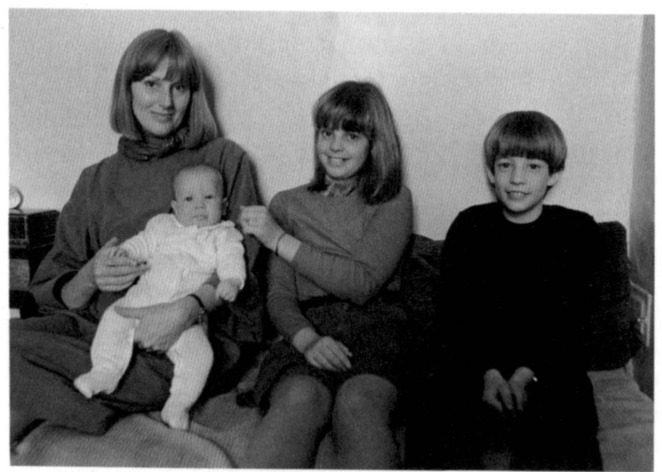

Clara Istlerová with Jan, Mariana, and Matěj
Karlín, Prague, 1984

But you eventually had three children.

Ten years later, in 1983, I had already been divorced for five years, my second son, Jan, was born. I was forty and a single mother.

                     Interview

How did you manage work at the same time as parenting?

I quit teaching and went on maternity leave. But I kept working. Freelancing made it possible. I did calligraphy for the Jewish Museum exhibitions, because at that time there were no digital printing possibilities. Actually, right after I came back from England, apart from teaching at the graphic design school full time, I worked with publishers Odeon, Československý spisovatel, Vyšehrad, Mlada fronta, and others. I designed whole series and individual books. Around 1977, I also got the opportunity to do film posters. Of course, with two small children, I would never have done so much work without the generous help of my mother.

Still, you were one of the few who managed to establish yourself in a field that until recently was the domain of men. When do you think that changed?

Let's talk about the nineteenth century, at the end of which we had Zdena Braunerová, the only woman to take up typography. The twentieth century, with its new conception of the role of women, also brought new possibilities in this field. The technical preparation of books for printing moved from the typesetting workshop to an office equipped with computers. Of course, this made it easier for women to participate in the profession and have a family.

But then you still weren't working in an office equipped with a computer. What did your working environment look like?

A table, a large board supported by books, and that was all. And an ordinary chair.

Music?

I didn't play music when the children were very little. I was even doing some calligraphy at the time—the large handmade papers had to be prelined with pencil first, and I wrote the texts in that grid. I calligraphed continuously between breastfeeding.

Did you work on anything else at home besides calligraphy?

I worked on books, design proposals, and planning entire editions. Back then, the job of a graphic designer-typographer was completely different. You would lay out the page grid, mark up the manuscript and front matter, and design the cover and binding. The typeset book, mostly monotype typesetting, came back as galley proofs in column, which I then cut and glued into a mock-up of the publication. At first, phototypesetting wasn't accessible to me, as there was only one location in Prague where it could be done. Rostislav Vaněk used it because he was doing many more things than I was. He designed graphics for Crystalex, cooperated with agencies that promoted our goods abroad. He introduced me to phototypesetting. But at that time, I was also in contact with Honza Malý, a photographer. I had printed alphabets, which he photographed and reproduced. I cut out the letters with a knife and glued them on white cardboard.

But it was just the name of the author and the title of the book. This he then rephotographed and enlarged to different sizes, which I continued to work with. At that time, apart from the color designs, black-and-white 1:1 drawings of the title page, cover, and binding were still being submitted to the publisher for reproduction. You had to think very carefully about what typeface to use. Of course, I've easily sometimes put a thick grotesque as a single letter in between a narrow antiqua, because in the folding and gluing, in the playing, you can do that kind of variation. But thanks to this somewhat complicated photographic phase, I came up with many tricks which of course you can now do playfully on the computer. When the letters were enlarged in a conventional enlarger, special effects were created by not having to completely develop the copy, for example. Something remained gray, something deep black. This is how I experimented with Honza, who gave me a lot of time. The relationship with an artisan, I would say, always marks



Interview

you. It enriches you with the dimension of his craft, you get to
know a different material. I know that if it weren't for his profession, I would never have figured some things out, and very
different books would have been made.

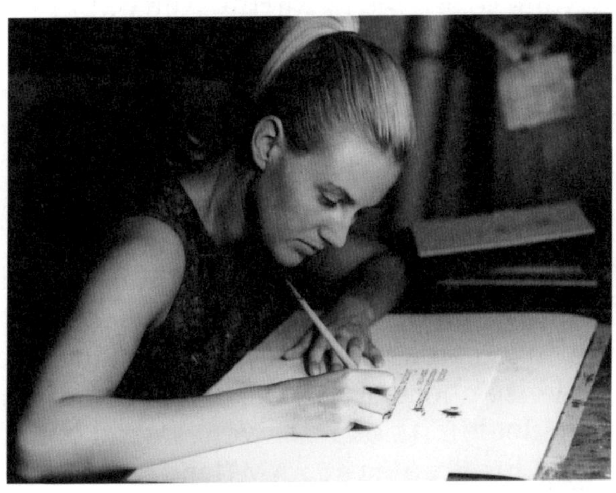

Clara Istlerová at work, 1976

Did Jiří Šuhájek influence you similarly?

Jiří was a glassmaker and enriched me with knowledge of
England and two children. And the experience of living with
a man in the same household. Because otherwise, my relations
with men were a bit random. Either for dinner or for work.
I experienced close cohabitation first with Jiří Šuhájek and
then later with Honza Malý, the father of my second son, and
even later with Karel Hvížďala. These are experiences ... not
as uplifting as work, but actually, if you avoid it, consciously
or unconsciously, you might be missing something at the end
of your life. Or not feel fully fulfilled. It's the only way to know
people's character and to be able to judge it better. If you don't
live body to body with someone, you'll never get there. But you
can, and I think you must keep your inner freedom even when
you live with someone.

How did you meet Honza Malý?

When I was teaching at the graphic design school he was a student ten years younger than me, and I was twenty-seven. He came to my classroom to get help selecting work for final exams. We also consulted the adjustments of his photographs. And then he came more and more often. When I got pregnant and had little kids, he came to see me in Karlín. And out of that, in time, a friendship developed … Even before I got divorced in 1978, we were still seeing each other, going out for dinner, for wine. That's where the later collaboration on the letters came from.

Did he ever give you advice on typesetting?

Absolutely. I certainly wouldn't have thought of a black-and-white edition for Československý spisovatel or Vyšehrad if we hadn't made variously sized enlargements of the glued letters. Thus, the black-and-white photograph was created, and in the end it was the most ideal in its expressiveness and clarity. When Honza continued his studies at FAMU, he consulted me on his semester papers. We influenced each other quite a lot.

How long did you live together?

Almost twenty years, until I met Karel Hvížďala. He called me in June 1997 and said he wanted me to edit his book. We knew each other from the time of the competition for the logo of *Týden* magazine, which he founded in 1993. And I said, "Yes, we can meet, but I'm on a break for two months, I'm going out with my kids. We'll call each other in the autumn." He was patient and didn't get anyone else. We met in September. In fact, it all began with this one book, *Výslech revolucionářů roku '89* (Interrogation of the Revolutionaries of '89). He was divorced at the time, I was long divorced. So, first dinners, concerts, theater, that kind of thing … I started to drift away from Honza.

Did you and Honza Malý ever consider getting married?

No, and we never said a word about it. I didn't even consider it important, and I still believe that it's better to stay unbound.

I don't think it has to be a problem for the kids as long as you speak with them openly about it. I think getting married only so everyone has the same last name is dumb. I was also always thinking about how he's ten years younger and that he'd meet some beauty one day.

But that didn't happen.

He found a girlfriend after I started the relationship with Karel, but I guess she was too serious for him. He was used to my approach, not being attached. He broke up with her in the end, unfortunately.

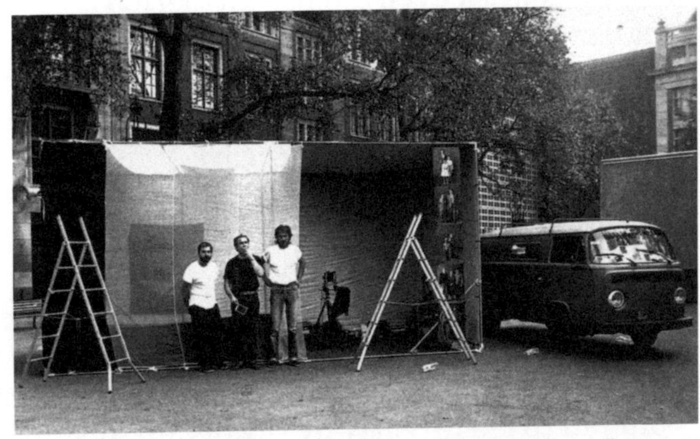

Ivan Lutterer, Jan Malý, and Jiří Poláček during *Český člověk* (The Czech Person), photographing everyday people in a makeshift studio, 1982

Honza Malý worked on *Český člověk* during the time you were together, right?

Yes. It was a great project and involved three photographers. Now Honza Malý and Jiří Poláček are dead, and Ivan Lutterer is dead, too. Lutterer ended up in America, where he went to do an internship at a university that gave him a scholarship to learn how to better restore old photographs. That interested him. And suddenly the announcement came that he was dead, that he had committed suicide. Neither Jiří Poláček nor Honza

Malý could believe it. It was very suspicious. Either there was some kind of nasty pressure on him, or it was possible that America was too harsh for him. God knows what happened there. Ivan was a strange man, a recluse, very withdrawn. This tragedy marked the boys, both Honza Malý and Jiří Poláček. They only went to take pictures one more time.

Were you a part of the *Český člověk* project?

No, I only did the cover of the publication, and I helped them choose photos and determine their sequence in the book. It took a long time because they had such a huge number of photos.

You did well in work even during the period of normalization?

I was lucky. During those stupid 1970s that everyone complains about, I found myself with really nice work.

Did you do mostly book design?

No, also exhibition catalogues. Karel Teige, the Ra Group, Devětsil. I got into work I wouldn't get into now. There's no such thing as exhibitions anymore. The graphic design of catalogues was always offered to me directly by the organizing institution. There were no design competitions back then. In the case of the Devětsil exhibition, which traveled from Prague to Brno, apart from the catalogue and the poster, I was partly involved in the installation. The basic composition on the cover of the catalogue also appeared on the poster in larger scale on a large panel in the entrance of the gallery. I didn't do any other exhibition installations. The exception was perhaps the collaboration with the Jewish Museum, for whose exhibitions I calligraphed both the large accompanying texts and the labels for the exhibits.

Is there any difference for you between the graphic design of books and catalogues?

                                   Interview

In the case of catalogues with historical content, the work is more or less defined by the chronology of the pictorial material. But I don't think this deprives you of the joy of creation. If a book—fiction or interviews—is accompanied by photographs, these should become an integral part of the whole typography of the book. The aim is to make the book look like an object—a whole in which the photographs wouldn't be merely illustration, an accompaniment, but an integral part of it—compositionally and in color.

How do you think about the text of a book
you are designing?

It is very important to focus on the subject matter as much as possible and to achieve the strongest possible effect in the greatest possible contrast of formal means. The form conditions the content. The form itself is important, because it provides a space to play out extreme contexts. There's a lot to be gained from the extreme, but the final solution is preceded by long reflection. It's necessary to think a lot first, to test—and then to design.

That sounds like pure formalism.

Yes, I consider myself a formalist. I'm fascinated by the contrast of white space and typesetting, free and closed shapes, light and shadow. I am attracted to a clear form that can create a spark. It's a great game, but always limited by the input: the format, the illustrations, especially if it's a children's book. When designing children's books, it was ideal to work with the illustrator in advance, before their work began.

Did you also meet with colleagues from your industry
in your spare time?

We had a group called Typo&. It was active and exhibited extensively from 1974. But I didn't participate in exhibitions until 1982. Here and abroad. If you can call Bulgaria or Russia "abroad"—at that time the Soviet Union was on the threshold of change.

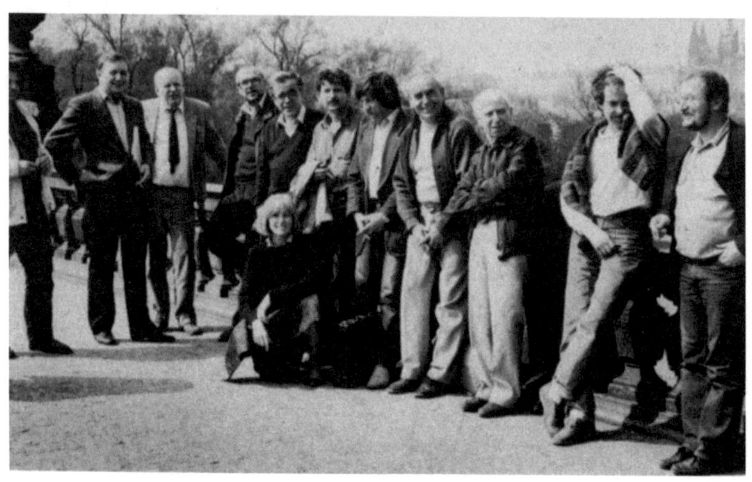

Typo& group on the Legions Bridge in Prague, 1989, archive of Alan Záruba

Under what circumstances and with what aim was the group founded?

We started from a situation in which, as an individual, you could hardly exhibit or promote anything. And so we joined forces. Most of us were graduates of graphic arts schools and UMPRUM, but we were joined by graphic designers from the older generation, such as Hlavsa or Jiří Rathauský, the creator of typefaces for the Prague metro, and from the 1990s onward, Professor Zdeněk Ziegler. Behind our activity was a kind of counterpressure on the situation and atmosphere that prevailed at that time. We borrowed and exchanged magazines and books that were hard to find. Nothing much came here from abroad in an official way. Those of us who had the opportunity to go to the West brought back inspiring printed matter. We even managed to order what was then, for us, an interesting avant-garde typographic newspaper, *U & lc* [a prominent typographic periodical founded in 1973], directly from a publisher in America.



Interview

Can you remember any titles?

*Graphis*, some issues of which specialized in book graphics, posters, or photography, and *Novum*. Or the yearly or biannual thick anthologies like *Art Directors Annual*. We got those occasionally. Of course, there was some bad stuff too, but we could get some sense of what was being done across the border, where the world of applied and book typography, photography, and illustration was going. Strangely enough, now that you have the opportunity to catch up on everything and go anywhere, you don't really think much about it.

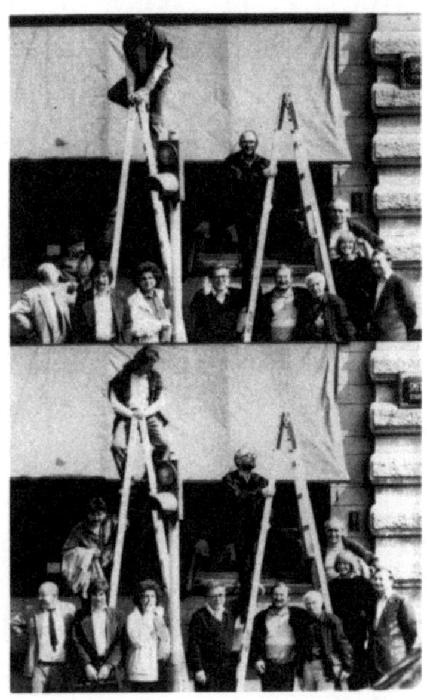

Typo& group, 1989,
archive of Alan Záruba

When I look at the work of Jan Solpera and Rostislav Vaněk, I think there's a lot of American influence (e.g., Herb Lubalin). In your work, there's more of a trace of avant-garde graphic design.

I, of course, looked at the Bauhaus and what came out of it. Although I also did cartoonish typefaces and actually started out with that, thanks to calligraphy. But that was brief, thanks to Honza Malý, who photographed and enlarged other fonts for me—in many copies, for example, old grotesques and antiquas from the 1920s and 1930s, which I then I experimented with. The resulting compositions were more in the spirit of the 1930s avant-garde than the 1980s.

And how did you get into film posters?

Zdeněk Ziegler[8] offered me the chance to design film posters in 1977 and recommended me to Czechoslovak Film. I remember that three different "definitives" had to be submitted to the commission for reproduction, i.e., color designs in A3 format. In those days, every work that was to be realized and paid for by the commissioner had to go to the so-called art approval committee at the Mánes building[9]—six to ten people, some of whom may never have held a pencil in their lives.

What did they decide?

They handled background screening, selection, and fees.

Even when they weren't from the field?

It was all very strange. But I was lucky, I never had any problems. Sometimes, on the other hand, when I went in with a fee for the layout for a catalogue, they said, "But that's not enough, you've made the whole layout with pictures and you're asking for five thousand." And they gave me a raise. And at that time five thousand was quite a lot. And they put a stamp on it. The stamp was the most important thing. The Union of Czechoslovak Visual Artists (SČVU) played quite an important role in the life of a visual artist of that time. It was—in a figurative sense—our employer and trade union organization, it took care of taxes and health insurance. It also had ancillary offices— the Czech Fine Arts Fund and the Works and Art Center under it. Zdeněk Ziegler sometimes sat on the committee, which was an advantage. There were about fifty graphic designers and architects waiting in the lobby. It took a whole morning to get a turn, just to get a stamp, without which the work would go in the trash. Terrible system. But he waved when he saw me there: "Come, come, Istlerová ..."

What have you tried besides designing posters?

Working with an architect. For example, I designed the signs for the Postal Newspaper Service (PNS), which were small daily newspaper shops, always located in very small spaces. They usually had banners on the façade of the building, and the sign had to be approved by an architectural committee, which decided whether it was appropriately placed and whether it disturbed the façade. I could have used any type of font. But it was necessary to first take a photograph of the building, its façade, and the entrance to the store, including part of the street. I then glued my design onto a black-and-white enlargement backed with cardboard. But I didn't do much of that kind of work, I didn't enjoy it.

Going back to Typo&. Did the exhibitions you held have a common theme or was it more about promoting your own work abroad?

We were just displaying our work. Some members were more focused on logos, such as Rostislav Vaněk, Milan Jaroš, or Aleš Najbrt. I didn't do logos, so I didn't participate in as many competitions as these graphic designers, who also designed orientation systems and manuals for logotypes. I exhibited completed books or black-and-white enlargements of designs and type compositions. We prepared and installed the exhibitions ourselves. We had the designs and the resulting works enlarged by well-known photographers. Later, when the quality was better, we used Xerox. Those who had printed books would exhibit them unfolded or as whole print sheets that we took from the printer. Our exhibitions were of interest to the public not only the professional public—and some became traveling exhibitions. When we were finished, we hid the semifinished pieces—paper boards with photographs or book covers glued on—and if there was interest, they were displayed elsewhere. One of us always had to travel with the materials to oversee the organization of the installation. For example, I spent a week in St. Petersburg in this way. I visited the Hermitage and experienced the city in the relaxed times of Gorbachev's perestroika. The woman in charge of the exhibition took me to Catherine the Great's residence. In general, St. Petersburg, with its classical buildings and bridges, is worth seeing. It was only November, but it was already cold and snowing. There was an atmosphere of a true Russian winter, as one knew it from literature.

How did you experience the November days of 1989?[19]

They were beautifully wild. In the Mánes building, the strike committee always gave us our tasks in the morning, they told us who was going where. Then we went in pairs around the factories and businesses in Prague to discuss and mobilize people.

What did you mobilize them for?

Mainly to go on a general strike. We went to the factories where we knew the working class could either remain completely on the sidelines or disagree with the changes that were coming. We persuaded them. It was interesting.

Did you also encounter disagreement?

I don't remember anyone throwing us out or not wanting to talk to us.

And who were you paired with?

I usually went with Jiří Žáček, my former classmate from graphic design school. I knew the area around Karlín, so I was assigned to this district. I remember that in Žižkov, in the snow and mud, we visited, for example, a machine tool company where they offered us hot tea.

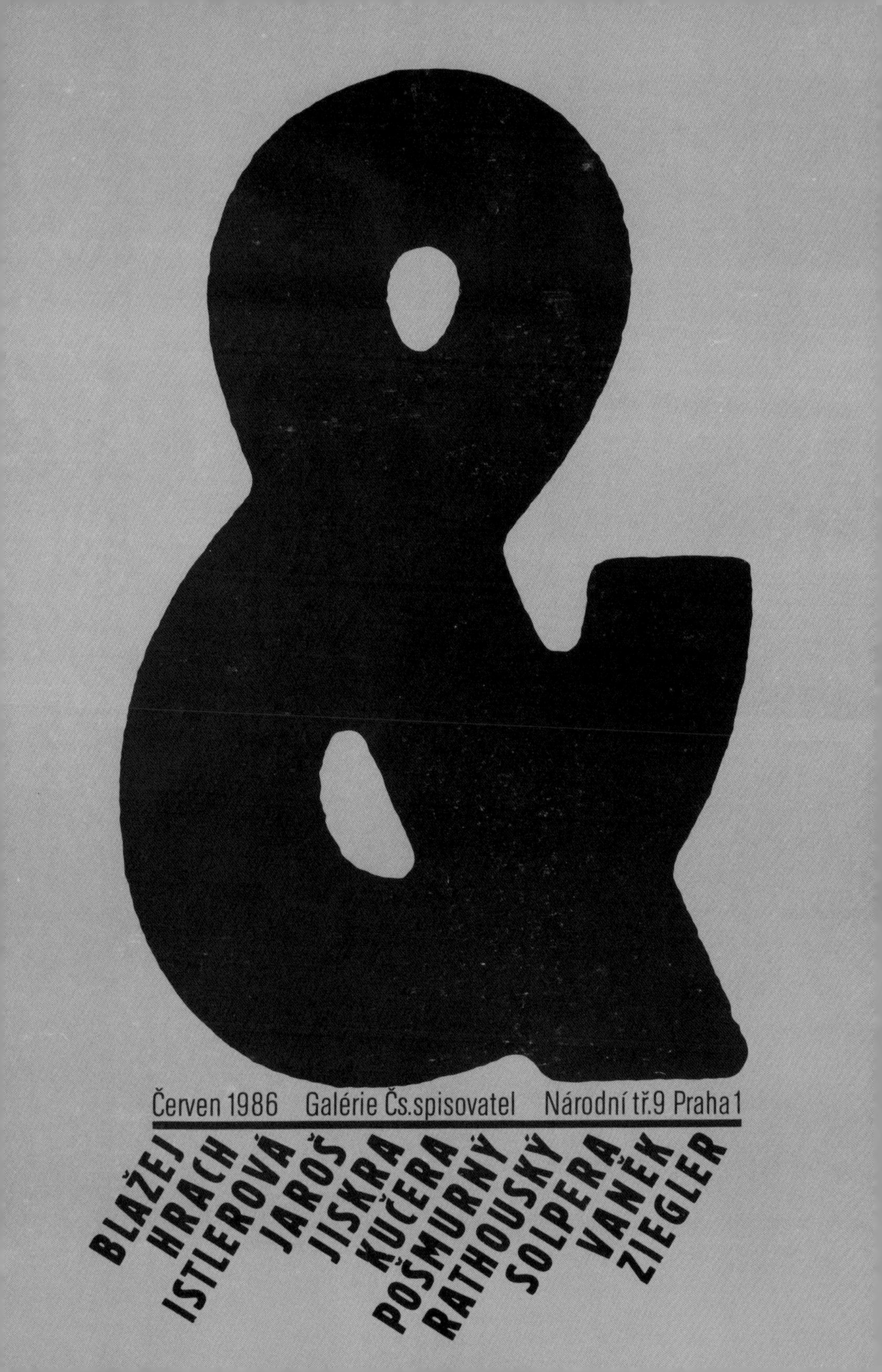

Červen 1986    Galérie Čs.spisovatel    Národní tř.9 Praha 1

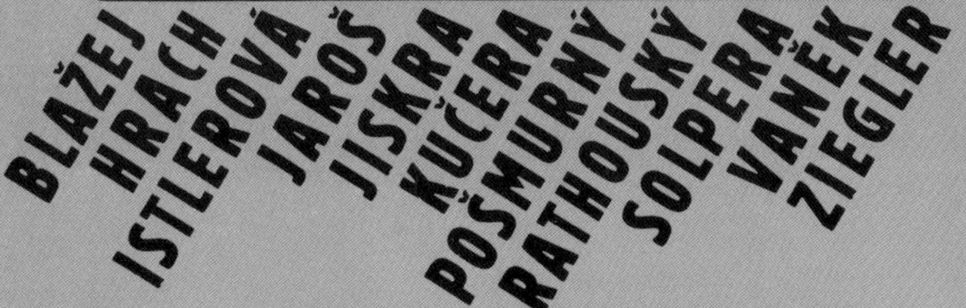

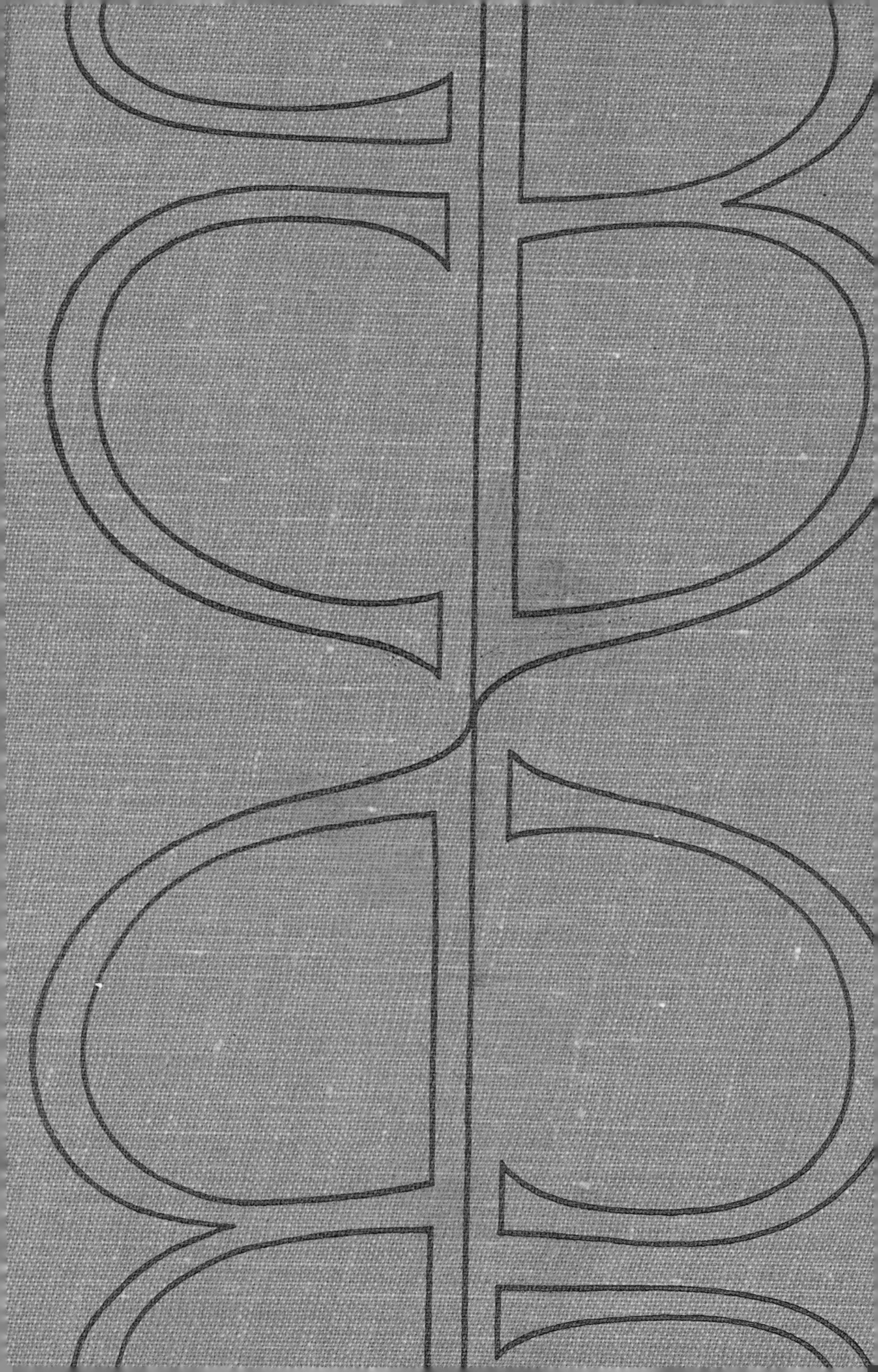

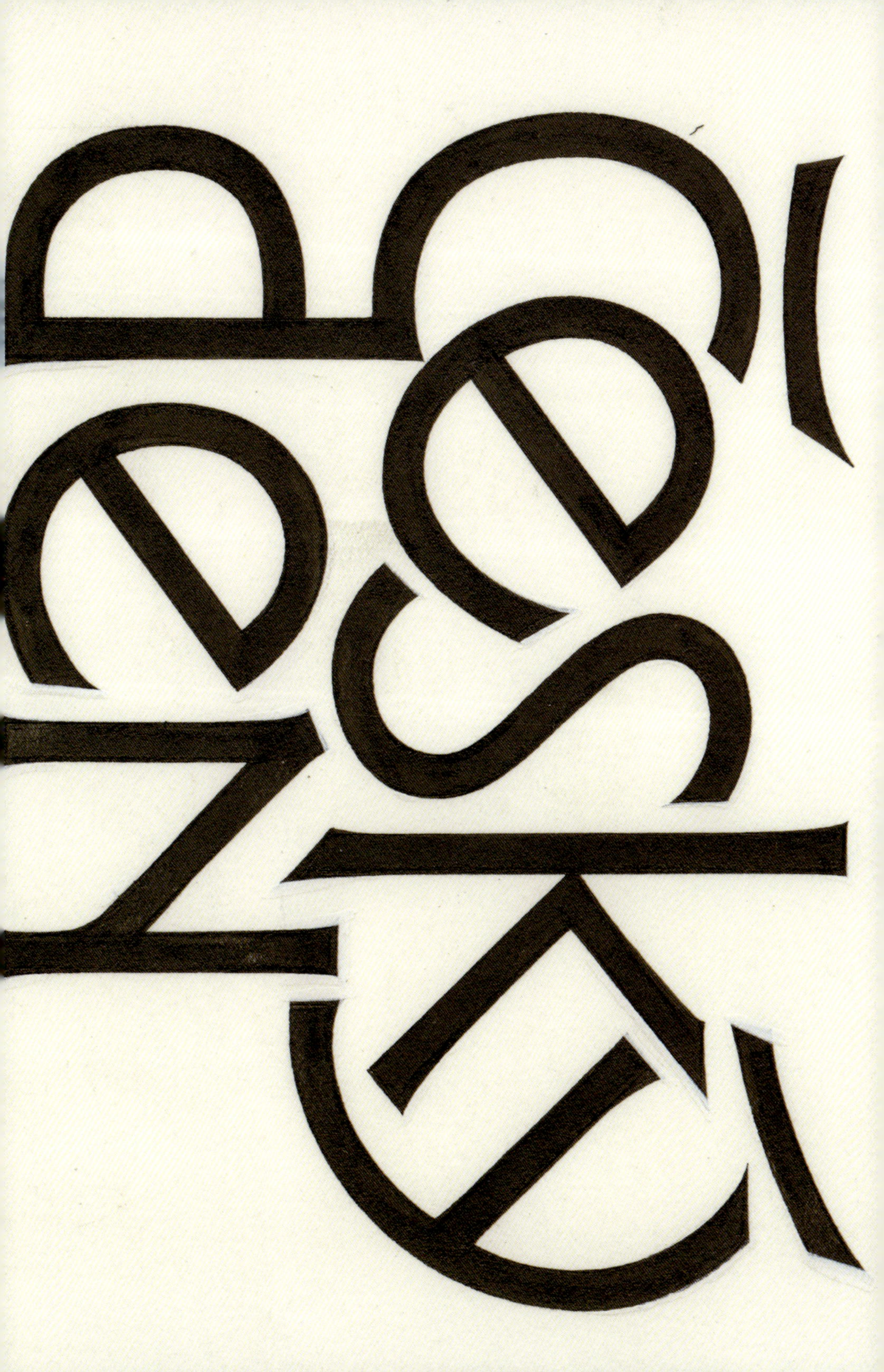

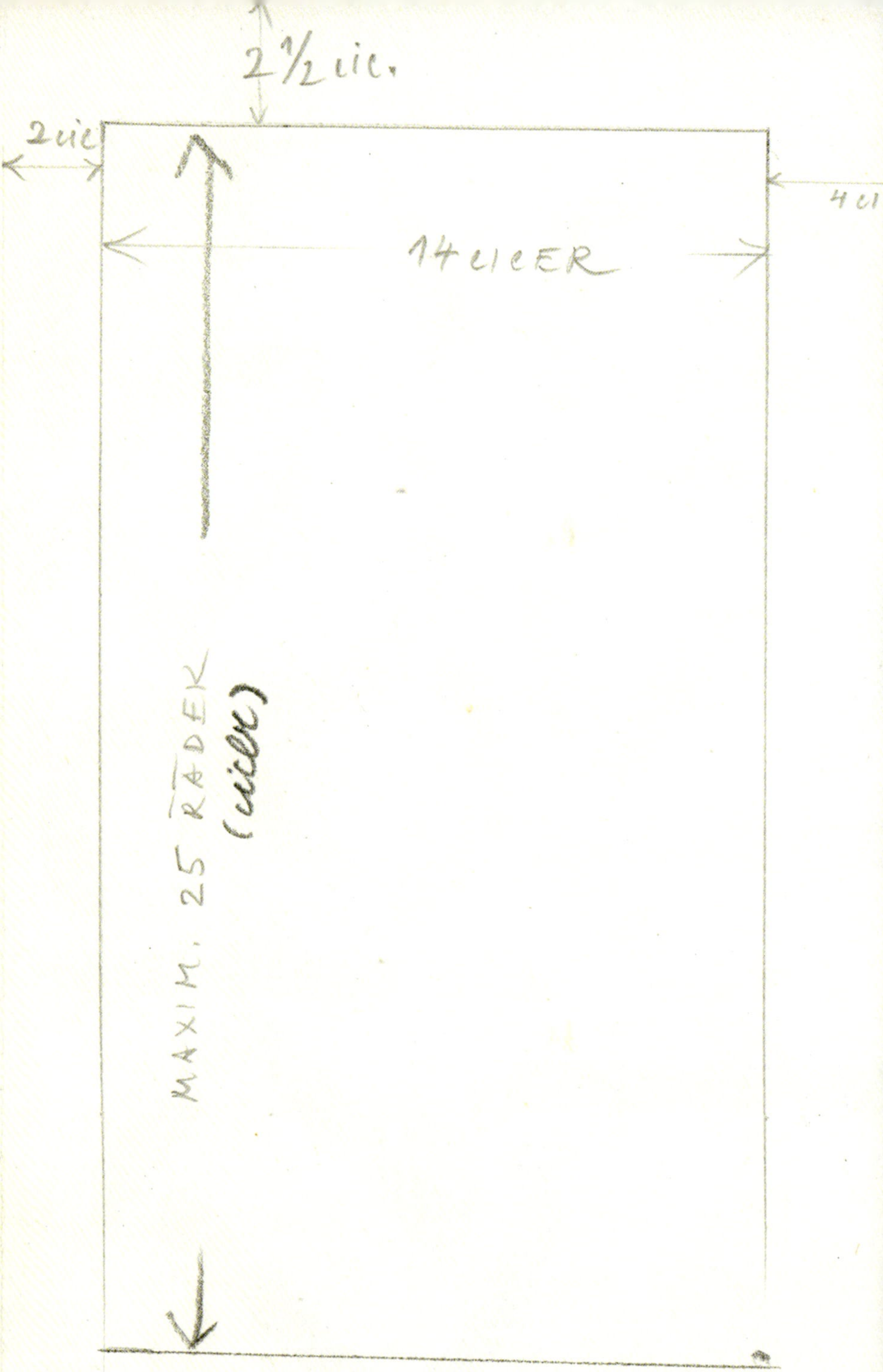

2½ cic.
2 cic
4 ci
14 CICER
MAXIM. 25 RÄDER
(cicln)

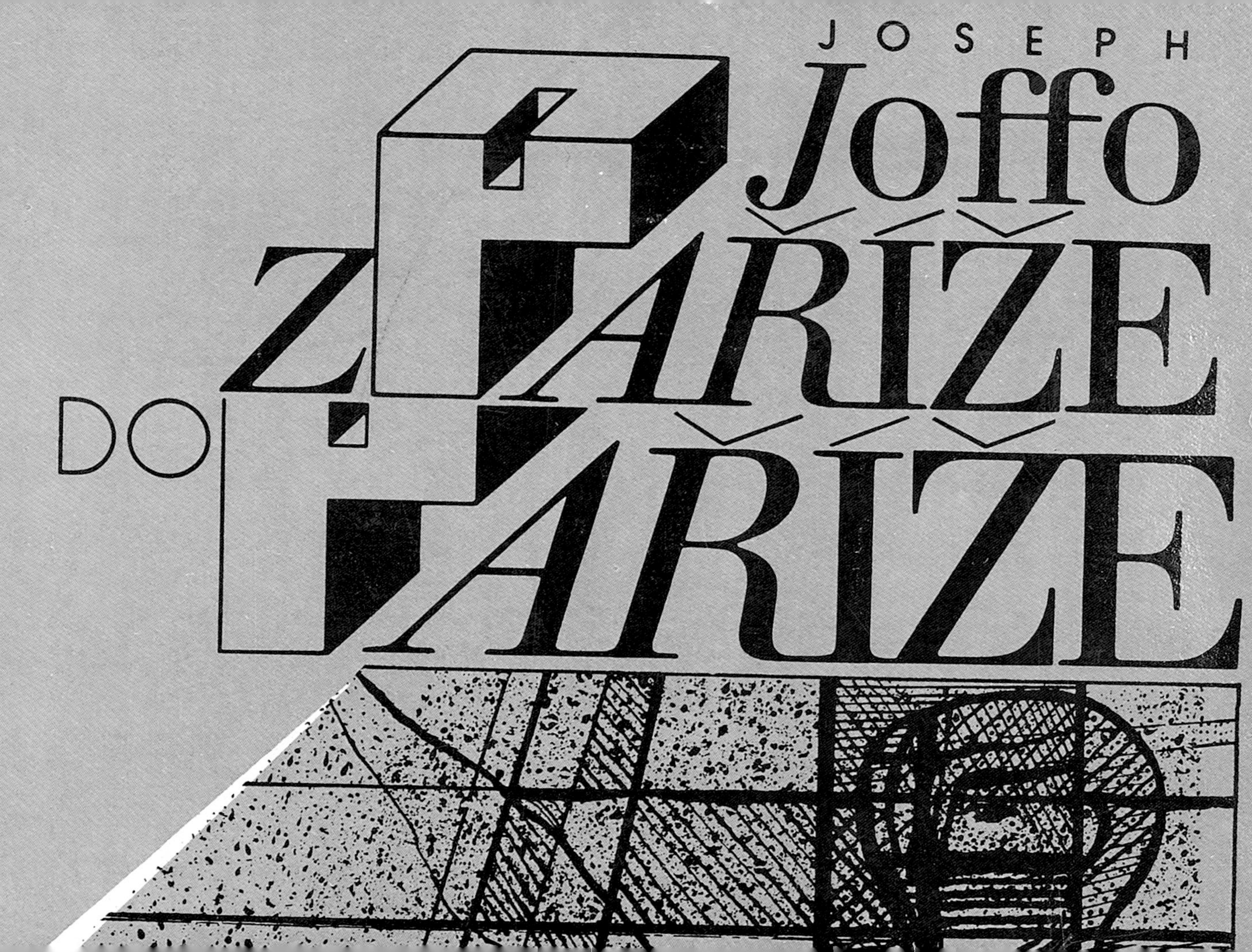

JOSEPH
Joffo
Z PAŘÍŽE
DO PAŘÍŽE

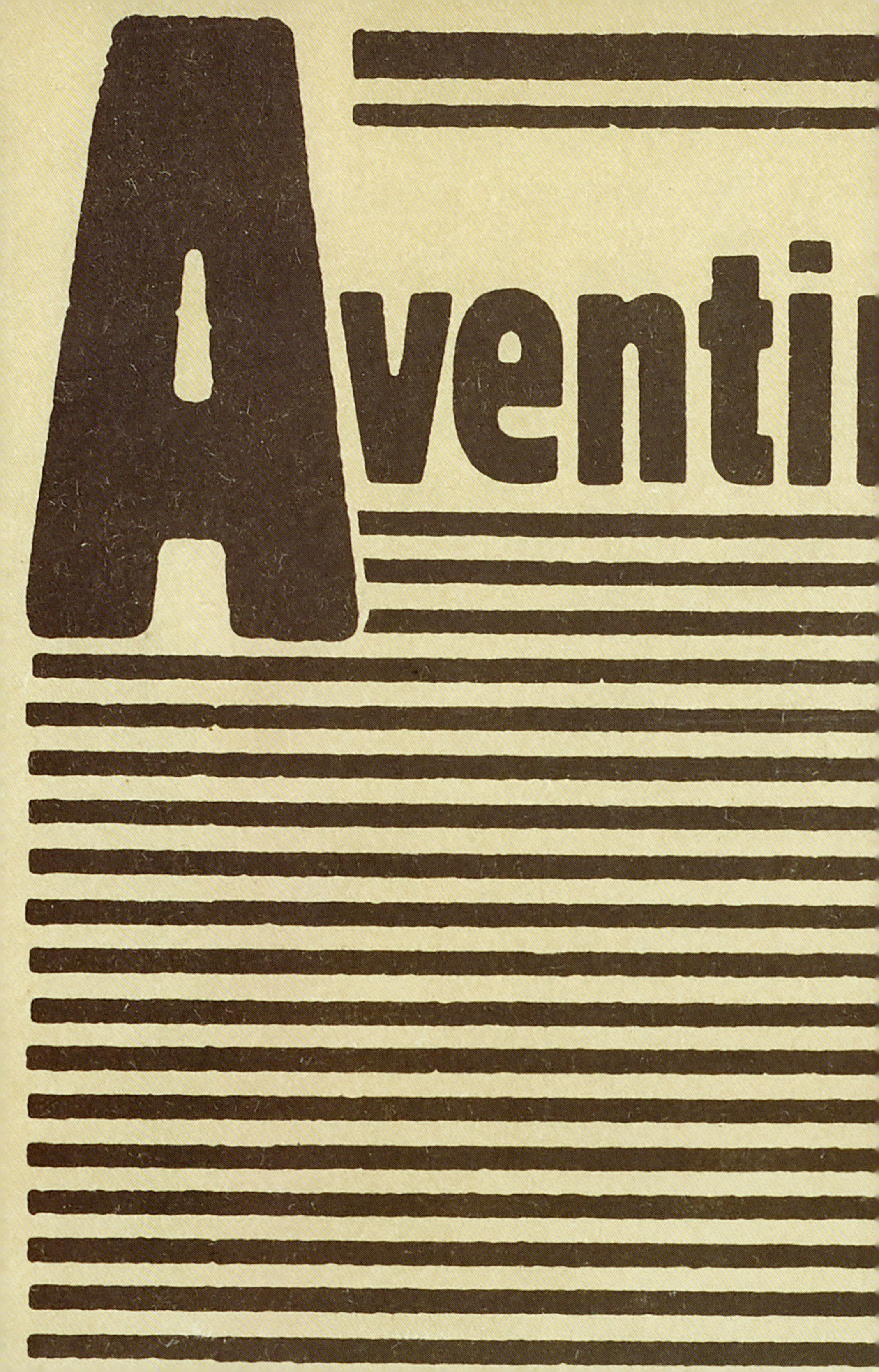
Aventi

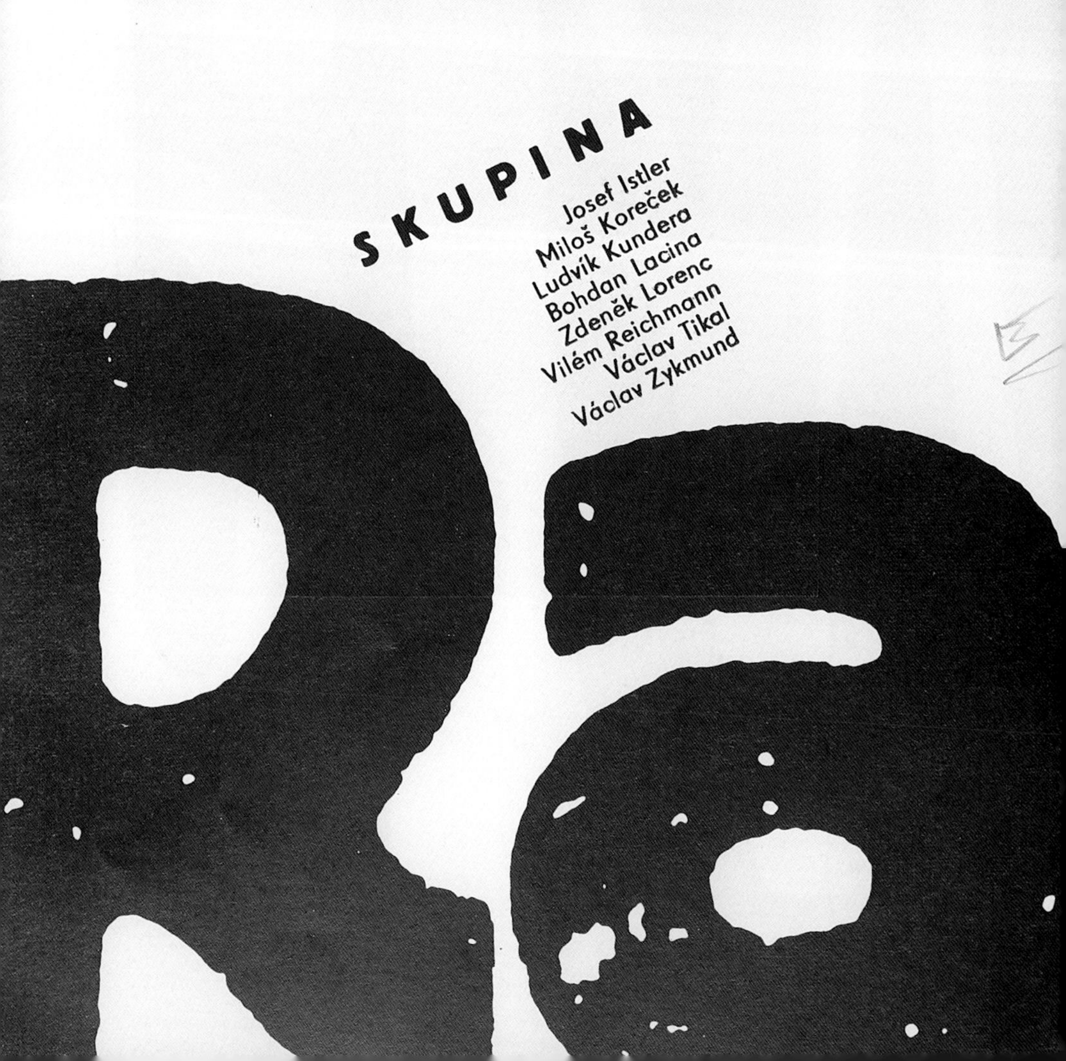

SKUPINA
Josef Istler
Miloš Koreček
Ludvík Kundera
Bohdan Lacina
Zdeněk Lorenc
Vilém Reichmann
Václav Tikal
Václav Zykmund

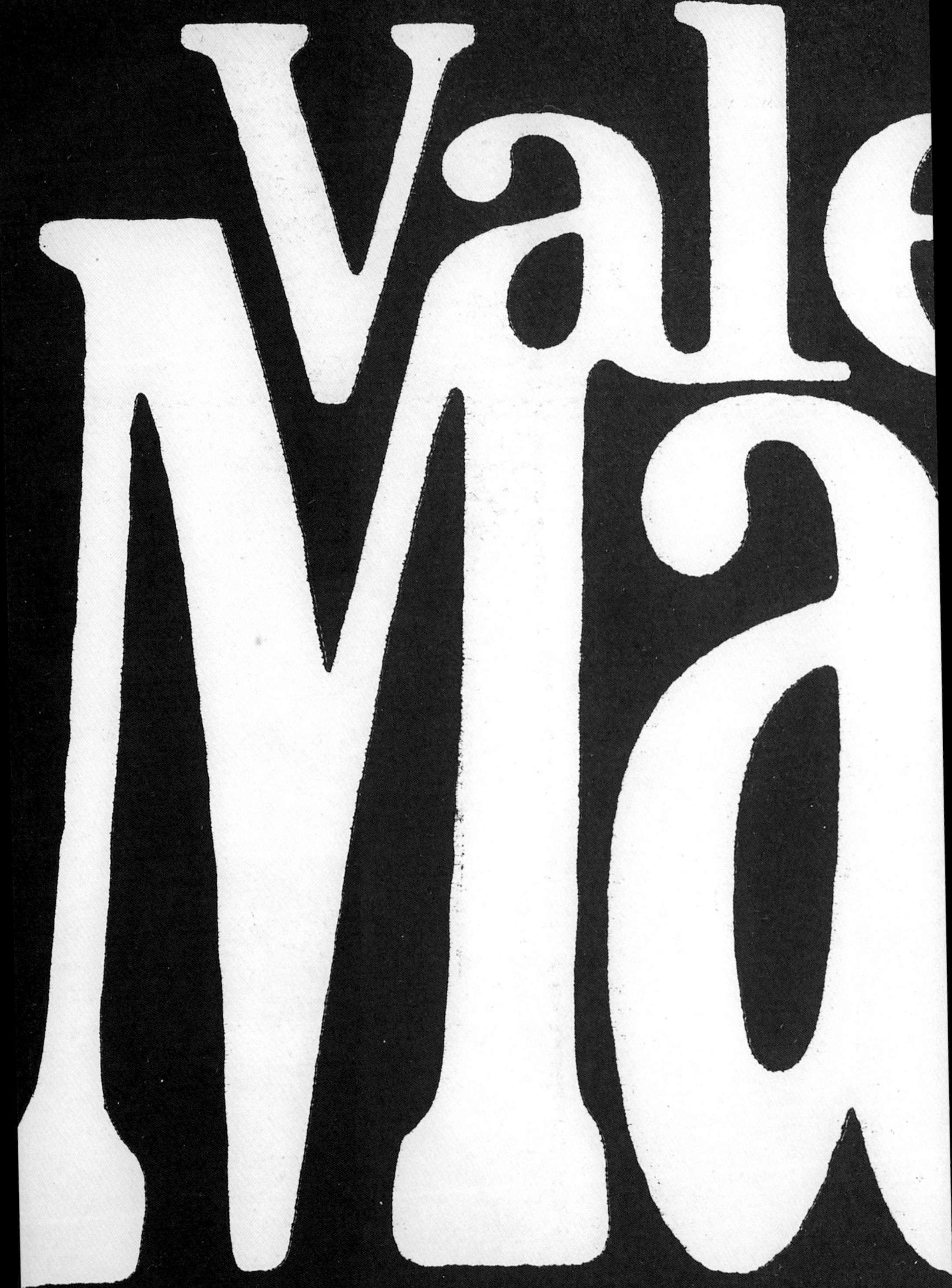

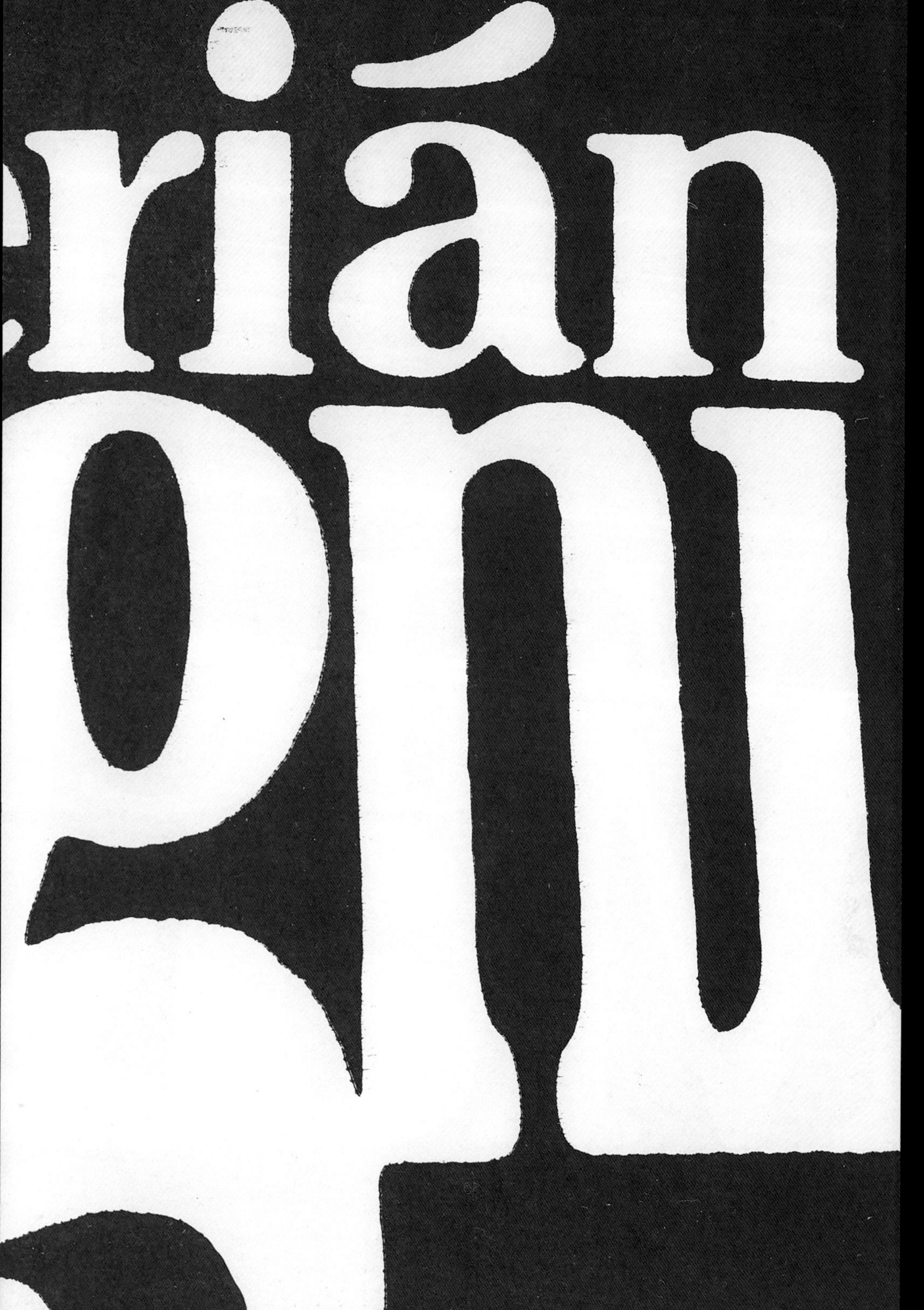

Valen
Mag

[4]

Tomáš Pešina
z Čechorodu
Mars na Moravě,
tj. o hrozných a krvavých
válkách, bouřích, rozbrojích,
bitvách, nepokojích a z nich
nastalých četných a neblahých
změnách poměrů, pustošení venkova,
plenění měst, boření posvátných
i světských staveb, ničení hradů
a městeček, spáleništích vsí
a zániku dědin a o jiných
takových neštěstích,
které Morava až
dosud zakusila
*Kniha čtvrtá*

Ten 2 vedle fuj
Ten jak když potí
Anglický tabák hnůj

Zde zamkněme se
Otočme dvakrát klíč
Každý svou lásku nese
Nic víc

HOTELY

Guillaume
Apollinaire

# TVRDOŠÍJNÍ

2. část

a hosté

užité umění

malba kresba

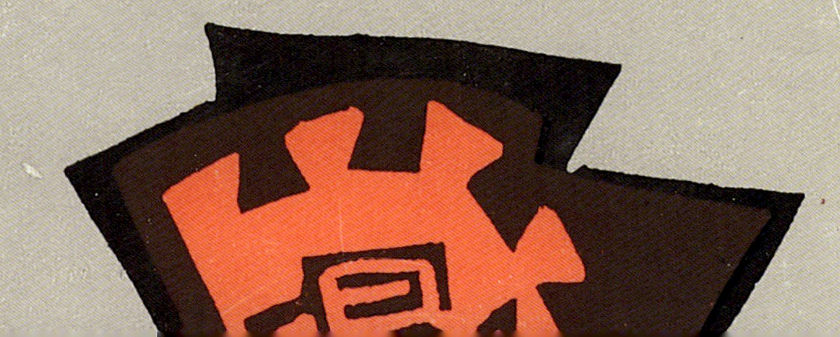

VYŠEHRAD
PRAHA
1989

# Jan Duns Scotus

Stanislav Sousedík

doctor subtilis

a jeho čeští žáci

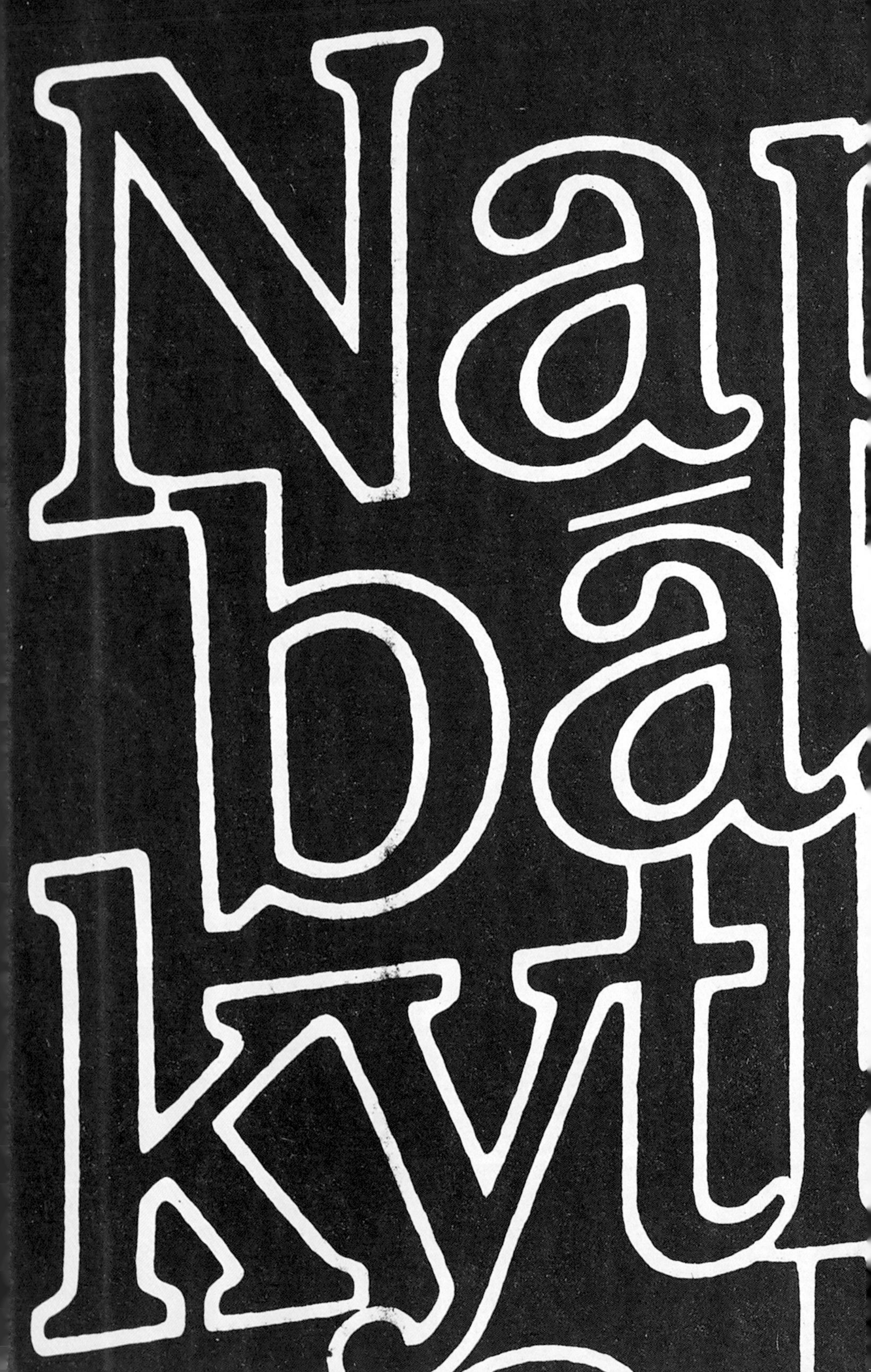

Were you also making posters and banners at that time?

Of course. Banners were made, leaflets proliferated, and there was even a competition for the branding of the Občanské Fórum (Civic Forum), which was won by the graphic designer Pavel Šťastný. During the demonstrations, our group met at Zdeněk Ziegler's, He had an attic studio with windows overlooking Wenceslas Square in Lucerna. We had flags, leaflets, and banners hidden there. We didn't miss any of the big demonstrations. The whole atmosphere was very nice. I don't understand why society is so divided now. But I guess we need to get stomped on, ugly, as much as possible to bring people back together. Maybe it's because everyone is doing so well. And they don't see the dangers lurking.

Are you still in contact with Zdeněk Ziegler? †

Not so much with Zdeněk Ziegler anymore. The last time I saw him was at the opening of an exhibition for his eightieth birthday at the Meda Mládková Gallery in Kampa. Zuzana Lednická, together with Najbrt studio, prepared and printed a catalogue for him, which also reflects his earlier works. We're no longer in contact, though. Maybe it's also because the TypoPlus, a kind of continuation of the Typo& group, started to be dominated by newly arrived young graphic designers, and we oldies have withdrawn a bit. I personally felt that I couldn't bring much new to the table anymore, even in discussion with them, because they had accomplished so much more. In the last few years, I've concentrated only on books written by Karel Hvížďala.[11] I've designed over twenty of them for him. And I hardly get to do any other work. Most recently, I edited *Cesta života*, and for Galén publishers, *Motomorfózy* by Václav Havel and *Vzpomínání* by Jiří Suchý.

† Zdeněk Ziegler passed away in 2023. This interview took place in 2019.

Has the character of your work changed much since 1989?

At the beginning of the 1990s, several larger and more demanding books were published—*Od moderny k funkcionalismu, Česká kubistická architektura 1911–1923, Český surrealismus, Gloria & Miseria – Praha v době třicetileté války* (From Modernism to Functionalism, Czech Cubist Architecture 1911–1923, Czech Surrealism, Gloria & Miseria—Prague during the Thirty Years' War)—rich in photographs and contemporary visual material. I was given an absolutely free hand by the publishers of the time as far as typography was concerned. Of course, I always respected the historical framework when creating the concept. Until 1997, I worked mainly with the Czech-French children's book publisher BRIO. They produced entire series in two or three languages. The most important thing in this work was the cooperation with the illustrators because they were the ones who gave the books their unmistakable character. These included Jean de La Fontaine's *Fables*, Alexander Dumas's *The Three Musketeers*, and the complete set of Andersen's fairy tales. We sat down with the illustrators and clarified the intent and execution. I usually first drew a mock-up of the whole book, i.e., placing the typesetting and illustrations in a precise space on the pages. I did this not only for my own idea of the composition of the pages, but also so that a break in the text would come out well in other versions. For example, I also prepared a mock-up of an entire book for Adolf Born, which he initially refused.

He didn't like this way of working?

He said I was restricting him too much. But my publisher approved it, so he couldn't protest. Plus, they paid very well. I was paid generous fees too. It was a nice job all round. If you have a clear idea of what a book should look like, you have to convince even such a distinguished gentleman as Adolf Born. But in the end we agreed: "Make me some sample illustrations and I'll put them in the break. Then we'll meet, I'll show you, and if you don't like it, we'll agree on another course of action."

               Interview

But he liked it. Perhaps because the meeting was attended by
Mr. Gründ, the French co-owner of Brio Publishing, who said,
"Excellent!"

How cooperative was Adolf Born?

Actually, I didn't interact with him that much. At the beginning
of the work on the book, we agreed on a certain number of illustrations, which were precisely numbered. Some of them were
small, complementary ones, which I could work with freely, as
well as cut-outs from the large illustrations, which I used to
complement and balance the typography.

In what form did he supply you with the illustrations?

He drew them, and then, numbered and specified for a certain
height or width, they went to the studio for reproduction.
I received them scanned and color-matched on a CD, which was
still used at the time as JPEGs for layout typesetting. After
the last proofreading, the illustrations were updated by me or
the studio to print quality and a digital proof was prepared.
Often one whole page of the press sheet for a press proof due
to the paper quality. The publisher at the time wanted to try
a lightweight offset softly toned paper, given the large scale
of the book and the nature of Born's boldly colored pastels.
Through this print test, which led to additional color correc-
tions of the drawings to achieve adequate quality in printing
due to the greater absorbency of the paper, I verified the impor-
tance of honest preparation of the materials, but also made
possible by good coordination between the publisher and the
printer. On several occasions I was also able to participate with
this publishing house in the Frankfurt International Book Fair
or in the Bologna International Children's Book and Illustration Fair. It was an interesting and enlightening insight into
the creation of books and the business around them.

How difficult was it to prepare the foreign-language
versions?

It was very challenging, but you learn from the challenge.
Plus, easy solutions deprive us of a certain joy of creative
activity. Only that which absorbs all our energy and requires
all our skills and abilities can bring us job satisfaction.

What computer were you working on at the time?

I'm still working on an Apple. I only encountered PCs in one
studio, when I was art director for a while at the fashion magazine *Cosmopolitan*. I joined them with the goal of earning
enough for a more powerful computer.

And when was that?

In 1993, '94. I was spinning my wheels quite a bit then.

You were a graphic designer at the magazine *Přítomnost*
in 1991–92. What was that experience like?

The name was taken from Ferdinand Peroutka's old *Přítomnost*,
which was published from 1924 during the First Republic and
edited by Jaroslav Stránský. It was high politics even then.
The articles in this renewed *Přítomnost* reflected ecological
problems, politics, social and societal issues, art. The editorial
board compiled the content and partly outsourced the texts.
The front page of the newspaper format and paper was always
dominated by a distinctive stylized drawing by Karel Nepraš,
symbolizing the central theme of the editorial or the main article. It was much enlarged, placed either centrally or horizon-
tally across the entire format. *Přítomnost* was at first biweekly,
but later, before the newspaper disappeared altogether, it was
published as a monthly.

How did you perceive the difference between working on
books for Brio and periodicals?

It was an enormous difference. But I thought, "You learn something from everything." It's like computers. I started with the

computer thanks to Mr. Vladimir Popp, the head of the photo desk at the then Rudé Pravo, who later opened his own studio at the turn of 1991/1992. One day he said to me: "You'll have to learn on the computer, otherwise you'll miss the boat. It won't work without it." For example, Zdeněk Ziegler and Rostislav Vaněk never learned and always preferred to work with students or studios where they made the breaks in the books according to their drawings. But it wasn't just a matter of having the courage to do it at all. My dad helped me financially with my first computer, and Honza Malý also contributed something, because he was shooting commercials and making money at the time. We took turns. Either I made money or he did. Computers and programs were super expensive in those days. I saw the move not only as an opportunity to try a new form of typographer's work, but also as preparation for the inevitable evolution. On the one hand, a sketch, an idea—that is, what you draw—on the other hand, a computer that offers many possibilities to change the typeface in a minute. But I wouldn't say that it's about making it easier. I think once you don't stick to your clear idea of the concept of the book, you get caught up in it. This happened to me on two jobs when I was designing and preparing annual reports for print. I got so caught up, I didn't know how to get out. Which was better, which of the many options that one had on the computer.

How do you think computers have influenced graphic design?

The computer doesn't invent anything, it just offers a plethora of perfect workmanship in an incredibly short amount of time. But the idea has to be born in the mind of the graphic designer. Whether with a pencil in hand or just by thinking. It's sometimes a bit tricky and deceptive to have so many variable means of processing at your disposal. It makes it all the more important to follow your own idea of the final form. I did eventually learn to work on the mentioned annual reports on the computer, though I often had stressful moments. I also worked on them with my son Matěj, who was studying at UMPRUM at

the time and was unusually creative. But as soon as I earned
enough money to buy a more powerful computer, I moved away
from it, also thanks to more interesting offers. But it should be
added that it's impossible to compare the seventies with the
present. The demands are different. The pace is faster. I think
the breadth of today's options both limits and defines people
a lot. It's easy to get swept away. If you don't say to yourself:
No, I'm not going with the flow, then you're more or less lost.

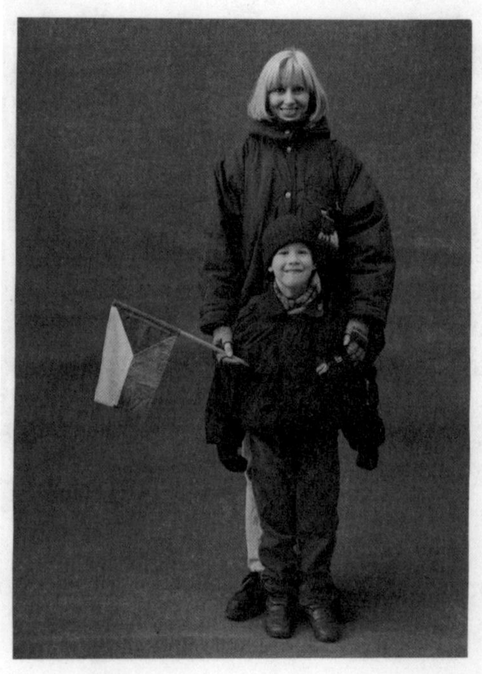

With son Jan at Hradčanské náměstí in Prague, 1990,
after Václav Havel was elected president

How did your parents feel about the changes of the 1990s?

Dad was unlucky. The first group exhibition he was allowed to
have in a long time took place in November 1989. The Union
of Visual Artists allowed him to exhibit his paintings in the
large exhibition hall of [the newspaper offices] *Mladá fronta*
in Spálená Street, which opened on November 13, the day of

                    Interview

his seventieth birthday ... and on November 17 the revolution broke out.

I guess nobody was very interested in exhibitions at that time.

Yes, everybody had other things on their minds. But a lot of people came to the opening, and Dad was a success. After many decades of work, he was finally able to exhibit publicly, and November came along just in time! My parents weren't too thrilled with the events that followed. After the experience of the World War II, when Dad was only barely saved from total deployment by a friend in Bulovka Hospital, and Mum was forced to quit her studies after the university closed, they were a bit jaded by life. They thought, "What can we expect from this?" I was already living in Dejvice, little Honzík was already born, the children were in school, I only saw my parents at birthday parties and Christmas. We kept the ritual of family celebrations together, but I was no longer in such close contact with them as I had been before. But I know that when I went to visit them or we saw each other, their reaction to the situation was lukewarm ... I didn't see any great enthusiasm from them. They were also getting on in years and not completely healthy. They'd been through the war, the bombing, the '48, the '68—I don't think they expected much from the changes.

Did your dad still go to pubs to meet his friends?

That was his life. Revolution or no revolution.

And I suppose he kept on painting ...

He was still painting or making prints. He was a hard worker all his life. But more foreign guests began to visit us—friends and gallery owners. He sold paintings abroad. Everything was looser in general. I discussed the situation a lot with my mother. Dad was never much for that. I never had any big discussion with him about politics. He always said everyone was an idiot, and that was the end of it. Unlike my dad, my mom was interested in everything, she read the newspaper every day and followed what was going on in the world until she was very old. She died when she was ninety-four, but even in her nineties, she was still interested in where the world was going, what was going on. Karel Hvížďala, who used to go to the Czech Radio building in Karlín, would visit her on those occasions and she would have high-level discussions with him. From her youth she was surrounded by intellectuals.

How did your group Typo Design Plus, which you founded after 1990, work?

We started that in 1994, partly to create a price list for graphic work. We wanted to prevent anyone from providing the same work we were doing but at dumping prices. And because more and more people were contacting us to ask for prices of individual graphic works. Shortly thereafter, the Supreme Audit Office (NKÚ) challenged us on the grounds that we were forming a cartel. They said we were imposing prices on the free market. Cartel agreements, for example, are made by oil companies who agree on a single price for oil. This, of course, distorts the natural competitive environment, but we weren't doing that. We only wanted to prevent severely reduced prices. We wanted to create a price list for graphic designers that would have a range of realistic prices for the graphic design, for the cover, for the poster, for the visual system, and for the logo manual. The rates of the complete price list were based on our experience and knowledge. Apparently someone tipped off the NKÚ that this was circulating on the internet, that Typo Design Plus wanted to dictate prices. But we didn't want that, we didn't want a monopoly, we wanted to give order to the evaluation of our work. So that the client also knows what to expect and what the real price of our work is on the market. At that time, the market was still developing. Many times, I got calls from aspiring graphic designers asking, "How much should I charge for a cover? How much should I charge for a poster?" Almost all of us had that experience, so we thought we'd design a price



Interview

list and put it on the internet under the Typo Design Plus group. We admitted authorship. It wasn't anonymous. We had to defend ourselves in court.

The Typo Design Plus group was formed from the Typo&?

Yes, the foundation remained, but many new members were added. Mostly graduates of UMPRUM and new students and those who were interested in socializing in a professional association. They always came to introduce themselves, brought works or even individual members of our group already knew them from school or from some cooperation and recommended them. It was a loose association.

The Typo& group used to put on exhibitions, what kind of activities did the Typo Design Plus group do?

In better times we used to publish yearbooks. Or quadrennials, which published a selection of the best work of the members over a given period. The typography was always done by one of us. Later on, when some of us got together in smaller studios, we each looked primarily after our own work.

What did you talk about at meetings?

There were discussions about work, experiences with commissioning bodies, and those who traveled brought news from the world of typography. In the days when exhibitions were being prepared, there were more meetings. Everything had to be planned, a preselection of works made, exhibition spaces secured, how much could fit, the period had to be determined, and who would exhibit the books, who would exhibit the logos, who would provide promotion, and potentially a small catalogue.

You also met with the young generation of graphic designers outside the Typo Design Plus group at UMPRUM, where you taught in the 1990s. Did you feel any shift in the perception of graphic design?

My time at UMPRUM was very short. But the spirit of the studio was completely different from what I experienced during my own studies at the school. Of course, there were many years in between. The way of communicating with the students was very open and intense and, I don't hesitate to say, inspiring for me.

What can typography students be taught at university?

By comparing different ways of doing typography, they can be taught to perceive the relationship of type and text to the surface, to illustration, and to photography. After learning about the history and development of typography and book-making, one can use examples of various print processes to demonstrate their qualities or flaws. This can help cultivate an appreciation and sensitivity for these aspects. The lecturer should teach students the art of defending their graphic solution or the method. Today, both the design and technical stages are at a completely different level than they were when I started, and teaching must take this into account. But even this progress should not neglect the unique input of the typographer, although it's a matter of individual character to what extent they'll experiment in their work and at the same time have the courage to defend their design with sufficient knowledge. It was difficult under the last regime and, given the great power of marketing, it's often difficult today.

Have you continued to work from home?

Always from home. I couldn't do it any other way with the kids. I completely ruled out having a studio. It would have been an unnecessary extra expense. That way I could take care of the kids after school, make sure they ate or did their homework. Eventually, when the kids grow up, those worries go away. Plus, I've never had a need for a car. I always thought: This thing has to earn its keep. I only changed computers when I knew I could afford it. Also, when you stay single, which I have been for years since my divorce in 1978, you count differently. In 2005, I mar-

                    Interview

ried Karel Hvížďala, who I'd been with since 1998, and he told me, "Let's get married, we'll be old soon and it'll be financially better for whoever stays."

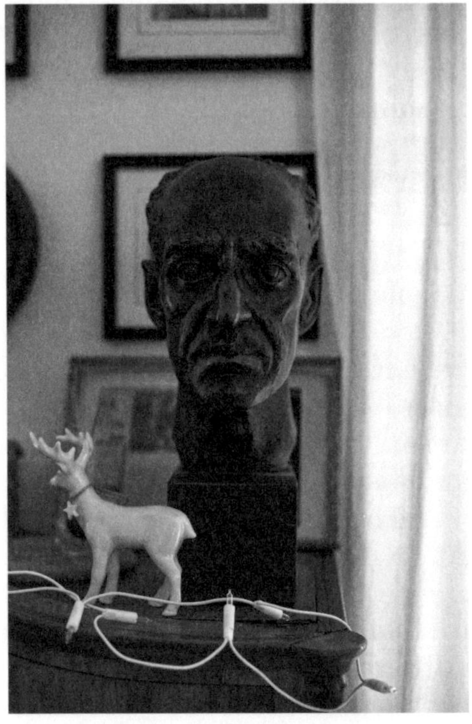

Bust of Clara Istlerová's father, Josef, made by Clara's brother Tomáš, in her apartment in Petřiny, Prague, 2019

If I count correctly, you've been married for twenty years.

Karel did the math recently, and it's true. I was with Honza Malý for almost as long, without counting anything, and I said to myself, "As long as it works, it works. When it stops, it's over."

A rational approach.

I don't know if it's rational or what it is. But it's a lot of what kind of family I grew up in. When I realized that each of those people end up living life on their own terms, there's not much you can do about it anyway. Just the opposite, the more one tries to influence a relationship, the more one knots it up and puts shackles on the other. Maybe that's true at work, too. The more boundaries you put internally, the more you strip yourself of your ability to regenerate and approach solutions with a different perspective. Karel says that the greatest happiness in his life was the fact that he was fired from everywhere and that's why he's remained internally free. This also applies to typography. I think the two vessels are absolutely inseparable—work and life. It's always mixed together. One influences the other.

And which people have influenced your work the most?

All the men who've entered my life have left a significant mark on my work. My first long-term relationship was with a bookbinder who was attending night school for graphic design. He bound several handmade paper books for me, which I then calligraphed text and created illustrations for the enjoyment of my family. That's when my idea of books was born. Marriage to a glassmaker opened a window to another world. Living with a photographer for nearly twenty years allowed me to work with writing in a different way: Phototypesetting was in its infancy and only concerned the main typesetting of text. It also taught me to perceive photography differently. Cohabitation with a writer added the final piece to the mosaic of working with a book. I now have the opportunity to be the first reader and critic of his manuscripts and see the book come together.

And what are you doing now?

You slowly fade from the scene. More and more generations are entering. Compared to my age, when people are twenty years younger, they're already fifty-five. They all have families to support. Graphic designers two generations younger already have their studios and their established businesses. They automatically get jobs that would have gone to me before. But it doesn't bother me at all. I've done as well as I could. I did books, maga-

                            Interview

zines, I designed stamps. I tried everything. I should devote the remaining time to my grandchildren because I was also helped with children at a certain stage of my life. One should give back. Karel says to me, "If you don't go out, you don't want to socialize, how can you have a job … People don't know you're still able to work." Working with publishers is a little bit tricky now, too. Instead of an art editor, the covers and layout are largely decided by marketing, who are mostly interested in sales …

How do you reflect on your work after almost fifty years of activity?

I don't reflect on my work. I don't feel the need to look back too much. What's important is the feeling you have of yourself and your family. An old person sees things differently. They're not so immersed in everything and take life with a grain of salt. But it's probably also because you always close each chapter you live, and then you enter the next one. But you definitely can't be afraid of change and new decisions. I'm not a fatalist, but things are as they should be.

NOTES

1    Karel Teige (1900–1951) was a Czech avant-garde artist, writer, and critic, and a key figure in the Czech modernist movement of the 1920s and 1930s. As a member of the Devětsil group, he worked as an editor and graphic designer for its magazine *Revue Devětsilu* (or *ReD*), which helped introduce modernist ideas to Prague. Teige was instrumental in connecting the Czech avant-garde with international figures like Le Corbusier, Man Ray, and André Breton, fostering a vibrant artistic dialogue in Prague. Though not an architect, Teige was a prominent architecture critic, advocating for scientific functionalism rooted in Marxist principles. His major theoretical work, *The Minimum Dwelling* (1932), explored ideas of functional, affordable housing. Teige's influence extended through his lectures at the Bauhaus and participation in the International Congresses of Modern Architecture (CIAM). Despite initial support for communism, Teige was later persecuted by the regime, and his works were suppressed after 1948. He died in Prague in 1951, following severe political repression.

2    Oldřich Hlavsa (1909–1995) was a prominent Czech graphic designer and typographer who significantly shaped twentieth-century Czech design. Trained as a typesetter, he developed a distinct style emphasizing typography as a core visual element, often on par with images and illustrations. Over his sixty-year career, he designed around 2000 books and contributed to the graphic identity of publishing houses such as Academia and Československý spisovatel, including notable series like *Klub přátel poezie*. His influential three-volume work *Typographia* (1976–86) encapsulates his innovative approach to typography and book design. Hlavsa received multiple awards, including the prestigious Leipzig Gutenberg Prize in 1991 for his contributions to book art.

3    The Strettis were a prominent Czechoslovakian family known for contributions to the arts and intellectual life. Notably, Jaromír Stretti-Zamponi, a painter and graphic artist, gained recognition for his evocative portrayals of Prague's landscapes.

4    Cadre of the Street Committee (*kádrování uličního výboru*) refers to the surveillance and vetting practices conducted by hyperlocal street committees in communist Czechoslovakia. These committees monitored residents' loyalty to the regime, assessing their political reliability and often influencing job opportunities, access to housing, and social status. This localized oversight system was a means of maintaining ideological control over daily life, with committees regularly scrutinizing individuals' backgrounds, beliefs, and behaviors to ensure conformity with state expectations.

5    The Secondary Industrial School of Graphic Arts (also known as the Secondary Industrial School of Graphic Arts in Prague, formerly the State Graphic School, colloquially Hellichovka) is a secondary and higher vocational school in Prague focused on photography, graphic design of printed materials, restoration, and printing technology. It is located on Hellichova Street under Petřín Hill in Malá Strana. The school was founded in 1920 and is named after the painter Josef Vojtěch Hellich.

6    On August 20–21, 1968, Czechoslovakia was invaded by the Soviet Union and most Warsaw Pact members to suppress the reforms of the Prague Spring, a period of political liberalization under Alexander Dubček that had begun earlier that year. This invasion marked a pivotal moment in the country's history, as it ended hopes for "socialism with a human face" and brought about years of repression. It remains a turning point in the nation's history, deeply impacting culture and inspiring intellectual and creative circles to preserve heritage and identity under harsh restrictions.

        Interview

7    Žižkárna is a colloquial term for the Higher Vocational School of Applied Arts and
     the Secondary School of Applied Arts in Žižkov, Prague. Founded in 1921, as the
     State Vocational School for Wood Processing, it focused on furniture and interior
     design, influenced by the Weimar Bauhaus.

8    Zdeněk Ziegler (1932–2023) was a renowned Czech typographer, graphic designer,
     and educator known for his significant contributions to graphic design. He served
     as a professor at the Academy of Art, Architecture and Design in Prague and held
     the position of rector from 2000 to 2003. Ziegler received numerous awards for his
     work, including recognition from international design associations

9    The Mánes building holds a central place in the history of Czech art as a symbol of
     the country's modernist and avant-garde movements. Constructed in 1928–30 by
     architect Otakar Novotný for the Mánes Association of Fine Artists, the building
     became a hub for artistic innovation and exhibitions. Its functionalist design reflects
     the association's progressive ideals, emphasizing simplicity and functionality. Over
     the years, the Mánes building hosted countless exhibitions, performances, and cul-
     tural events, fostering connections with European avant-garde artists and playing
     a pivotal role in establishing Prague as a center of modern art in Central Europe.

10   The November Days of 1989 refer to the pivotal events of the Velvet Revolution in
     Czechoslovakia, which led to the end of forty-one years of communist rule. The move-
     ment began on November 17, 1989, with a peaceful student demonstration in Prague
     that was violently suppressed by the police. This sparked widespread protests and
     a surge of public support for democratic reforms. Over the following weeks, millions
     of people took to the streets, demanding freedom and democracy. The revolution cul-
     minated in the resignation of the communist government on December 10, 1989, and
     the subsequent election of Václav Havel as president. This period marked a signifi-
     cant transformation in Czechoslovakia's political landscape, transitioning from
     a totalitarian regime to a democratic state. The Velvet Revolution is remembered as
     a nonviolent uprising that emphasized civil rights and the power of collective action.

11   Karel Hvížďala (b. 1941) is a Czech journalist, writer, and playwright known for
     his interviews with Czech dissidents, including *Long-Distance Interrogation* with
     Václav Havel. After emigrating to West Germany in 1978, he collaborated with Radio
     Free Europe and exile publications. Following the Velvet Revolution, he returned
     to Czechoslovakia, co-founded the magazine *Týden*, and served as editor-in-chief of
     *Mladá fronta DNES*. His works, exploring themes of democracy and media, earned
     him the Egon Erwin Kisch Prize (2003) and the Ferdinand Peroutka Award (2007).

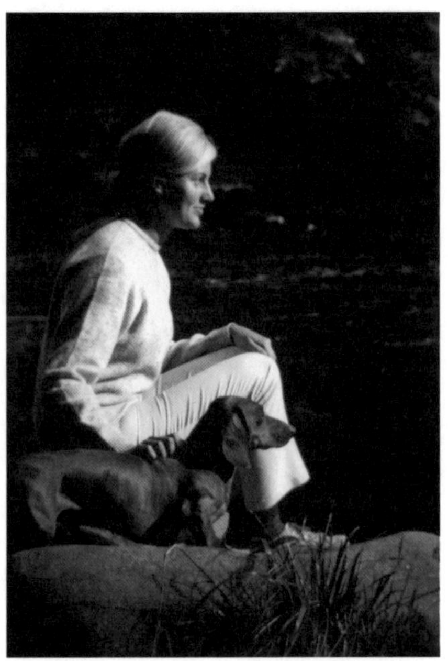

Istlerova in the Jizera Mountains
with the dachshund Sepl I, 1963



Interview

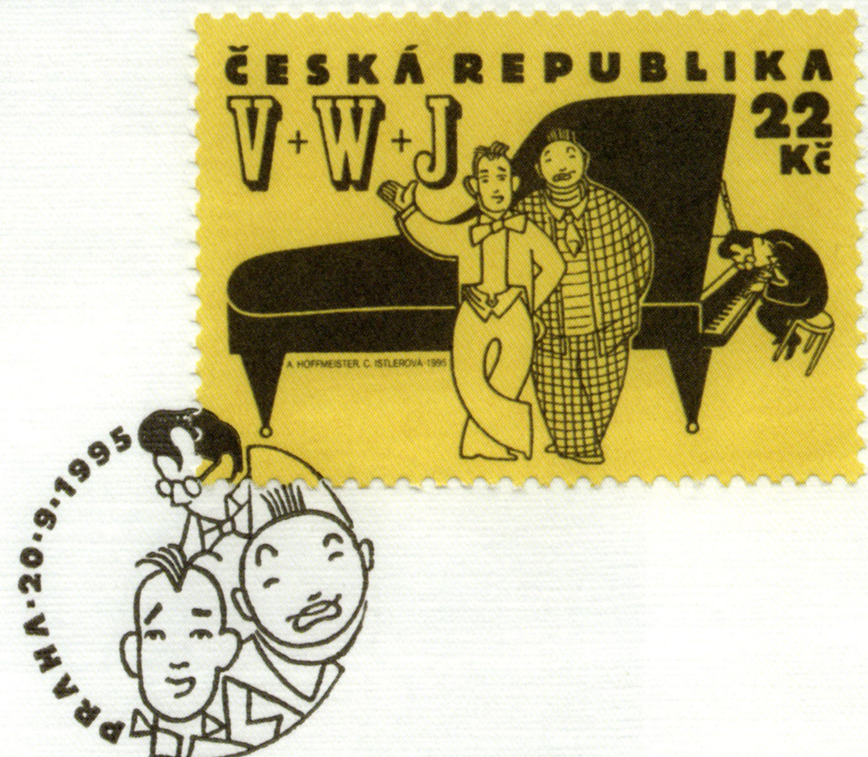

ČESKÁ REPUBLIKA
V + W + J
22 Kč
A. HOFFMEISTER C. ISTLEROVÁ·1995
PRAHA·20·9·1995

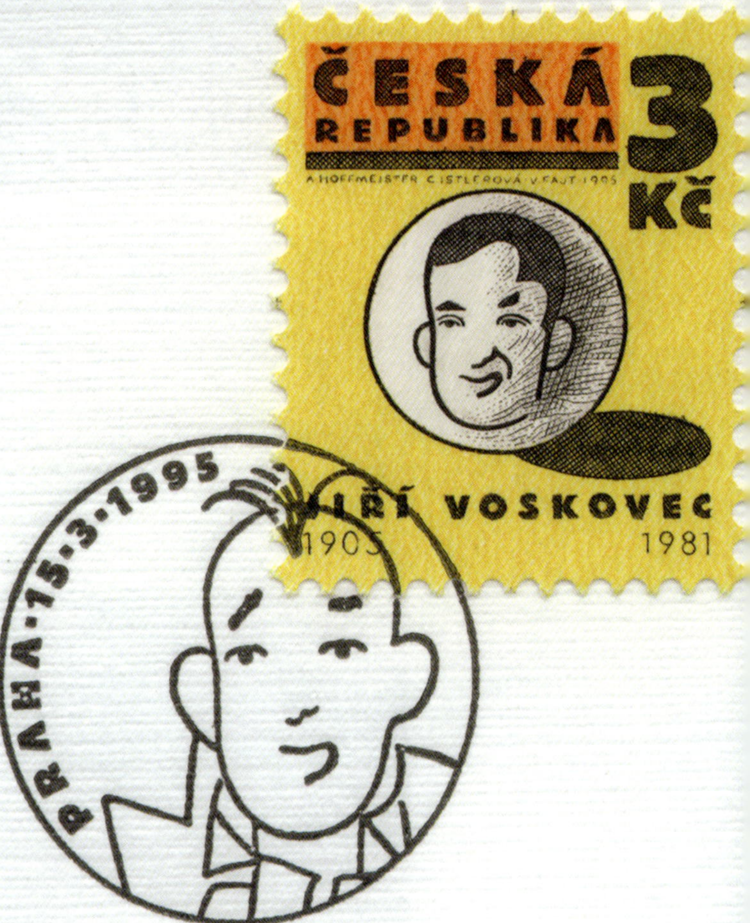

ČESKÁ
REPUBLIKA
A. HOFFMEISTER C. ISTLEROVÁ V. FAJT 1995
3 Kč
JIŘÍ VOSKOVEC
1905
1981
PRAHA · 15 · 3 · 1995

# Od moderny k funkcionalismu

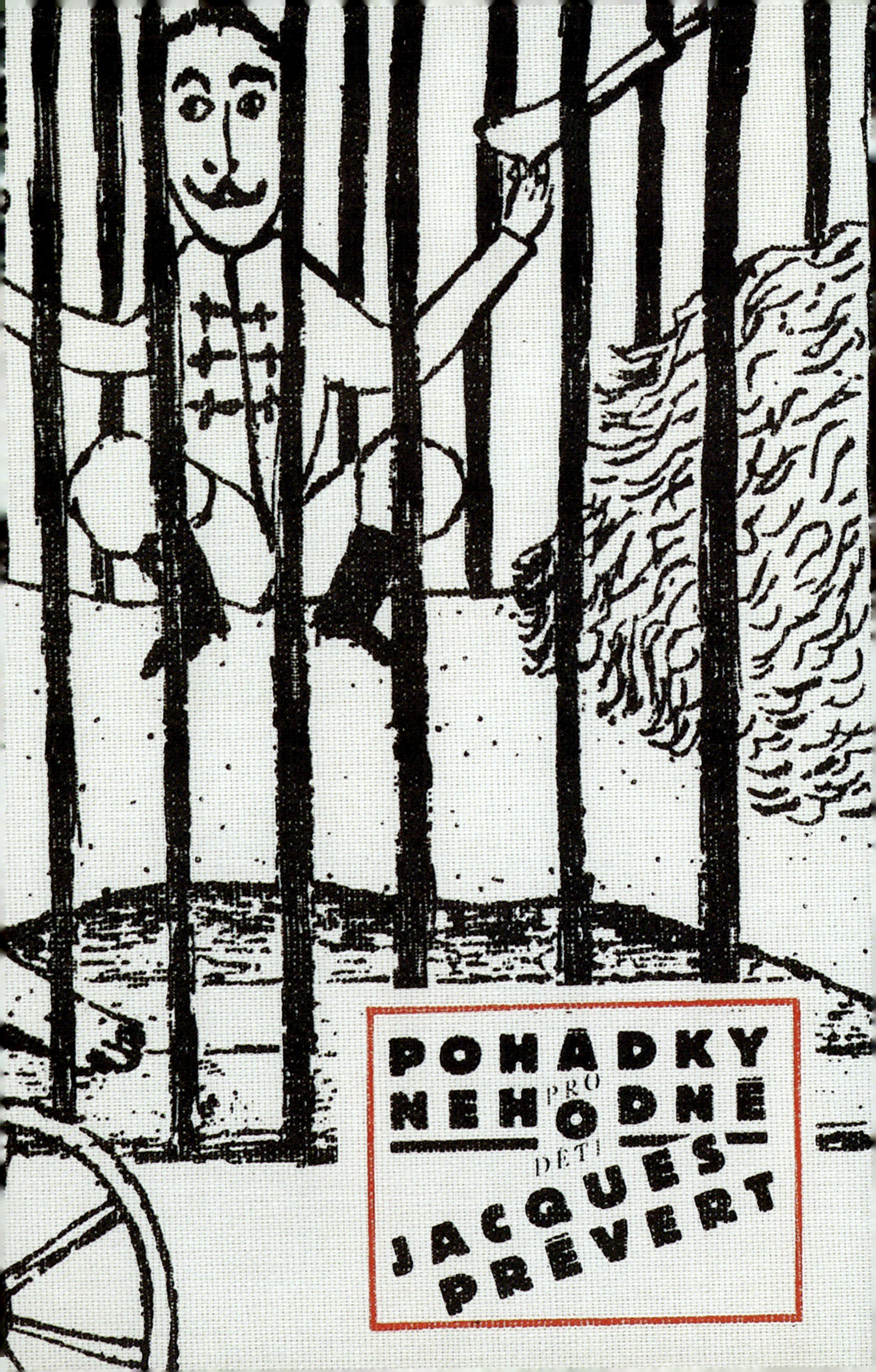
POHADKY
NEHODNÉ
PRO
DĚTI
JACQUES
PRÉVERT

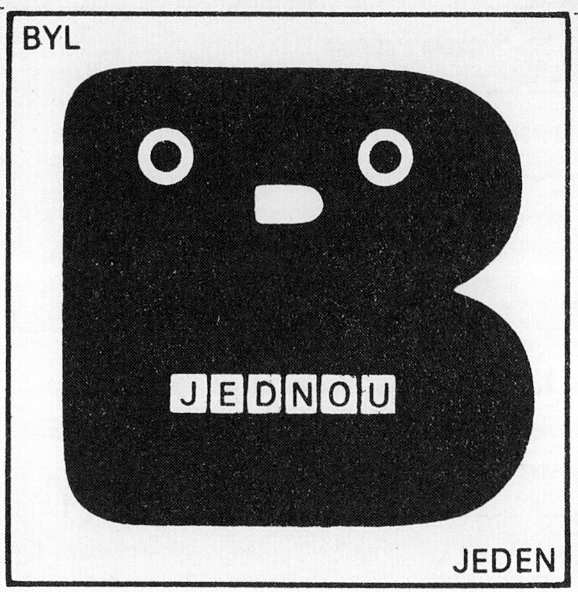
BYL
JEDNOU
JEDEN

# 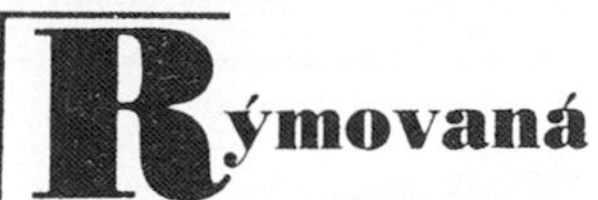ýmovaná

To není nenávist co k tobě mám

já tebou prostě

pohrdám

Nechtěla jsem být manželka

chtěla jsem bejt tvá milenka . . .

Až potom

když jde do tuhýho vidíme oba ty kilometry

lásky složené

z milimetrů

a centimetrů po dobu dvacetipěti let

R Ý M   je v talóně a

M L Á D Í   taky.

To není nenávist co k tobě mám

je mi jen nevýslovně smutno a

Ž I V O T

frčí dál

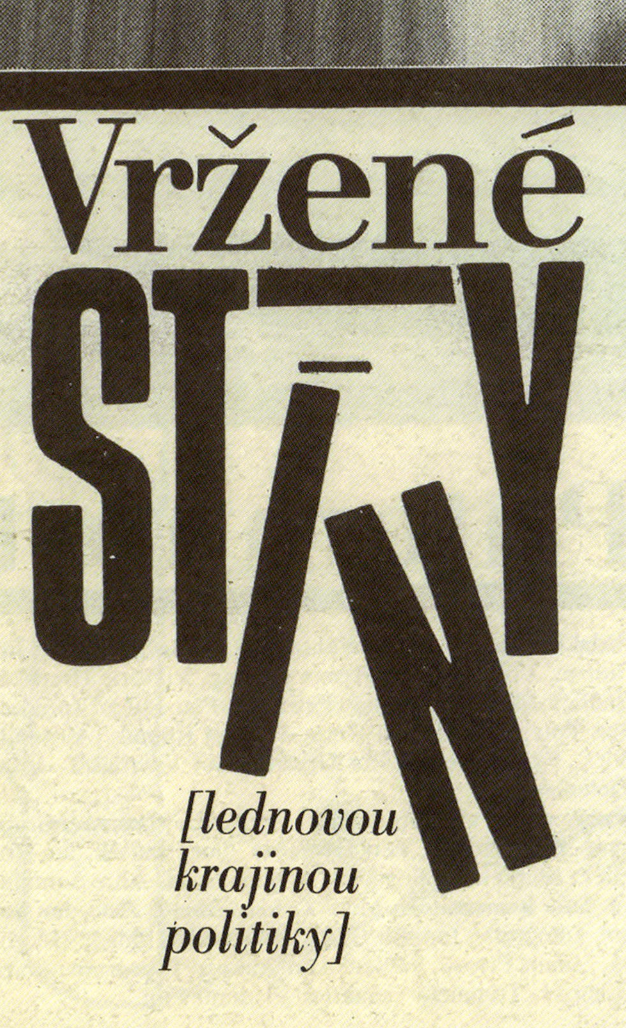

# Vržené STÍNY

*[lednovou krajinou politiky]*



nabízí více
ed závorku,
e »zakláda-
o podoben-
ch obrazech
a o jejich
láme vrže-
izovat jako
ní chceme
olitice, jak
olitiky glo-
fóru, takto
, je nám tak
A jestliže tu
ním smyslu

měr. Nikoli žal
mentátoři – sp
tickou mapu s
částí procesů š
ba ne hned po
o jejich dopad
soudný nepoch
domácí politik
vém sněmu vý

Řekli jsme p
nost vydávat,
tomnosti z mís
spektra. Cháp
cí a sdílíme př
řování je vzore

kterou jsme díky mnohonárodní podobě celého kon-
fliktu, a tedy i díky našemu vlastnímu angažmá pociťo-
vali o poznání intenzívněji, než nám ji mohou pro-
středkovat masová média. O litevském dramatu, o tě-

rvní republiky

# 1939

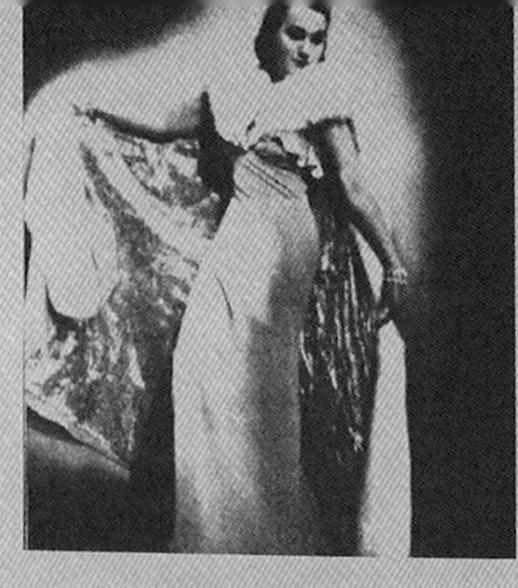

18

rvní republiky

Tichý kormorán
šíře 65 mm
isovatel

# **A** NA RUBÁŠI ZÁPLATA . . . . .

Tělo moje stůj při mně,
i ve chvíli umírání!
Že by to bylo vono?
Takhle vobyčejně?
DIAZEPAM
NITRAZEPAM
CHLORPROMAZIN
MEPROBAMAT
a před tím víno. Hodně dlouhé ííííí.
Při zavření očí mi uletěl vršek lebky. S leknutím jsem si sedla.
Do mozku mi narážely ryby. Ostré, tvrdé, špičaté ryby. Když
jsem zavřela oči, viděla jsem rty. Ohromné. Metrové i menší.
Nikdo se nesmál. Žádné rty se nesmály. Ale všechny detaily
jsem na nich                             viděla –
                                        vrásčité
                                      popraskané
                                      sešpulené
                                FUJ! Přesná fantazie.
                                  Šla jsem k tobě.
                                Že eště nechci umřít.
                                   Budila jsem tě
                                   Rušila jsem tě
                                Potřebovala jsem tě
                                Cože? Řekl jsi COŽE?
                          Která svině z tebe udělala takovou svini!
                             Budím tě. Ruším tě. Potřebuju tě.
                             Heleď se: V čem mi dáš do rakve?
                             Které šaty jsou moje nejkrásnější?
                                 Jak vypadá rubáš?
                               Kde koupit střih na rubáš?
                                    Ach Bože!
                   S narozením jsem neměla žádné starosti a teď tolik!
                                  MAMINKO!

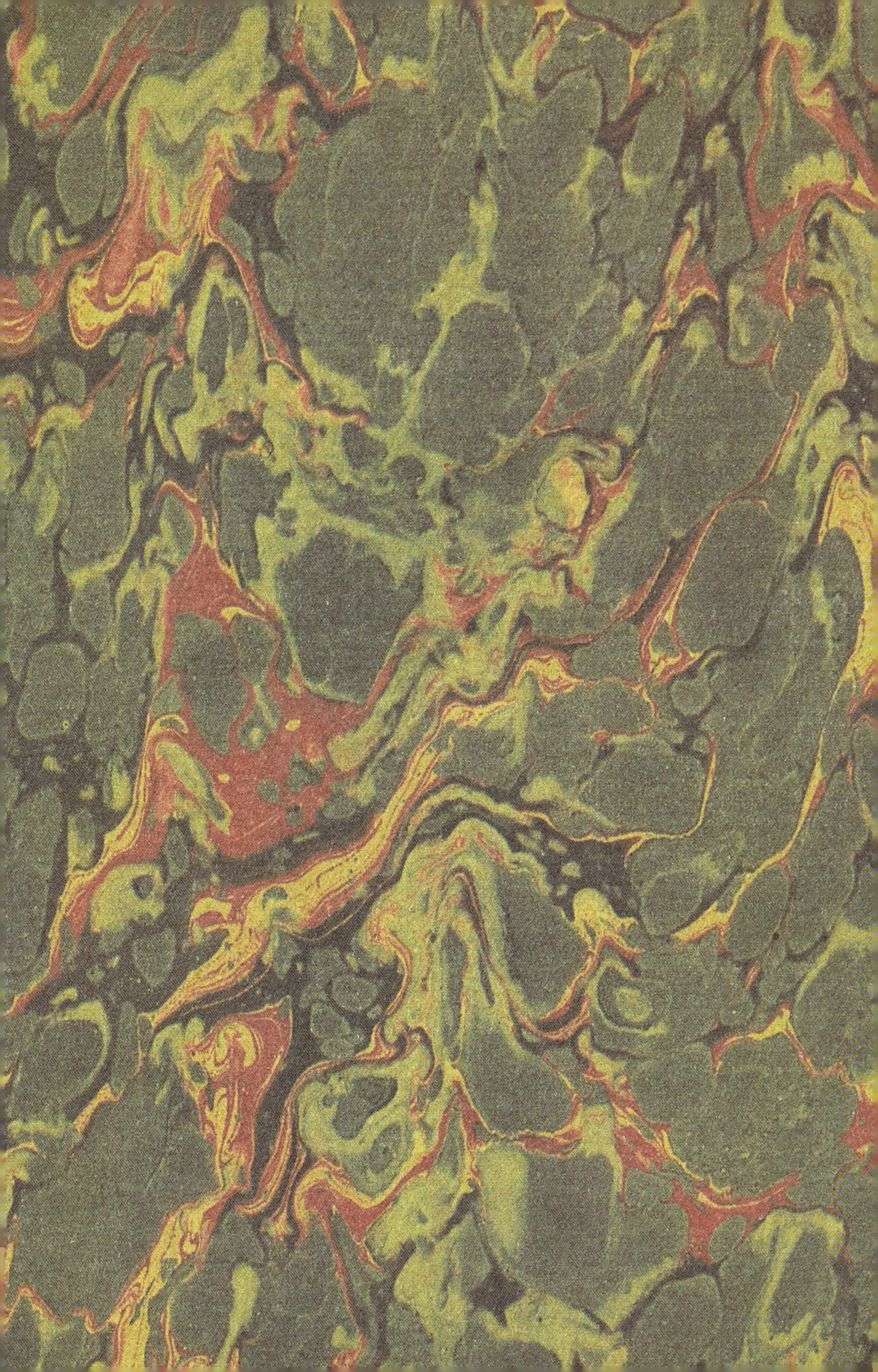

# HAVEL

# LANDOVSKÝ

# SUCHÝ

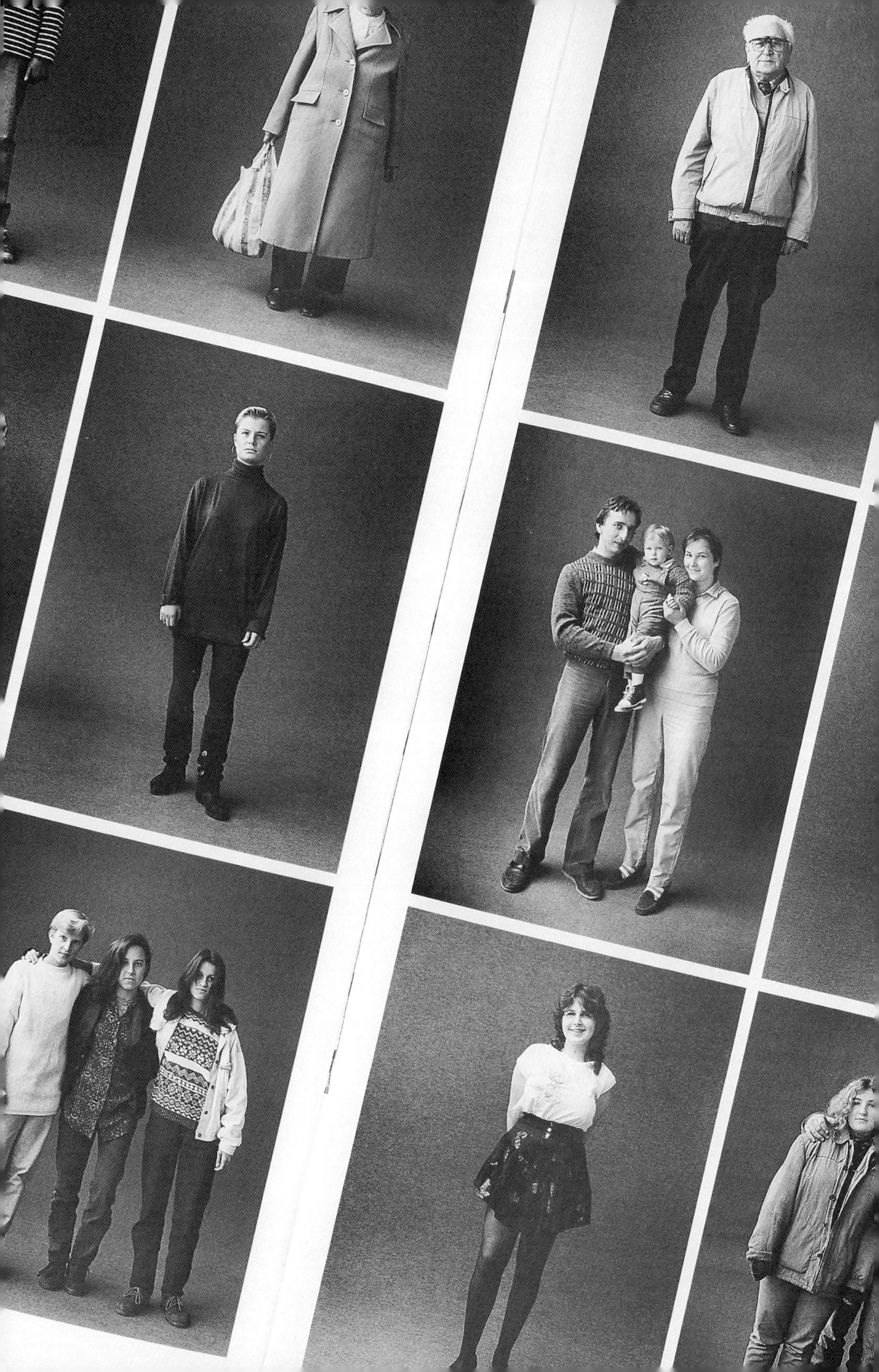

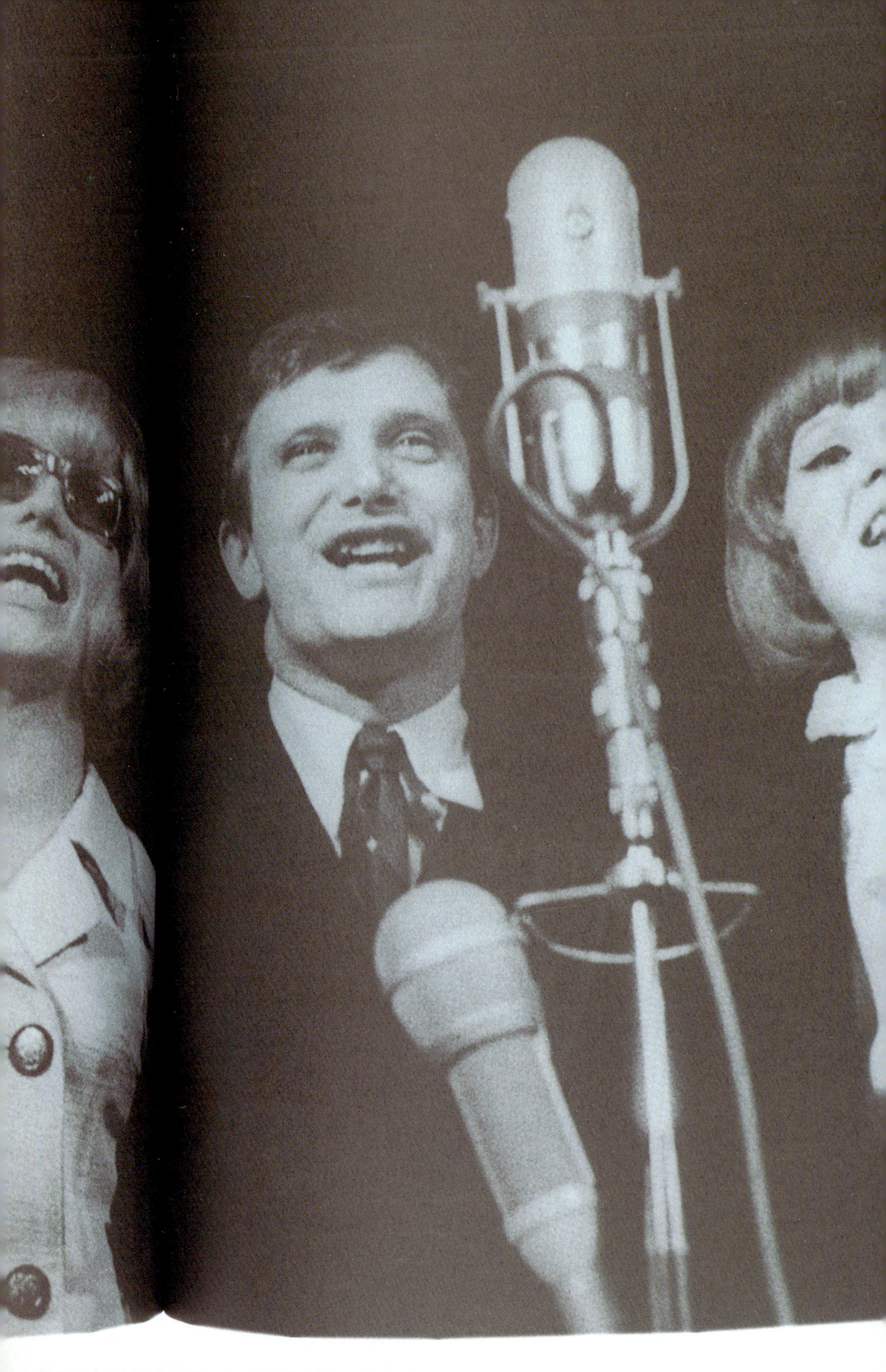

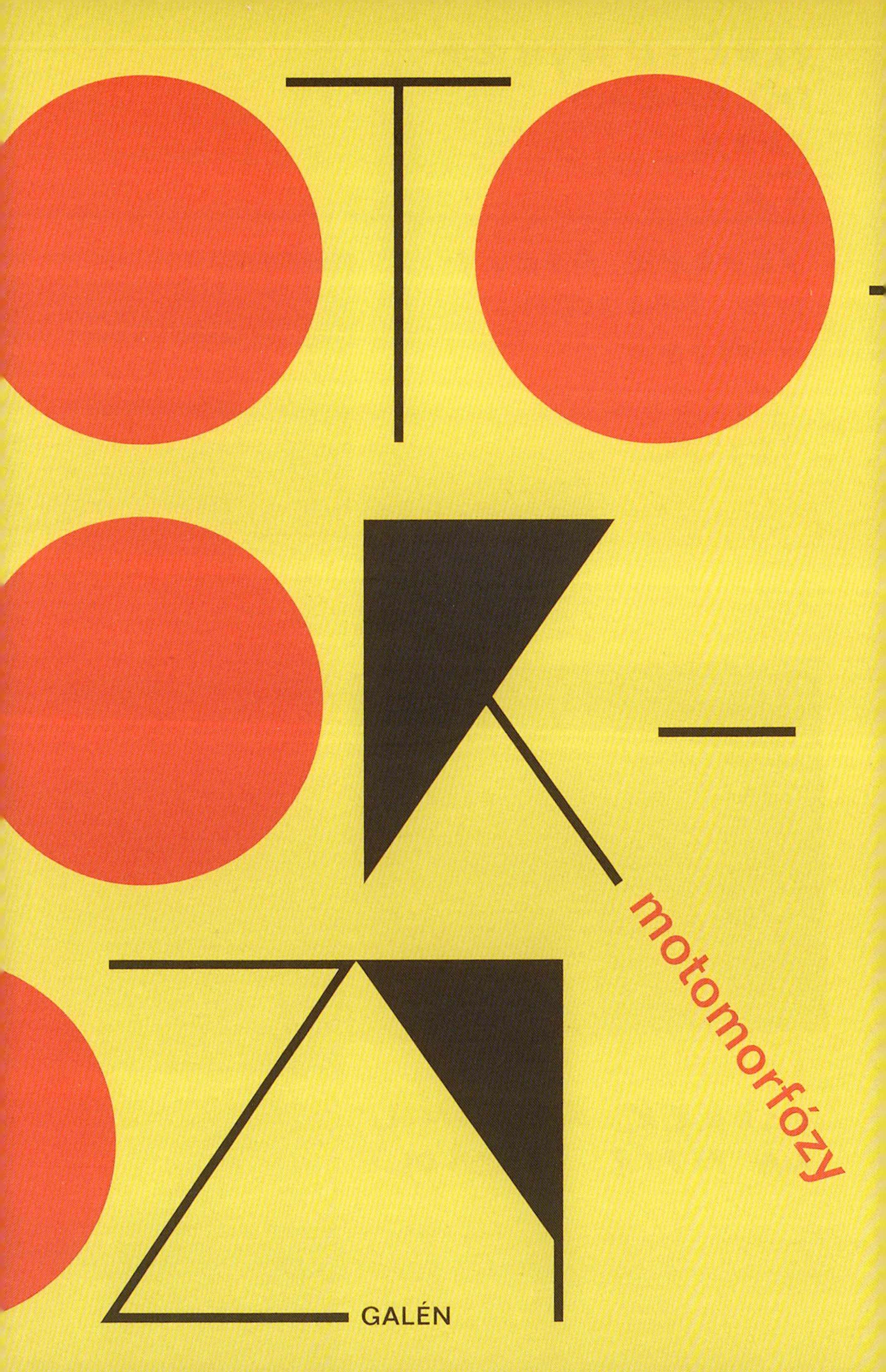OTO KAZA
motomorfózy
GALÉN

OLDŘICH NOUZA
SKLENĚNÝ
PARK
ČS

VZOREK BARVY
NA OBÁLKU
+ TISKU
VEŠKERÉHO
TEXTU

VZOREK KARTONU
NA PAPÍR. VAZBU

# On Books
## Clara Istlerová

01      The Reflexe edition, Vyšehrad publishing, 1982
        · 135 × 205 mm

The Reflexe series (commonly referred to as the "black edition") owes much to the photographer Honza Malý and his
patience with me. Once when I was gluing the letters together
and I watched Honza illuminate negatives in the enlarger after
shooting them, I suddenly noticed that when I tilted the paper
under the enlarger, amazing things appeared in the shape:
unexpected sweeping lines of type or its various, artistically
interesting deformations. These random features then became
one of the inspirations for the layout of this edition.

The artistic conceit of the cover and binding mainly reflected
the treatment of the book's title. The entire edition was black
and white. The book block was a classically prescribed typesetting, based on the Baskerville typeface. But in each book, the
typesetting of the texts was individually designed, based on the
needs of the manuscript, which of course I always read first. It
opened a window into another world, and for that I was grateful.

The book *Boëthius – Poslední Říman* (Boëthius – The Last
Roman) was the first one to be published, the one that started
the whole series. It was the only one with a laminated binding
and no dust jacket.

It has been two or three years since I was asked by the publisher if I would agree to allow the continued use of my foun-
dational design, although they no longer had the funds for the
graphic design and would do it themselves. I gave them my con-
sent, but did not follow up on the results. It was always respect-
able, intelligent literature, so why should it not be published?
I had no idea, however, that a big investor subsequently "swal-
lowed" Vyšehrad publishing house and implemented cost-saving
measures on the designs.

                   On Books

# Boëthius
# Poslední
# Říman

Boëthius

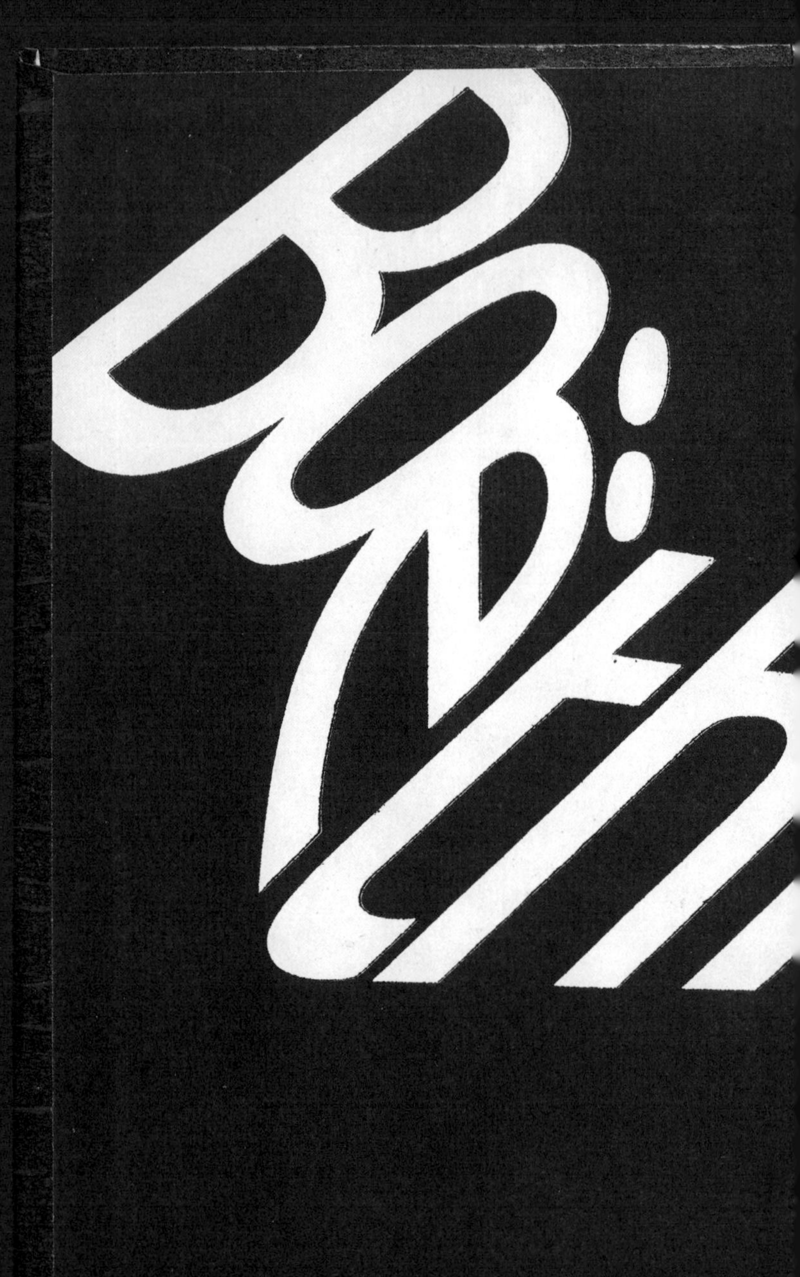



On Books

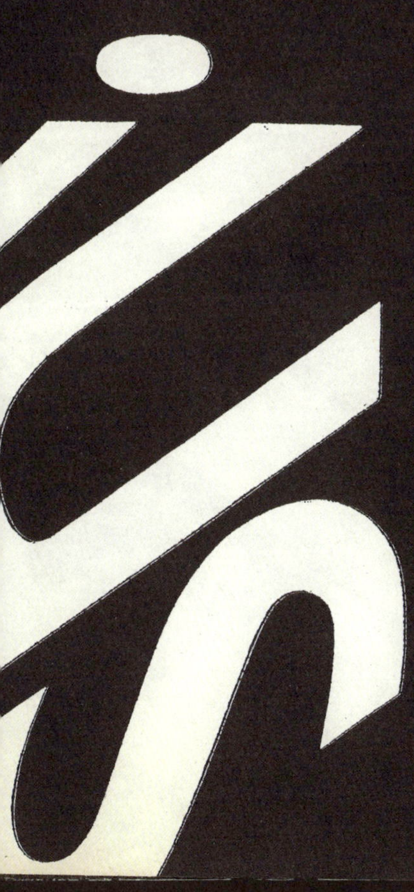

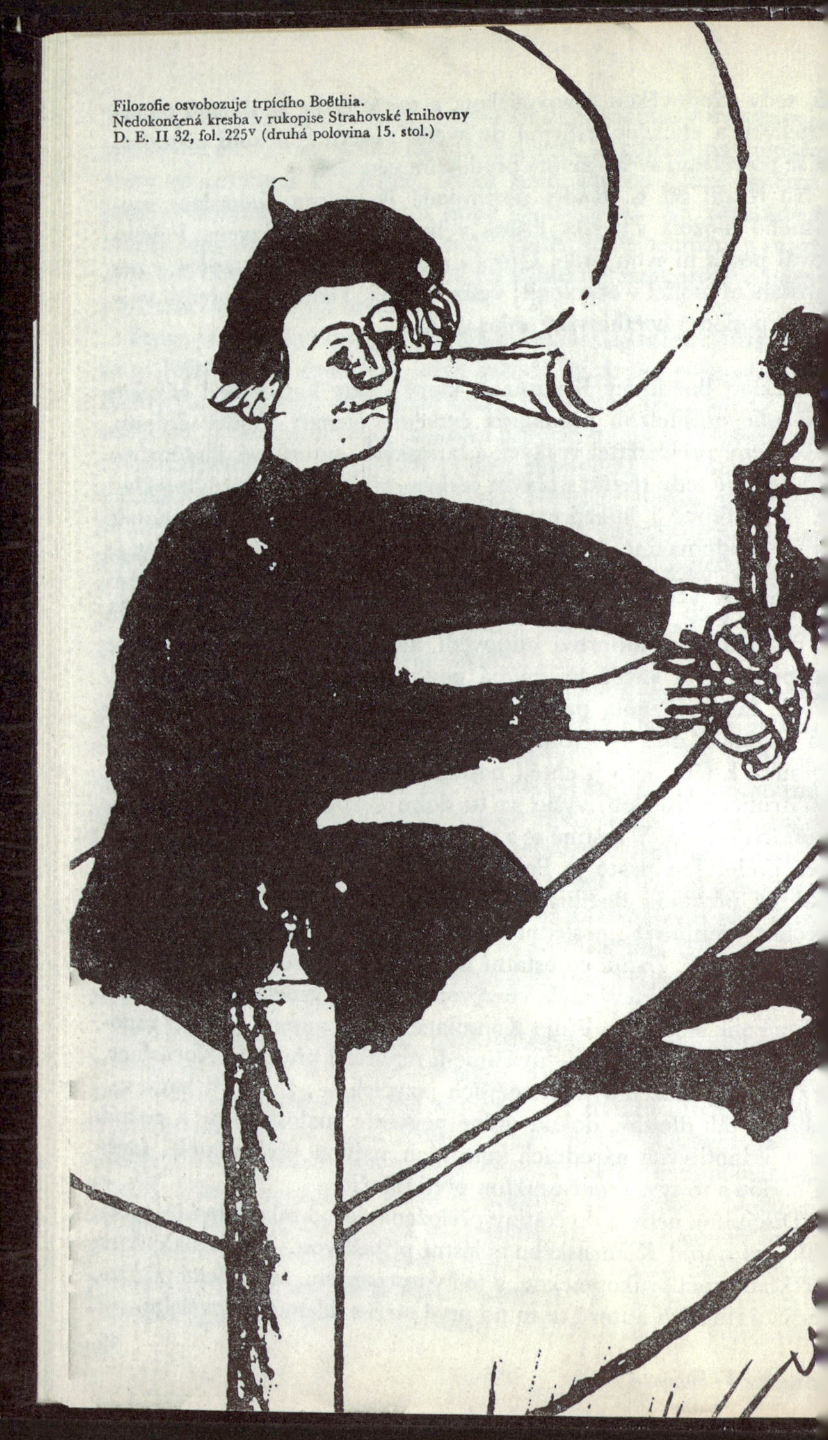

Filozofie osvobozuje trpícího Boëthia.
Nedokončená kresba v rukopise Strahovské knihovny
D. E. II 32, fol. 225ᵛ (druhá polovina 15. stol.)



On Books

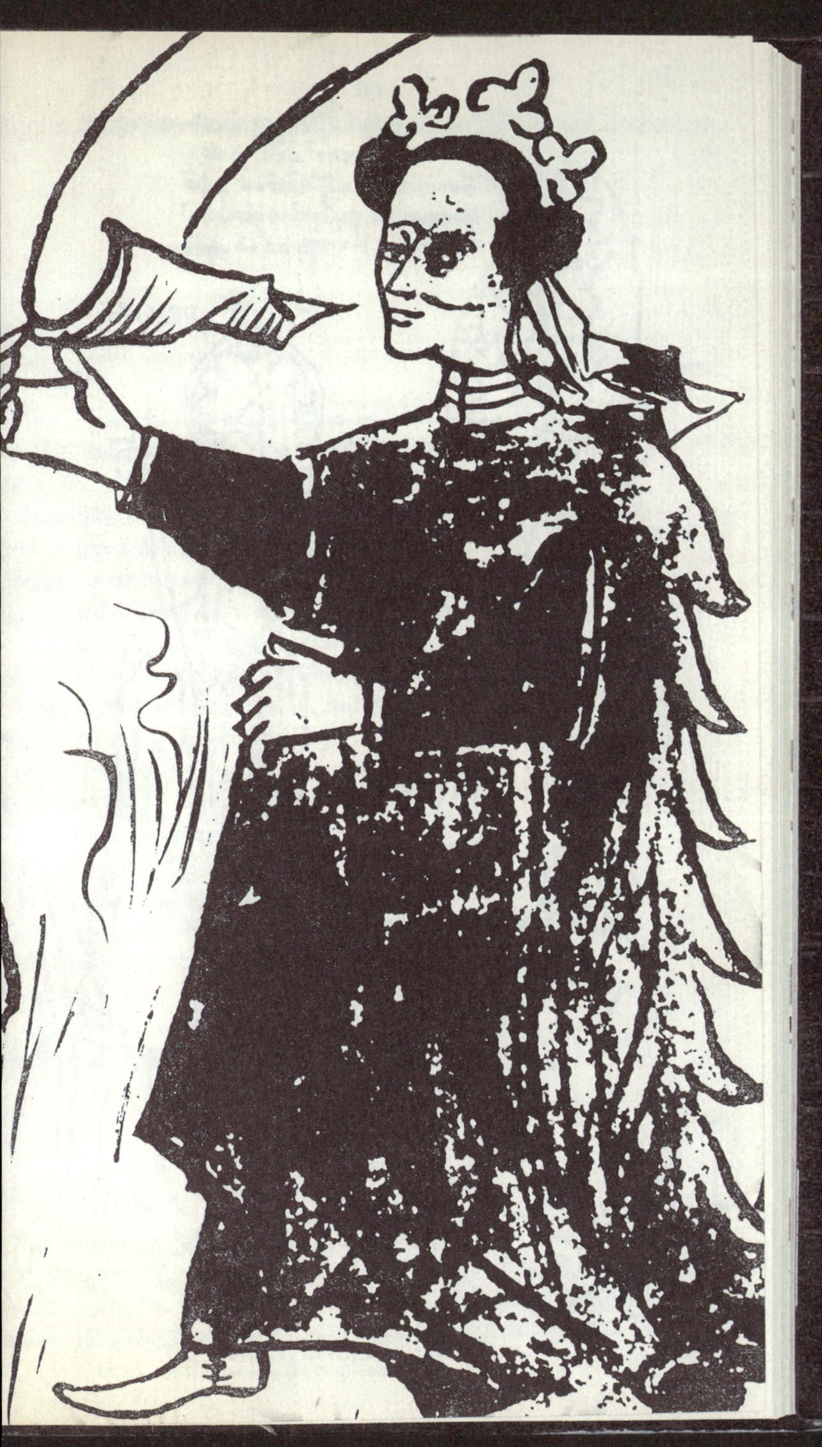

 *Devětsil: česká výtvarná avantgarda dvacátých let*
(Devětsil: Czech Artistic Avant-Garde of the 1920s), 1986
205 × 290 mm

The catalogue for the 1986 Devětsil exhibition should not have
been created. It was not planned. In the end, we agreed to put
a little money into it. Due to the low budget, the catalogue was
printed near the Chuchle racetrack, where there was a small
printing house with old presses. The catalogue was approved
when I told them that a black-and-white print would be enough
to provide basic information about Devětsil and the set of
exhibited works, but at the same time the cover really had to
be something special. And I persuaded them, which took a long
time, to use a thick box cardboard, screen printed. They didn't
believe it would work or that it would be possible to bind it.
Eventually, there were some willing people in that dingy, dirty
building near Chuchle who actually did it. I was on press every
day. Once the people at the print shop saw how extremely interested I was in it, they adapted. Their interest was aroused and
the whole thing turned out quite well. Then the catalogue sold
out within the first three days of the show!

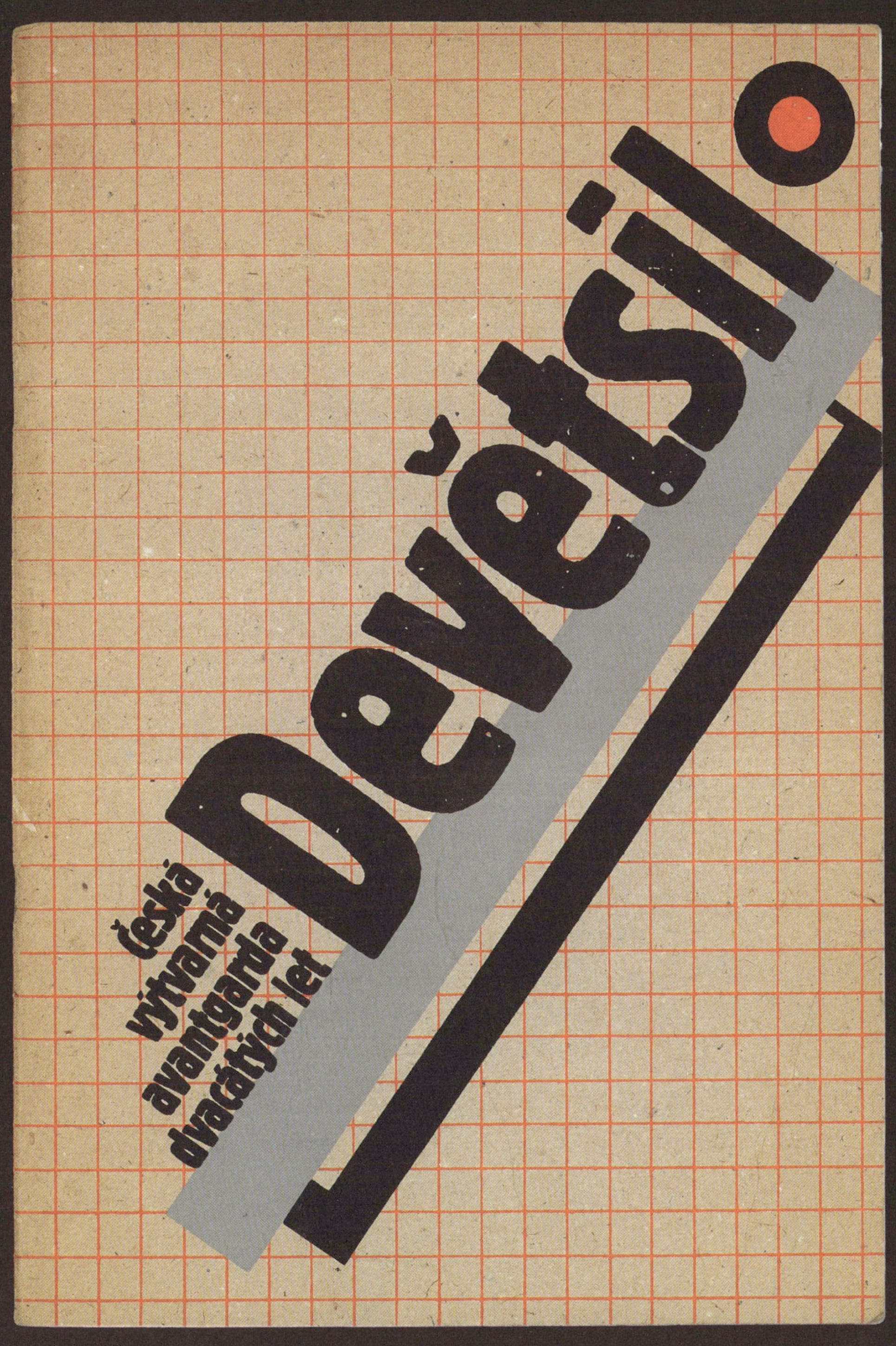

Devětsil
česká
výtvarná
avantgarda
dvacátých let

PÁSMO - DISK - PÁSMO - DISK - PÁSMO

Pouze moderním lidem!

JSME POSTRACHEM:
ctihodných kritiků / středoškolských profesorů / zpozdilých vysokoškolských literátů, konjunkturních literárních bab

NAŠIMI PŘÁTELI JSOU
moderní básníci / mladí intelektuálové / revolucionáři bez výhrady a bystří dělníky

P. T. reakcionáři se zdvořile žádají, aby leták pohodili na veřejné ulici, u holiče, v kavárně a pod.

Po přečtení leták předplatte Pásmo. První ročník. 14 čísel 45 Kč. / Jednotlivé číslo Kč 3.30, po 1. červnu 1925 Kč 3.60

# LA VIE

## (ŽIVOT)

### L'ART NOUVEAU – CONSTRUCTION
### ACTIVITÉ INTELLECTUELLE
### CONTEMPORAINE

**DIRECTEUR**

**J. KREJCAR**

PUBLIÉ PAR **UMĚLECKÁ BESEDA** (UNION D'ARTISTES)
[SECTION DES ARTS PLASTIQUES]
PRAGUE, TCHÉCO-SLOVAQUIE, 1922

Na pražskou reprízu výstavy Devětsilu se nepodařilo získat
řadu děl z majetku Národní galerie v Praze, uvedených v ka-
talogu. Pořadatelé výstavy se za toto, jimi nezaviněné
nedopatření omlouvají.

Na stole stojí džbán a oblost břicha
a křivka válce je tak krásná! Stolní deska
dělí světlo a stín. „Staří a mladí,“ říká si
pekař Jan a šťastná pohoda má jej k tomu,
aby opakoval tato dvě slova do nekonečna.
A potom, když vše je živé a všechno září
a krátký stín se choulí u paty věcí jako
za poledne, Marhoul klade ruce do klína
a usíná.

Vladislav Vančura, **Pekař Jan Marhoul**.
Praha 1925, s. 19.

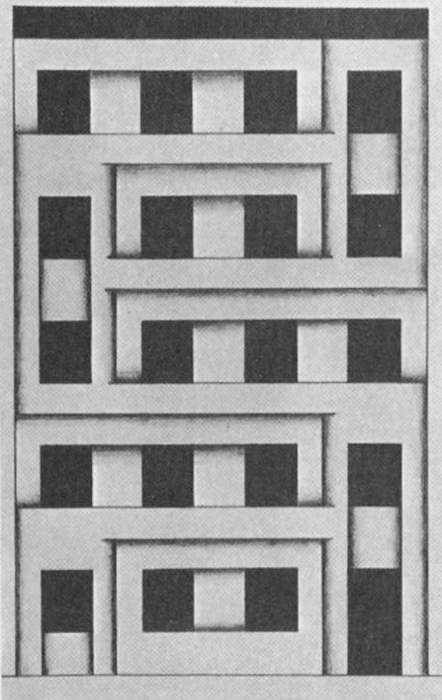

Vít Obrtel.
návrh nájemního domu,
1921

Vít Obrtel,
návrh domu umění v Ostravě,
1923 (č. k. 232)

Mezi umělci, kteří podepsali prohlášení Devětsilu z prosince
1920, byli dva, kteří se kromě dalších výtvarnických oborů zabývali
také architekturou — Alois Wachsman a Josef Havlíček. Od Wachsmana známe několik kubistických architektonických náčrtů už z pre-
devětsilského údobí. Kubistický styl pak poznamenal i Havlíčkovy
a Wachsmanovy projekty náhrobků či celých hřbitovů z počátku
dvacátých let, publikované ve Stylu (1921—22) a v Časopisu československých architektů (1922). Od svých nejbližších vzorů, jimiž
nepochybně byly poválečné projekty Vlastislava Hofmana, se práce
prvních devětsilských architektů liší jakousi záměrnou naivitou
kreslířského podání, ve které se patrně měla zračit programová záliba
Devětsilu v nejprostších věcech, „mlčenlivých soudruzích“. Zá-
měrně naivní — asi tak v duchu Seifertova Města v slzách — byly
i komentáře, jimiž Havlíček a Wachsman své náčrty doprovázeli.
„**Člověk umírá, opouští obyčejně život s tváří vyzařující takový
zvláštní klid,**“ píše Wachsman v Časopisu československých architektů (s. 15). „**Na ten jsem vzpomínal, dělaje tento náhrobek.**“

Okouzlení nejprostšími věcmi však zároveň probouzelo jakousi
magii věcnosti, snahu o nové, v podstatě už nekubistické zpevnění
architektonického tvaru. Ještě lépe než u Havlíčka nebo Wachsmana
lze tento přerod pozorovat v tvorbě Bedřicha Feuersteina, umělce
dosud činného v okruhu Tvrdošíjných, který spolu s Jaromírem Krej-
carem zaujal v Devětsilu během roku 1922 opuštěné Wachsmanovo
a Havlíčkovo místo. Bělostné válce a masívní krycí desky, z nichž se

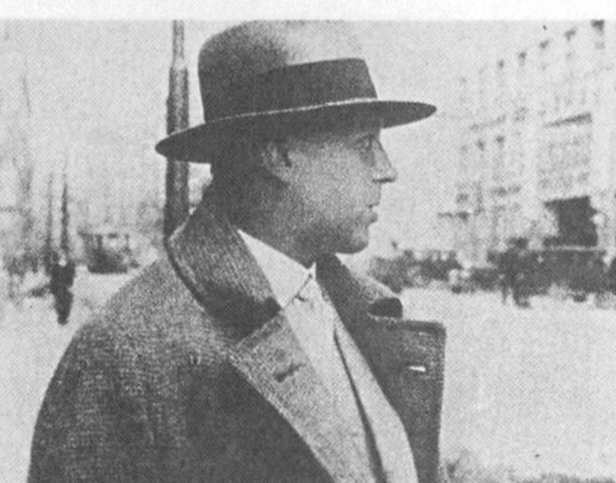

Fotografický
snímek
Víta Obrtela
asi 1926

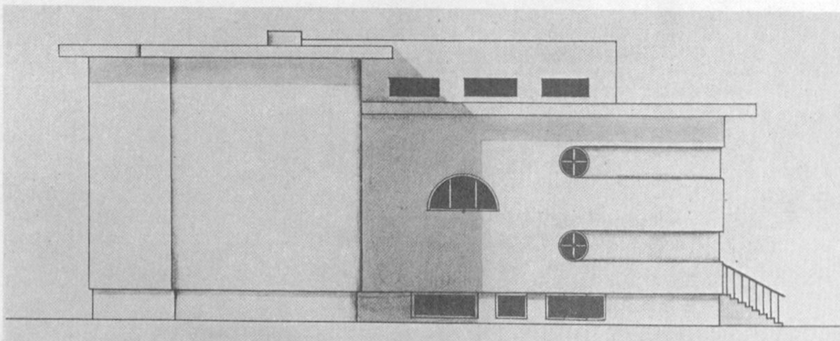

# <u>DEVětsilu</u>

skládá dynamická konfigurace Feuersteinova krematoria v Nymburku (1922–24, spoluautor Bohumil Sláma), mají už jistě blíž k puristické Le Corbusierově definici architektury jako souhry sluncem ozářených geometrických pratvarů než k Hofmanovu kubismu, jehož snad jediným pozůstatkem tu jsou meziokenní reliéfní kříže v čele a na bocích oválného „tamburu". Historik architektury Vladimír Šlapeta (v Umění 1981, s. 310) správně postřehl, že geometrizující tvarosloví nymburského krematoria silně ovlivnila klasicistní či empírová architektura éry Velké francouzské revoluce. Klasicistním „pantheonským tématem" je zde zřejmě i základní figura kolonády před oválnou obřadní síní.

Tento empírový ráz, prostupující i jiná Feuersteinova díla, byl dlouho přičítán umělcovým osobním zálibám. Teprve nyní se nám tradice empíru a klasicismu začíná v dějinách avantgardní architektury jevit jako jeden z jejich nejdůležitějších inspiračních zdrojů. Vedle svých náhle aktuálních kvalit prostoty a jednoduchosti mohla být ideovým vůdcům Devětsilu empírová architektura blízká i svými „revolučními" asociacemi. Výmluvný je už zájem, jaký **„vyspělému revolučnímu empíru"** věnoval Karel Teige v Revolučním sborníku Devětsil (1922, s. 5–18 aj.). Ozvěny empírové tradice lze jistě vycítit i v dvoubarevném Fragnerově a Linhartově soutěžním návrhu divadla v Olomouci (1922), vystaveném na Bazaru moderního umění v roce 1923. Téže tradici jsou poplatné také práce „čestného člena" Devětsilu, pamětníka kubistické Skupiny výtvarných umělců Josefa Chochola (Inženýrská komora v pražské Dittrichově ulici 19, 1923–25) anebo soutěžní Obrtelův projekt domu umění v Ostravě (1923). Připomeňme, že Vít Obrtel dodnes pokládá za **„josefínskou"** – čili empírovou nebo klasicistickou – v podstatě celou devětsilskou produkci z let po svém vstupu do sdružení (1923). Nebyli to tedy ani Chochol, ani Feuerstein, ani sám Obrtel, kdo u nás první došli k puristicky strohému stylu, nýbrž císař Josef Druhý.

Wachsmanův a Havlíčkův kubismus, stejně jako Feuersteinův novoklasicismus, bychom mohli chápat jako dvě rozličné odpovědi na otázku po **„novém umění proletářském"** v oblasti architektury. Je nutno zde uvést ještě další experiment tohoto druhu, Krejcarův pokus o obnovu strohé kotěrovské moderny s jejím „pravdivým" obnažováním tektonické kostry domu i jeho cihelného či betonového materiálu. Krejcar užil tento způsob v soutěžním projektu

Staré pokolení dělníků a noví příchozí vzbouří se pod ranami a šviháním, měděné mračno klidu se otevře bleskem.
Závora chudáctví je zlomena a těsné místo se šíří v prostor. Bude protknuto veselými cestami ze severu k jihu a z východu na západ.

Vladislav Vančura, **Pole orná a válečná**. Praha 1925, s. 212.

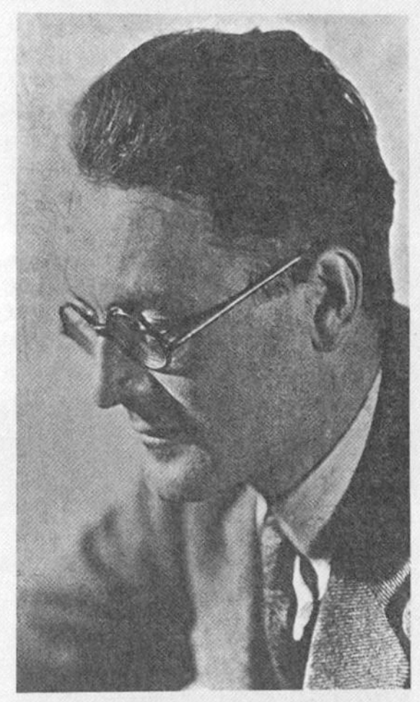

Fotografický snímek
Evžena Linharta,
asi z konce 20. let

Evžen Linhart,
návrh řadových rodinných domů,
1923–1924 (č. k. 235)

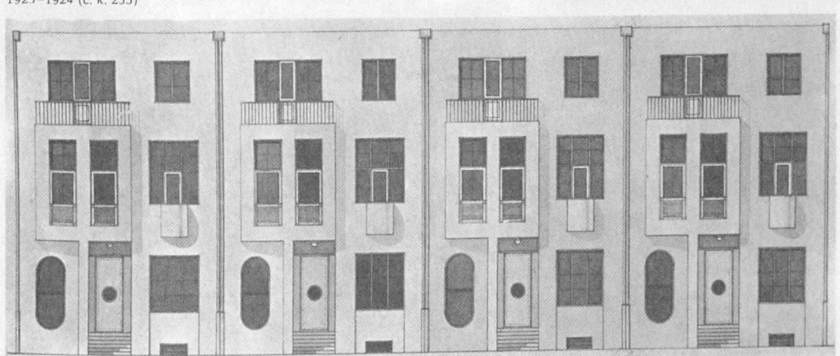

03    Josef Brukner, *Ostrov, kde rostou housle*
      (The Island Where Violins Grow), 1987
      125 × 190 mm

At the beginning of this project, the art editor of Albatros publishing house wanted to make an exceptional book. We agreed
to use reproductions of black-and-white and color drawings and
paintings by various abstract painters from around the world
as illustrations for the poems. For the printing, I suggested
a smooth, gently tinted office paper produced by the paper mills
in Větřní, which would bring together the typesetting and the
pictures and would not appear as harsh as it might on smooth
white offset paper. Because of this, I had to approach the director and convince him that the printing really would come out
nicely, that the color pictures would be in the appropriate
tones, and that the black-and-white ones would maintain their
quality. I said, "Okay, Mr. Director, I accept personal responsibility that it will turn out well."

First, as was my custom, I prepared a complete mock-up of the
book. The publisher supplied the photographs, only some had
to be reproduced again. The manuscript went into typesetting,
which I then glued into the pre-drawn mock-up. When the book
went to the final stage, I was told that it would be printed in
Český Těšín! Which would involve a seven-hour train journey
… I arrived there in the evening, booked a hotel by the station,
and got up in the morning for my shift at the printing house,
where I examined every sheet with the printer. With this offset, 80-gram paper, the back of the sheet behaved completely
differently than the front when printed. Plus, the paper produced a lot of dust, so no sooner had a couple of sheets gone
through than each roller had to be cleaned. That meant rerunning a certain number of sheets before the desired color was
stable. The printer was understandably desperate because the
old rollers were totally warped and each one held the color at
a different intensity. Today, with every new offset four- or five-
color roller there is a computer that shows the percentage of

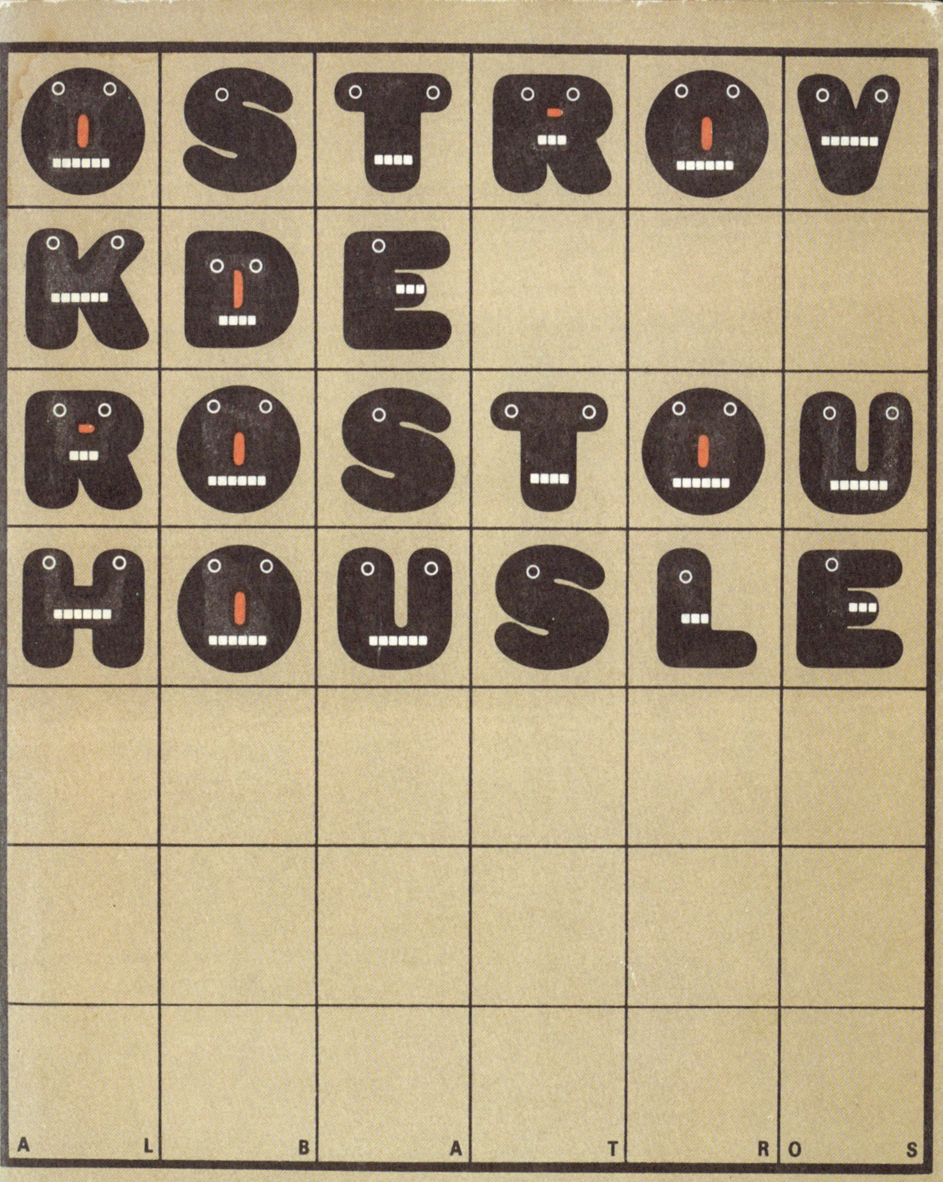


OSTROV
KDE
ROSTOU
HOUSLE
ALBATROS

color that is on the roller, and you just tap to add more. Back
then, the printer still had to run around the whole machine and
use a spatula to apply the ink from the can to the roller or to
the paint well. He was a great, dedicated guy. Fortunately, the
printers didn't rotate shifts. That might have resulted in a very
different result for part of the printing, with visibly differently
colored sheets alternating in the book. For the cover I used
font Seymour Chwast's *Bestial Bold*, which was photographed,
enlarged, then glued and then photographed again. It turned
out well beyond expectations and the book was awarded at the
Bologna Children's Book Fair.



On Books

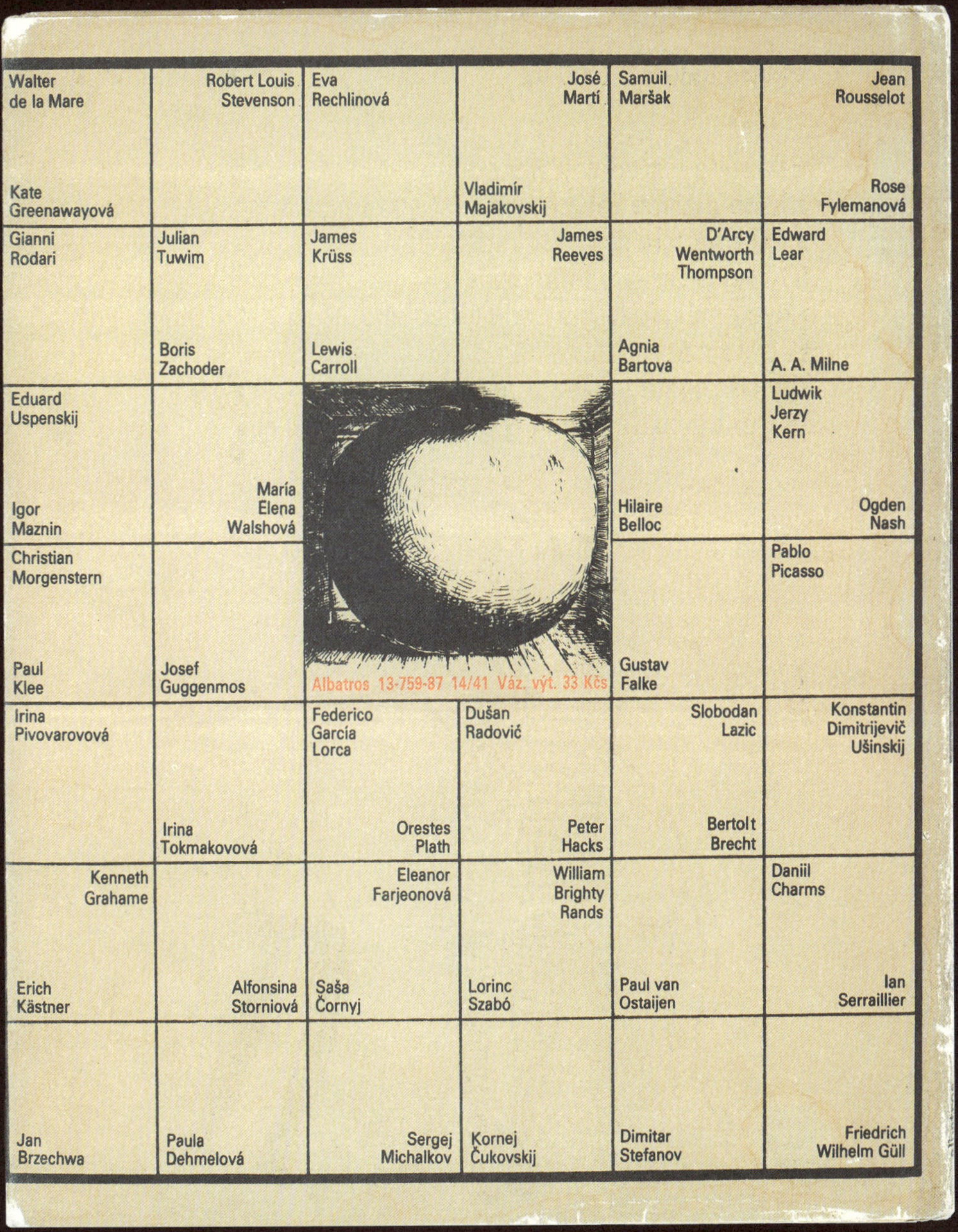

Walter de la Mare

Robert Louis Stevenson

Eva Rechlinová

José Martí

Samuil Maršak

Jean Rousselot

Kate Greenawayová

Vladimír Majakovskij

Rose Fylemanová

Gianni Rodari

Julian Tuwim

James Krüss

James Reeves

D'Arcy Wentworth Thompson

Edward Lear

Boris Zachoder

Lewis Carroll

Agnia Bartova

A. A. Milne

Eduard Uspenskij

Ludwik Jerzy Kern

María Elena Walshová

Igor Maznin

Hilaire Belloc

Ogden Nash

Christian Morgenstern

Pablo Picasso

Paul Klee

Josef Guggenmos

Gustav Falke



Irina Pivovarovová

Federico García Lorca

Dušan Radović

Slobodan Lazic

Konstantin Dimitrijevič Ušinskij

Irina Tokmakovová

Orestes Plath

Peter Hacks

Bertolt Brecht

Kenneth Grahame

Eleanor Farjeonová

William Brighty Rands

Daniil Charms

Erich Kästner

Alfonsina Storniová

Saša Čornyj

Lorinc Szabó

Paul van Ostaijen

Ian Serraillier

Jan Brzechwa

Paula Dehmelová

Sergej Michalkov

Kornej Čukovskij

Dimitar Stefanov

Friedrich Wilhelm Güll

**Hilaire Belloc**

Pavián

Pavián je roztodivný tvor,
žije na pláních jistých hor
a ukazuje tam prý holý zadek.
(Omluvte prosím tento řádek.)
Kdyby měl ale knír a chodil v obleku
— ovšemže po ulici a ne po větvích stromů —
shledali byste možná v úleku,
že z oka vypadl pánovi Tomu a Tamtomu!

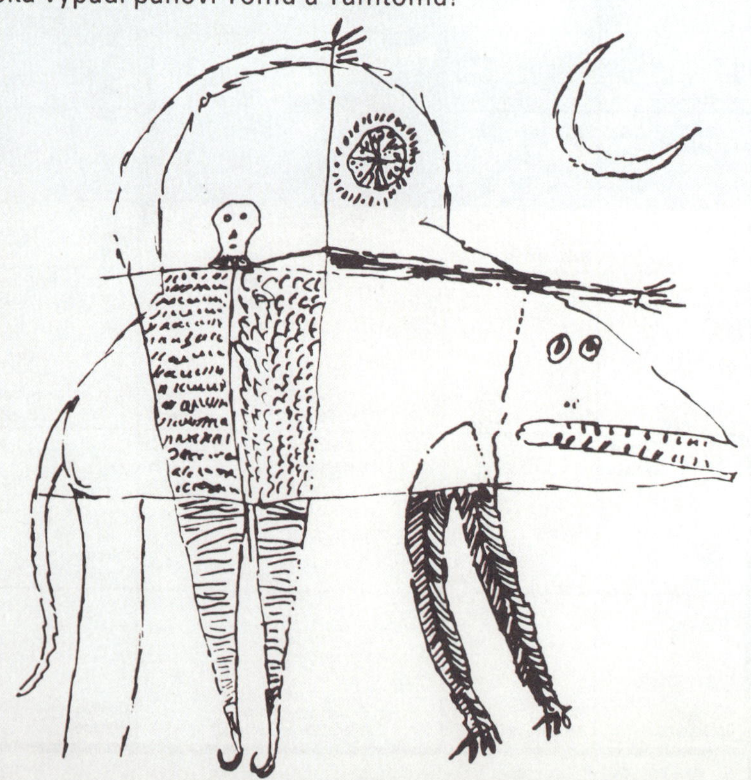

Victor
Brauner
kresba
1964

**Ogden Nash**

## Vepř

Paul Klee
Zvěřinec
na procházce
1926

Ten skromný vepř, pokud se nepletu,
nám dává šunku, špek a kotletu —
a sám si odtrhuje od huby:
obědvá slupky od brambor a otruby.

## Žralok

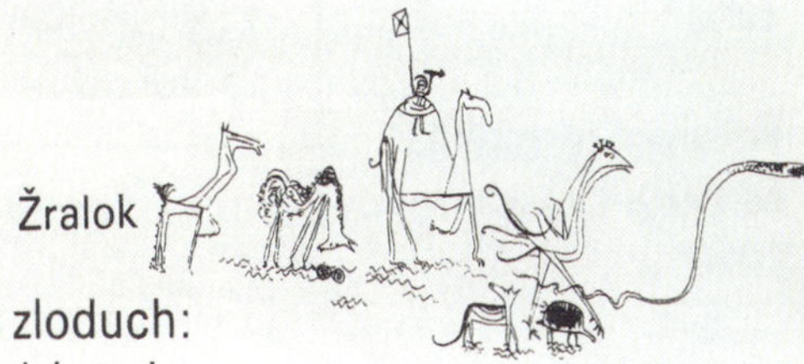

Tvrdí páni vědci, že žralok není zloduch:
který jenom klidně sní a přitom loká vodu.
To já vím své, pokud jde o žraloka:
nejdřív mě klidně sní a potom vodu loká!

Saul Steinberg
kresba

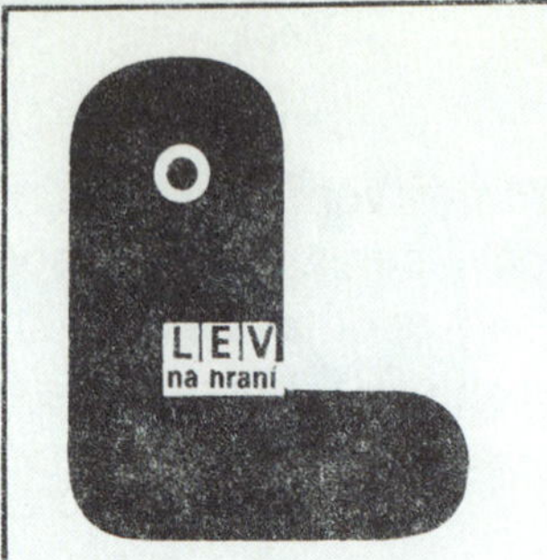


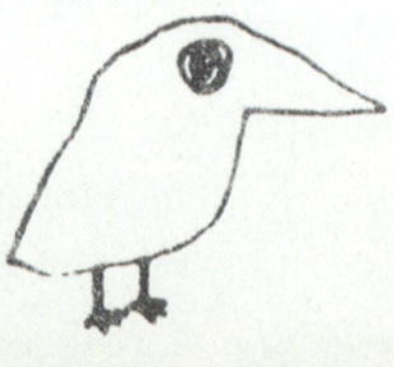



On Books

**D'Arcy Wentworth Thompson**  Vrabčák

Jeden zvídavý vrabčák
vymyslel jednou, proč asi
papoušci mají dlouhý zobák
a lišky dlouhé ocasy.

Liška místo rukávníku
ohon nosí, když je zima —
a papoušek dlouhý zobák
na šňupavý tabák prý má!

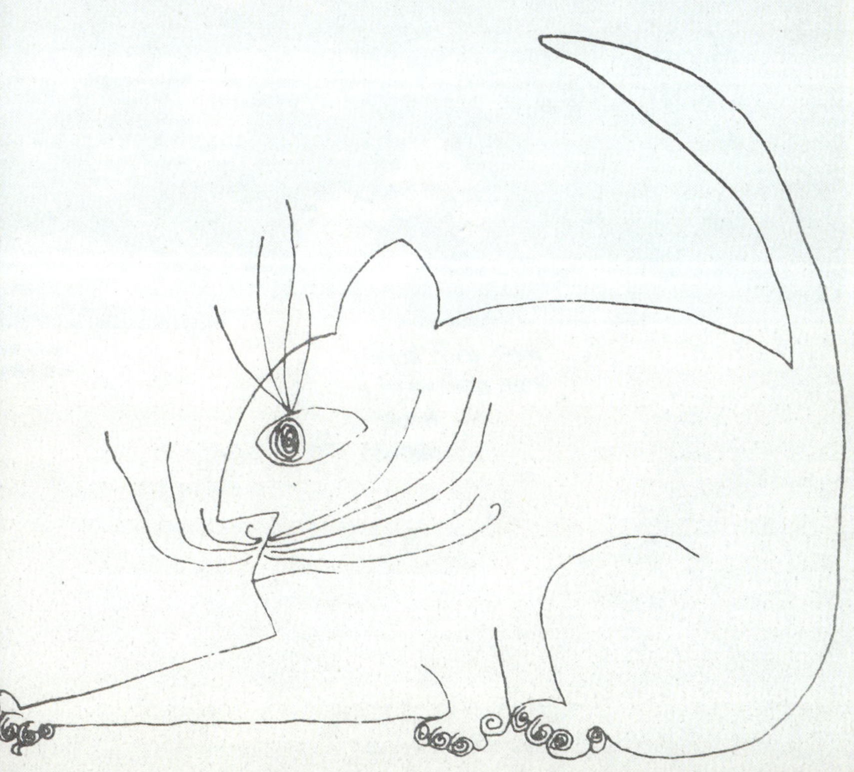

*Přítomnost* was produced in the printing house of the former *Rudé právo* newspaper near the Masaryk railway station, where there was a phototypesetting department headed by Vladimír Popp, who was willing to help me. The entire issue, page by page, was glued by hand from the columns of phototypeset text and captions prepared by me. After the editorial board met, we knew what the content of each issue would be and the main "opener," i.e., the illustration we would ask Karel Nepraš to draw. I prepared a sketch of the front page, giving him the exact size he had to fit his drawing into. Each issue always focused on one theme, so Karel created a symbolic dominant drawing based on the texts, which, because it was large and distinctive, was supposed to tighten the whole cover artistically. I created the graphic design of this, first fortnightly and later monthly, from the beginning. First, a stable header with a masthead was created, and then the concept, including how the layout would be modified from issue to issue. We then stuck to that.

And it was a hustle. As a rule, there was little time for typesetting and processing, because not everyone always met the agreed deadline for submitting texts. A standardized, light blue, preprinted 1:1 type area was prepared into which I pasted the rubberized typesetting. I counted the manuscripts classically: it comes to here, done, the next article follows. I had two or three fonts that were used and varied. This way, I sometimes glued the newspapers together late into the night or quietly into the morning—I often collapsed from hunger. It was two o'clock in the morning and I still hadn't finished.

After 1993, the money ran out at *Přítomnost* because it did not achieve the sales they expected. It's a shame, because there were great, smart people working there.

# Přítomnost

politika
historie
ekonomie
ekologie
věda
umění
cena 7 Kčs

II. ročník / 1991

9

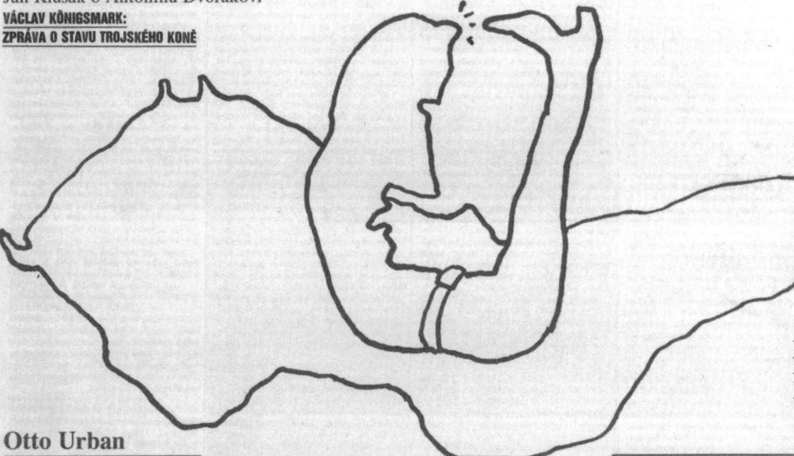


## Otto Urban

# Časové úvahy o české společnosti 1 9 9 1

Není pochyb o tom, že česká společnost dnes prochází jedním z nejrušnějších a nejvýznamnějších údobí svých moderních dějin. Určitým způsobem uzavřená a relativně stabilně strukturovaná česká společnost posledních desetiletí se rozpadá, rychle se mění jak vnější, tak vnitřní podmínky její existence. Společnost se otevřela, a tím se také vytvářejí předpoklady pro to, aby se v mnohem větší míře a plnosti projevily její dosud skryté a nevyjádřené možnosti. Nastřádaný potenciál se uplatňuje s prudkostí jarních vod, které zcela přirozeně přinášejí vedle čistých proudů také zakalené toky.

Jistě, v době, která více otázek nastoluje než řeší, není snadné se v širokém řečišti orientovat. Nechceme-li však jen bezvládně plout anebo vychytrale naskakovat vždy právě na tu nejvzedmutější vlnu, potřebujeme určitý celistvější a přehlednější – byť zdaleka ne »úplný« a zcela »jasný« – obraz současnosti. Přesněji řečeno »obrazy současnosti«, protože v podmínkách názorové tolerance a plurality je »jednota vidění« protismyslná. Moderní doba navíc již dávno nezná vševznalce – polyhistory; autor žádaného obrazu je navíc více či méně determinován profesionálně, tedy předmětem, poznávacími metodami a specifickým pojmovým aparátem svého oboru. Což se týká beze zbytku i métier historika. Ten má při pohledu na současnost v širších souvislostech posledního půlstoletí jen jednu možnou výhodu: ví o něco více o předpokladech, předchozích tendencích a vývojových možnostech – jakým však směrem a v jaké podobě se ty které možnosti naplní či nenaplní, to ví stejně málo jako kdokoli jiný. S využitím svých profesionálních znalostí a způsobů pohledu na minulou i současnou realitu formuluje spíše konkrétní občanské postoje a náhledy. Nic víc, a nic méně. Historik české společnosti nemůže nevidět, jak obtížně tato společnost dnes hledá svou vlastní totožnost, a přitom se až křečovitě snaží o začlenění do širšího společenství. Účelná integrace předpokládá subjekt, který si je vědom své identity – nevybraněné a beztvaré společenství se časem nevyhnutelně rozpadá a ztrácí svou vlastní podstatu. Nikdo tedy českou společnost 1991 nezbaví povinnosti, aby hledala svou podobu a místo jak ve vlastní zemi, tak v širší Evropě.

Téma »česká společnost a Evropa« je v našem chápání nadále až příliš zatíženo ideologizovaným viděním »rozpolcenosti« Evropy, viděním bezděčně černobílým. Chceme »zpět do Evropy«, aniž si uvědomujeme, že jsme geograficky i politicky věru nikdy jinde nebyli. Rozpůlení Evropy na »atlantické společenství« a »ruský orbit« (W. Lippmann, 1944) po druhé světové válce bylo logickým dobovým vyústěním určitých tendenci a trendů celoevropských; neznamenalo také konec jednotných společných evropských dějin, dávalo jim jen jinou dimenzi.

To, co se v posledních desetiletích dělo na východě našeho kontinentu, bylo stejně »evropské« jako to, co se dělo na jeho západě. Stačí si jen dostatečně uvědomit autenticky evropský původ všech teorií a ideologií »sociálních experimentů« po roce 1917. Vědecký socialismus nevynalezl žádný ruský mužik, ten byl jako teoretický produkt výsledkem evropského filosofického, politického a sociálního myšlení a jednou z koncepcí moderní občanské společnosti. Na této základní skutečnosti nic podstatného nemění »ne-evropské« praktiky a případné ideové »příměsi« z jiných civilizačních a kulturních oblastí. Konečně, nebyl také nacistický »sociální experiment« výlučně evropským jevem? Nesmírné draze zaplacená zkušenost s nejrůznějšími totalitními variantami »reálného socialismu« od nacionálního až po stalinistický je společnou evropskou zkušeností a nesmazatelným kusem společných evropských dějin. Chápeme-li se odpovědnosti, pak ji – byť v míře nestejné – nese celá Evropa. Z tohoto hlediska se do nové Evropy vracíme všichni, totiž do Evropy, která najde svou novou tvář a podobu, své pozitivní mravní a kulturní hodnoty. Jen takové evropanství má smysl a může být více než prázdným a nadutým projevem neblahého a neodůvodněného europocentrismu.

Většině z nás je zřejmé, že totalitní politické systémy jsou trvaleji neslučitelné s občanskou společností a v přímém protikladu s principem občanství. Politickému a mocenskému systému však přisuzujeme někdy jednostranně zdůrazněný význam a dostatečně nediferencujeme mezi tímto systémem a skutečným společenským vývojem v plné šíři. V dějinách jsme dosud nepoznali ideální »otevřenou« státněpoliticky organizovanou společnost, stejně jako hermeticky »uzavřenou« společnost totalitní. Pětačtyřicet let »dvojí Evropy« neznamenalo a nemohlo znamenat naprosté přerušení všech vazeb, v obou »částech« žily a rozvíjely se – i když snad v jiné podobě a rozdílné intenzitě – humanistické a demokratické tradice stejně jako tendence protikladné. Nebylo by na místě a nebylo by šťastné přehlížet, že vzdor protivenství a nepřízni byla v posledních desetiletích vytvořena ve východní Evropě také řada materiálních a kulturních hodnot, které tvoří společný vklad do pokladnice evropského bohatství. Otázkou a úkolem je tyto hodnoty přesně rozpoznat a charakterizovat. Leckteré dnešní žalobné psaní o »neúspěších socialismu« až průhledně připomíná negativní závislost na těch, kteří léta letoucí psali o jeho »úspěších«. Ztotožňováním politického systému a společnosti paušálně znehodnocujeme výsledky práce bezpočtu lidí jen proto, že se uskutečnily v rámci určitého »systému«. Ty výsledky mají svou hodnotu, byť byly třeba jako »úspěchy« přivlastňovány nositeli politického systému. Česká společnost se v průběhu uplynulých čtyř desetiletí pronikavě změnila a neschopnost rozlišit pozitivní a negativní stránky těchto změn může vést k mravní kocovině a znesnadnit hledání jakékoli identity. Využívá česká inteligence naprosto jedinečné příležitosti svobodného projevu k tomu, aby tlumočila věcná a nezávislá stanoviska vedle nezbytně zaujatých postojů odpovědných politiků?

Diferencované hledání a objasňování vztahu k Evropě a evropanství a současně k vlastní nedávné dějinné zkušenosti jsou součástí nejobecnějších podmínek nalézání vlastní identity české společnosti 1991. Z nich pak do značné míry vyplývají již konkrétnější, speciálnější a mnohem praktičtější problémy,

Josef Jedlička

# O politické sentimentalitě

### aneb

# JAN RATKIN

»Stříbrný vítr« je úkaz povýtce privátní. Budiž mi tu proto dovoleno úvodem i poněkud hořké privátní konstatování, že jej – aby se tak řeklo – už dávno neslyším. Popadne mě sice občas pošetilá touha vyjet si – ne tedy snad rovnou s baletkou do Benátek, ale třeba jen někam k řece, dívat se, jak se horská voda pění ledovou tříští. Pohřichu já sám nejlíp vím, že tenhle jarní nepokoj, který posléze skončí rodinným výletem s fotografováním na louce s blatouchy, nemá se »stříbrným větrem« vůbec nic společného.

Jsem si jist, že moji vrstevníci, a tím spíše pak lidé ještě o jednu generaci starší, vědí přesně, o čem je tu řeč, jako vím téměř bezpečně, že u mého syna vyvolá už jenom sama ta secesně poetická ražba shovívavý úsměv a že pro lidi kolem třicítky je »stříbrný vítr« pojem spíše literárně-historický, nadaný jednou menším a podruhé o něco větším obsahem. Není se vlastně čím chlubit a také se nikterak nehonosím, když věcně zjišťuji, že na pokraji šedesátky patřím patrně k poslední generaci v řadě dvou nebo tří pokolení, jejichž citovost a základní vztah ke světu, to jest k autoritě, k sociálním otázkám i ke kultuře velmi významně poznamenal slavný román Fráni Šrámka.

Jan Ratkin, chlapecký hrdina Stříbrného větru, nepatří sice mezi postavy českého literárního Olympu jako Švanda dudák či Josef Švejk, není postavou příkladnou jako babička či odstrašující jako v nejednom pojetí Kondelík, ale nabízí se čímsi zřejmě zcela výjimečně k tomu, aby se s ním čtenáři celé jedné epochy ztotožnili. Poprvé Šrámkovi generační druzi, kteří v něm nacházeli – jak o tom svědčí dobové prameny – věrné zpodobení svých vlastních pubertálních zmatků a krizí. Podruhé o něco mladší pokolení poválečné, jehož příslušníci už chápali Jana Ratkina jako časného předchůdce své lyrické revolty proti akademickému a skrupulózně zkostnatělému světu už skomírající rakousko-uherské monarchie. Ještě o pár let později vyrostl Jan Ratkin se svým přítelem Zachem a učitelem Ramlerem na typ obecný a – jak se tenkrát zdálo – na jednou provždy platný model živelného, zbrklého, ale i upřímně idealistického a zapáleného mládí.

Ve chvíli, kdy se na dospívající lidi začínal pomalu klást stín druhé světové války, objevili se Ratkinové tragičtí, kteří ve svém literárním předobrazu snadno našli rysy odpovídající jejich vlastnímu pocitu mládí zmarnělého a nenaplněného. Odtud byl pak už jenom krok k časům, které pamatuji, kdy se Stříbrný vítr četl jako zpráva o šťastnějším světě velkých citů a vášní, pro něž v současném světě místa stále ubývalo, i jako melancholické poselství o nezadržitelně uplývajícím mládí, přelévajícím se nenávratně do věku rozumu a přežila.

I na pouhý první pohled není těžké vycítit, co společného mají všechny tyto rozdílné konkrétní realizace literární postavy rozprostřené po rozloze dobrých třiceti let. Otázka, která se dnes nad Stříbrným větrem klade, musí však směřovat k tomu, co to bylo za historické okolnosti, z nichž vyrostla postava tak životná a reprezentativní, a jaká to byla vlastně mentalita, která si po tak dlouhou dobu mohla vždycky znovu najít v Janu Ratkinovi své autentické ztělesnění. Neboť je to povýtce historická otázka, jak prostě plyne už z toho, že se tato figura posléze z jedné generace na druhou vyčerpala a přežila. Proč se tak stalo, to je otázka další. Touto cestou se pak snad bude možno přiblížit k zjištění, o než tu vlastně vskutku jde – jaký dosah a důsledky mělo ratkinovské citové a názorové východisko pro životní praxi několika pokolení, a jak určil mýtus »stříbrného větru« sociální a politické poměry nejkritičtějšího období našich národních dějin.

Román Stříbrný vítr nelze kriticky číst, aniž při tom vnímáme jeho tichý tragický generální bas, jímž se zážitek první světové války. »Mám vás rád, Ratkine,« říká v intimní chvíle hrdinův přítel, na bazarovsko střižený nihilista Zach, »vy jste – horké srdce. Nemyslete si, i já mel v sobě svatý oheň. Každý lepší chlapec má v sobě svatý oheň…« – což je ostatně věta, kterou zatím pouze vytkněme, abychom se k ní mohli vrátit. Zach pokračuje: »…rozbíhá se takový chlapec, rozbíhá, na každém trnu kousek masa zanechá… Nu což o kousíčky masa, ale i šat se potrhá, to je ta nepravost, šat se potrhá a na to jsou staří přísní…« Jistě nic nebrání, a také ve skutečnosti tomu nic nebránilo, aby se toto slavné místo interpretovalo jako bolestné zrání jinocha, věčný boj mladistvého idealismu o sebe sama proti nepřízni a výsměchu přízemně praktického světa dospělých. Ale v souvislostech celého románu vyúsťují všechny lyrické pasáže o bolestiplném mládí v poněkud překvapivou pointu: když Jeník Ratkin, náhle dozrály prvním milostným naplněním, zazpíval vstříc »stříbrnému větru« svou velkou chválu života, zdvihne jedlovou větvičku a hodí ji do skalní rozsedliny se slovy, která jsou zároveň poslední větou knihy: »Na tvůj hrob, Jene Ratkine, a pošetilý!«

Opět tu jistě nemůže být námitek proti obvyklému výkladu, že v té chvíli se Ratkin vymaňuje z pubertálních zmatků, melancholicky se loučí se svým »dětinství krásným věkem«, aby se pokusil pronést své »planoucí srdce« světem jako muž. Ale v dobových souvislostech má toto loučení tragičtější i definitivnější přízvuk. Tak se nám ze scény ztrácí i Hans Castorp, neklidný hrdina Mannova Kouzelného vrchu, a zahlédáme ho potom už jenom klopýtat přes drátěné překážky mezi zákopy válečného bojiště. Pro tisíce Ratkinů nedopadla ta jedlová větvička pouze na symbolický hrobeček chlapeckých pošetilostí, ale na počertech skutečný hromadný hrob s nehašeným vápnem kdesi v Haliči, u Verdunu nebo na Piavě. Byl to věru krutý první krok do dospělosti, který učinili oni původní Ratkinové, a není divu že ti, kteří to přežili, vkládali do posledních slov Stříbrného větru tolik politického obsahu jako do proslulého výkřiku »Hovno!«, jímž končí jiný, výslovně antimilitaristický Šrámkův román Tělo. Programové utonutí v živočišné smyslovosti, jak jej líčí Tělo, a chvála Života ve Stříbrném větru není ostatně původem nic jiného než obranná reakce mladého organismu proti nevčasné a absurdní smrti.

Je-li však Tělo dílo v pravém smyslu slova dobové, to jest nadšeně přijaté, po krátkou dobu silné působící a rychle vzaté z oběhu, účinek Stříbrného větru byl méně prudký, zato pronikavější a nesrovnatelně trvalejší. Šrámek jím totiž nabídl válkou zaskočené a rozvrácené generaci, ale i několika dalším vlnám mladých lidí, sevřených mezi úzké kleště dvou světových katastrof, životní hledisko, výklad událostí, na svůj způsob cosi jako ideologii, která se, po pravdě řečeno, prokázala jako osudná.

Válka je především brutální intervence do nejsoukroměšího života člověka. Nejenže jej ohrožuje v samé podstatě, ale brání, aby byl prožíván se vším, co vytváří jeho plnost – zbavuje jej přede vším ostatním jeho rozměru citového a lyrického. Ze zorného úhlu války (což platí o jakékoli společenské krizi, tedy i o té, kterou způsobuje diktatura) se jeví každý spontánní projev jako nejvýš žádoucí, každá osobní aktivita, byť to i bylo nejkrutější hoře lásky, jako štěstí. Válka, která je cosi výsledně mimořádného, zostřuje smysl pro všednost, válka, která je povýtce »protilidová«, dává vyrůst citu pro společenské a třídní rozdíly. Souhrnem všech těchto kladných životních hodnot, vybraných a sežazených skrze válečný zážitek, je mládí – ovšemže mládí samo o sobě, ale což teprve takové mládí, které jsme nemohli naplnit, z něhož jsme nemohli přirozeně dospět, což teprve ono mládí, kterému nebyl dopřán čas, aby se prosadilo se vší svou nevinností a reformním idealismem proti okoralým srdcím a zvápenatělým mozkům původců absurdní války!

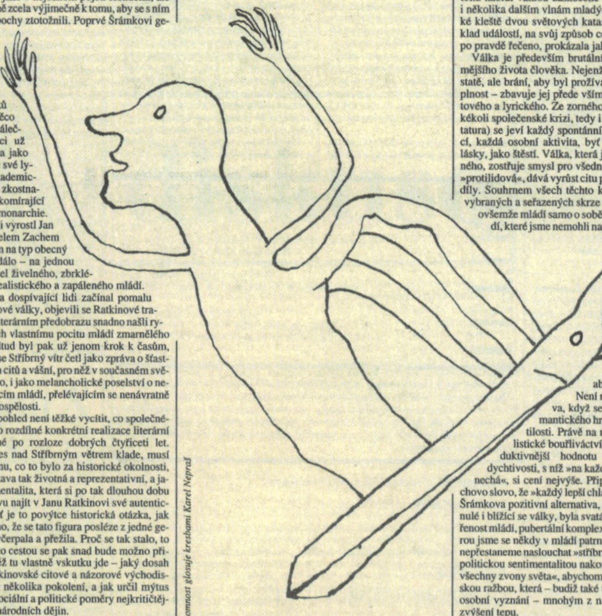

Není radno věřit Ratkinovi doslova, když se odvrací s úsměvem od romantického hrobečku své chlapecké pošetilosti. Právě na ní si zakládá, právě to idealistické bouřliváctví má za společensky nejproduktivnější hodnotu a právě své mladické dychtivosti, s níž »na každém trnu kousíček masa zanechá«, si cení nejvýše. Připomeňme teď znovu to Zachovo slovo, že »každý lepší chlapec má v sobě svatý oheň«. Šrámkova pozitivní alternativa, kterou nabídl obětem uplynulé i blížící se války, byla svatá nevinnost a riskantní otevřenost mládí, pubertální komplex, to jest věrnost přísaze, kterou jsme se někdy v mládí patrně všichni zavázali, že nikdy nepřestaneme naslouchat »stříbrnému větru«. A také víra, že politickou sentimentalitou nakonec přece jen »rozhoupáme všechny zvony světa«, abychom se vyjádřili jinou šrámkovskou ražbou, která – budiž také to řečeno v zájmu věci jako osobní vyznání – mnohým z nás dodnes způsobuje lehké zvýšení tepu.

Mnoho mladých lidí meziválečných pokolení tuto ratkinovskou alternativu přijalo a vzalo za svou. Alespoň ti »lepší chlapci«. Zatímco si pak jitřili rány a ještě na stará kolena se vychloubali jizvami utrženými při tom rozevlátém běhu trním a hložím, ti »horší chlapci« se honem koukali ze svých romantických škrábanců vylízat. Zatímco oni proklamovali spásu světa lyrickou obrodou, tito začínali okoušet, jak chutná moc. A zatímco jedni mnoho přemýšleli o tom, jak z rudých blůzek, rozvlněných pevnými ňadry mladých fabriček, sešít velký prapor revoluce, ti druzí se přičinlivě šplhali na místa sekretářů a generálních sekretářů. Ovšemže oni Ratkinové byli lepší – proto také většinou zahynuli na ten či onen způsob v soukolí světa; ale hynuli i proto, že měli romantickou a sentimentální víru v samospád dobra.

Ve věku globálních a totalitaristických manipulací, jaké nastaly po druhé světové válce, si nelze tuto víru zachovat. Poučili jsme se (a ne-li my, tedy najisto naši synové), že nestačí planoucí srdce, aby se rozhoupaly zvony práva a spravedlnosti, natož pak mocní tohoto světa. Víme, že dobro může zvítězit jenom tehdy, když bude silnější než zlo. A v této chvíli teprve definitivně doznívá »stříbrný vítr«. Protože jsme zestárli, ale i proto, že jsme zmoudřeli.

A proto naposled větvičku na tvůj hrob, Jene Ratkine, bohužel včerejší a velmi pošetilý!

# Přítomnost

politika
historie
ekonomie
ekologie
věda
umění
cena 7 Kčs

červenec 1990/2

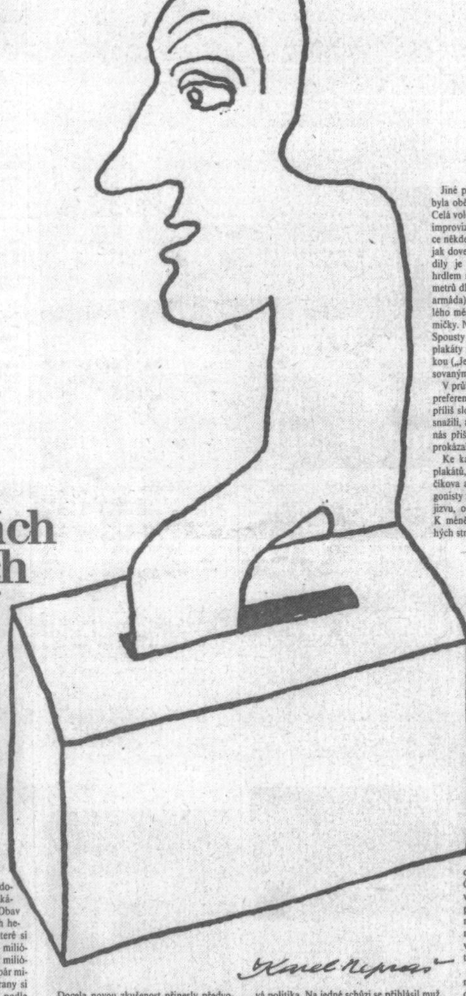


# Ve volbách a po nich

**V**olby jsou za námi a při všech možných výhradách dopadly dobře. Poražené strany se zlobí, vítězné už mají plné ruce práce, ale lidi mají radost. Po dlouhých letech jsou tu zase legitimní parlamenty, vláda, prezident — začátky právního státu. To je jeden důvod k radosti; druhý je ten, že ze všech zúčastněných obstáli nejlépe právě sami voliči.

### KAMPAŇ

Obav před volbami bylo víc než dost: z množství politických stran, tedy jak se říkalo „stran a hnutí"; z toho, jak jsou navenek neurčité a jak se sobě podobají. Odkud berou peníze na tolik plakátů? Proč vlastně jsou a kdo je v nich? Obav z demagogů, obav z účinnosti líbivých hesel a podbízení. Co tu bylo stran, které si myslely, že mají své jisté: půl druhého miliónu rybářů, milión zahrádkářů, přes půl miliónu družstevních zemědělců a hezkých pár miliónů těch, co mají rádi pivo. Jiné strany si zase řekly — co tak asi každý chce? A podle toho dělaly kampaň. Intelektuál, uvyklý despektu k „obyčejným lidem", nechce ani věřit, že obojí nakonec tak špatně dopadly. Není to div? Podceňování voličů a snaha vytloukat kapitál z nadávání na jiné se — aspoň tentokrát — nikomu nevyplatily.

Docela novou zkušenost přinesly předvolební schůze. Jednoduchá polarita „komunisté — nekomunisté" tu, pravda, hrála velkou roli: na každé z asi čtyřiceti schůzí, které jsem absolvoval v Praze, padla otázka, zda jsem byl někdy členem. Ale pak už přicházely takové otázky, jako by tu už byla opravdová politika. Na jedné schůzi se přihlásil muž, který mi položil šest stručných otázek, test na tělo, jaký by si žádný politolog nevymyslel: od jaderných elektráren přes pomlčku a hromadnou dopravu až po můj názor na zákaz potratů. Co otázka, to problém. Odpovídal jsem asi patnáct minut, a ty byly perné.

Jiné překvapení, aspoň pro politika-začátečníka, byla obětavost a nápaditost pořadatelů a aktivistů. Celá volební kampaň odshora dolů byla jedna velká improvizace. Nebylo nic. Plakáty, místnosti, dokonce někde prý ani volební plenty. A tak se lidé činili, jak dovedli. Kde nebyly plakátovací sloupy, nahradily je betonové kanalizační trubky, postavené hrdlem na zem. V Děčíně natáhli horolezci tři sta metrů dlouhé lano z věže zámku (kde sídlí sovětská armáda) na protější skálu za řekou a před očima celého města na něm věšeli vlajky a také ovšem sedmičky. Někde měli domácí koláče s čísly z hrozinek. Spousty doma dělaných plakátů, vedle nich unylé plakáty made in Austria s barevnou rodinnou idylkou („Je nám spolu dobře"), oživované ručně dopisovanými naivistickými veršíky.

V průběhu kampaně jsem začal přicházet na chuť preferenčnímu systému, který se zpočátku zdál být příliš složitý. Díky němu se totiž všichni kandidáti snažili, a byl jsem na předvolebních schůzích, kam nás přišlo víc než mělo. Ostatně i výsledek voleb prokázal, že preference nebyly zbytečné.

Ke kampani patřilo i strhávání a přestříkávání plakátů, nepochybný stín však vrhla teprve Bartončíkova aféra, která bohužel místo smutného protagonisty zasáhla voliče jeho strany, zanechala v nich jizvu, oslabila jejich důvěru v prostor veřejnosti. K méně pěkným rysům patřilo i obviňování druhých stran, že jsou to „převlečení komunisté", a tažení proti „malým stranám". Nakonec se ukázalo být zbytečné; nevím, komu pomohlo, ale vítězům jistě uškodilo. Kapitola sama pro sebe byla kampaň v televizi, dlouhá bílá přerušovaná čára banalit a skoro urážlivého podceňování diváků. S jakým napětím jsme — právě před rokem — sledovali naproti tomu televizní čtvrthodinky polské Solidarity! Když se nakonec podařilo sehnat dohromady dva diskusní večery, bylo divákovi jasné, proč se jim strany tolik bránily. Dvě podivné jedenáctky málo rozhněvaných mužů, kteří se dvě hodiny o překot hlásili o slovo, a když je dostali, deklamovali učebnicové triviality. Oba experti OF tu měli věru lehkou práci.

### VOLBY

Žádné pohromy, provokace ani velkoplošné podvody, které před volbami tolik strašily v hlavách i v novinách, se nakonec nekonaly. Klidný, sváteční a trochu nudný průběh vlastních voleb přinesl výsledky, které však přece jen překvapily. Především volební účast. Čím to asi bylo? Dlouholetý zvyk povinných voleb možná udělal své, ale okolnost, že při poměrně složitém systému prakticky nebyly neplatné hlasy, svědčí spíš o skutečném zájmu. Že si tak málo lidí popletlo barvy hlasovacích lístků a že skoro všichni dokázali ze třikrát patnácti vybrat tři, není samo sebou.

Ještě větší překvapení byla kroužkovací mánie. Co tolik odborníků před volbami tvrdošíjně popíralo, to se nakonec stalo. Ve většině krajů se kroužkovalo, a to i na kandidátkách KSČ, víc než polovinu hlasů některých stran museli vzít komisaři do rukou dvakrát a někteří televizní hrdinové nasbírali hodně přes čtvrt miliónu kroužků. Řada herců, kteří chtěli jen „tlačit" v pozadí, najednou spadla

05      Jiří Teper, *Milovaný obraz* (Beloved Image), 1991
        125 × 180 mm

The book *Milovaný obraz* (Beloved Image) was created at the
instigation of two crazy guys who commissioned me to do
a typographic treatment of their friend's poems. At that time,
phototypesetting already existed, and through other books,
I came across the aforementioned Vladimír Popp, a man who
worked in the printing house of *Rudé právo* [the official newspaper of the Communist Party of Czechoslovakia]. He headed
the phototypesetting department and was willing to work with
me on the book. Finances weren't very important to me at that
time, because I was getting 2500 CZK for a mock-up of a similar
book, which was quite a lot of money at that time. But with this
type of work, money was not usually discussed much. I got the
manuscript and made a mock-up: I drew in pencil how I wanted
the composition of the two pages to be. I created a frame—a format, a mirror of the paginated typesetting, and I placed the
texts of the poems in this type area. I tried to compose spreads
in such a way that there would be movement or, on the contrary, stillness. I then prescribed the manuscript, the type of
font—alternating between antiqua and grotesque—the size of
the font, the spacing, the line spacing. Then I was given a print-
out of the photosetting, which was rubberized underneath with
a special glue and protected by a layer of thin paper. I cut this
typesetting and glued it onto the prepared layout pages of plain
white paper. These were then reproduced and went to print. The
paper I chose was a good quality offset chamois, tinted paper, the
same for the paper binding, and blue for printing all the text.

The basis of such work at that time was scissors, paper, and
great patience. In this case it was still a thin book, so it was
not extremely difficult. The book *Od moderny k funkcionalismu*
(From Modernism to Functionalism) was a whole different
animal. The book went on to win an award at the Frankfurt
International Book Fair in the World's Most Beautiful Books
competition.

                     On Books

Jiří Teper

# Milovaný OBRAZ

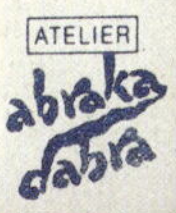

Každý člověk
má prý nad sebou hvězdu
Když zemře
hvězda vyhasne
Dál jen některé . . .
astra Homéra . . .
. . .Alberta Schweitzera . . .
Víme proč!

Ale hvězdy jsou
strašně daleko
Jaké mám tedy štěstí
že tě svírám v náručí
ve kterém se ještě chvěješ
bezradností
spadlých
z nebe

A já tě všechno naučím!

38

A Ť S E S T A N E

Stane se
a máte pocit
že vám život
utíká skrz prsty
a naskočíte do prvního vlaku
který jede kolem
Vaše jízdenka může být
dávno prošlá
Novou jste ovšem
nestačili koupit
Tam kde se dřív stavělo
se už dneska projíždí
A možná jedete úplně
jiným směrem
Ale viděl kdy kdo
průvodčího toho vlaku?
Zná někdo jeho strojvůdce?

39;

**Mám takový strach**

Dívám se do tváří přátel

Na jejich živá gesta
                    Přimhouřené oči
Ústa která se otvírají
                    Jazyk a zuby
Ruce ve vlasech
                    Vlasy padají do čela
Ty se protáhneš
                    Ruce se dotknou

**Oči zaostří**

Ústa nadechnou

Někdo se rozesmál
                    Stejně jako včera

Jako předevčírem

**Mám takový strach**



On Books

Barman už pro dnešek skončil
Ale ještě se baví s kolegou
Počítá nějaký účet
Přerovnává skleničky
Prohlíží proti světlu
Kouří jednu cigaretu za druhou
Vyklepe po sobě popelník
A zase kouří
Konečně se jde převléct
Ale ještě něco podotýká
Ještě si zapálí
Postojí u baru
Otevře kolegovi coca-colu
Před hodinou měl telefon
Matka zemřela
Ještě vysype popelník
Nějaký účet
Ještě si zapálí
Nakousne větu
Opře se
Mrkne
Ještě mrkne

103.

Barmanovi
se nechce
**odejít**

For Aleš Lederer, I came up with the graphic concept for his Střed series, including the logo, but he only let me design part of it. Then he said that I was too expensive and that he would do a simple layout himself or with the help of someone cheaper … However, he paid me about 1,500 CZK for the layout of a single book, i.e., for a mock-up of the book, cover, and reproduction materials. At that time, I glued the texts to the bookplate from the individual letters on paper and Honza Malý then created the appropriate sizes photographically. So, it was quite a demanding and meticulous job. The colored backing on the cover was made of special paper à la old-fashioned endpapers and was imported from Switzerland. So, in the end, I have a somewhat tenuous relationship with these books. I have not followed the series any further, so I do not know how they handled it.

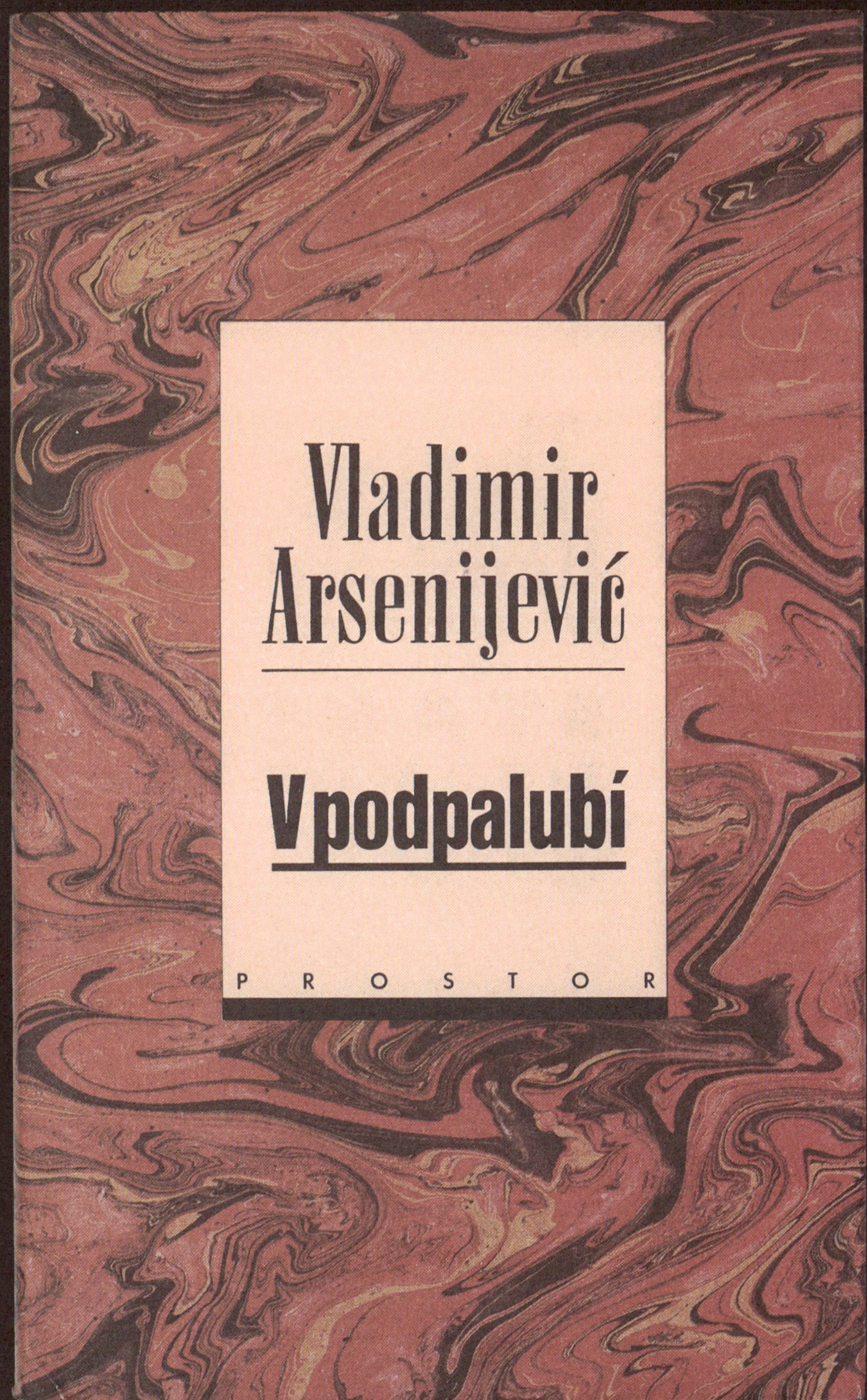

Vladimir Arsenijević
V podpalubí
PROSTOR

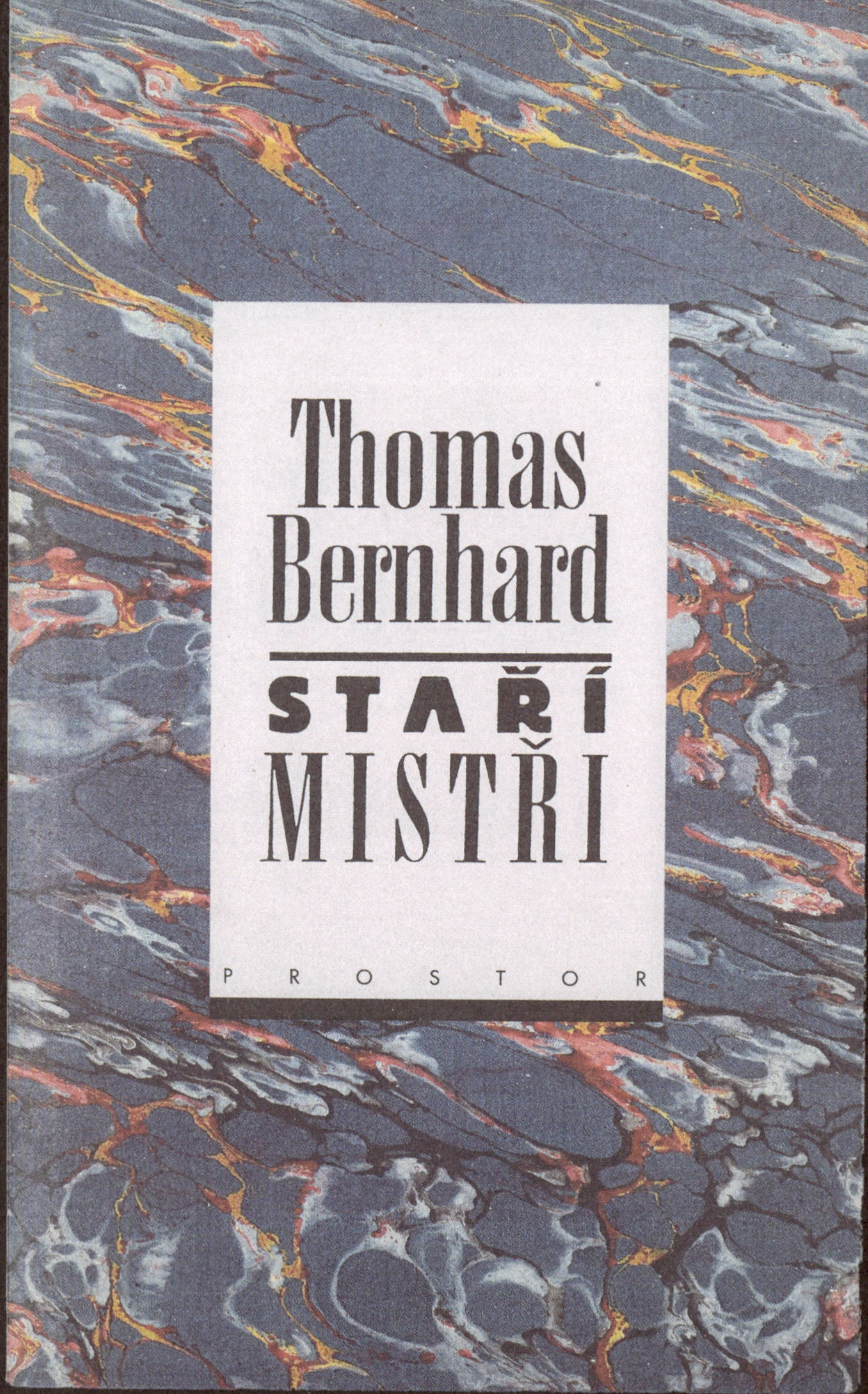




On Books

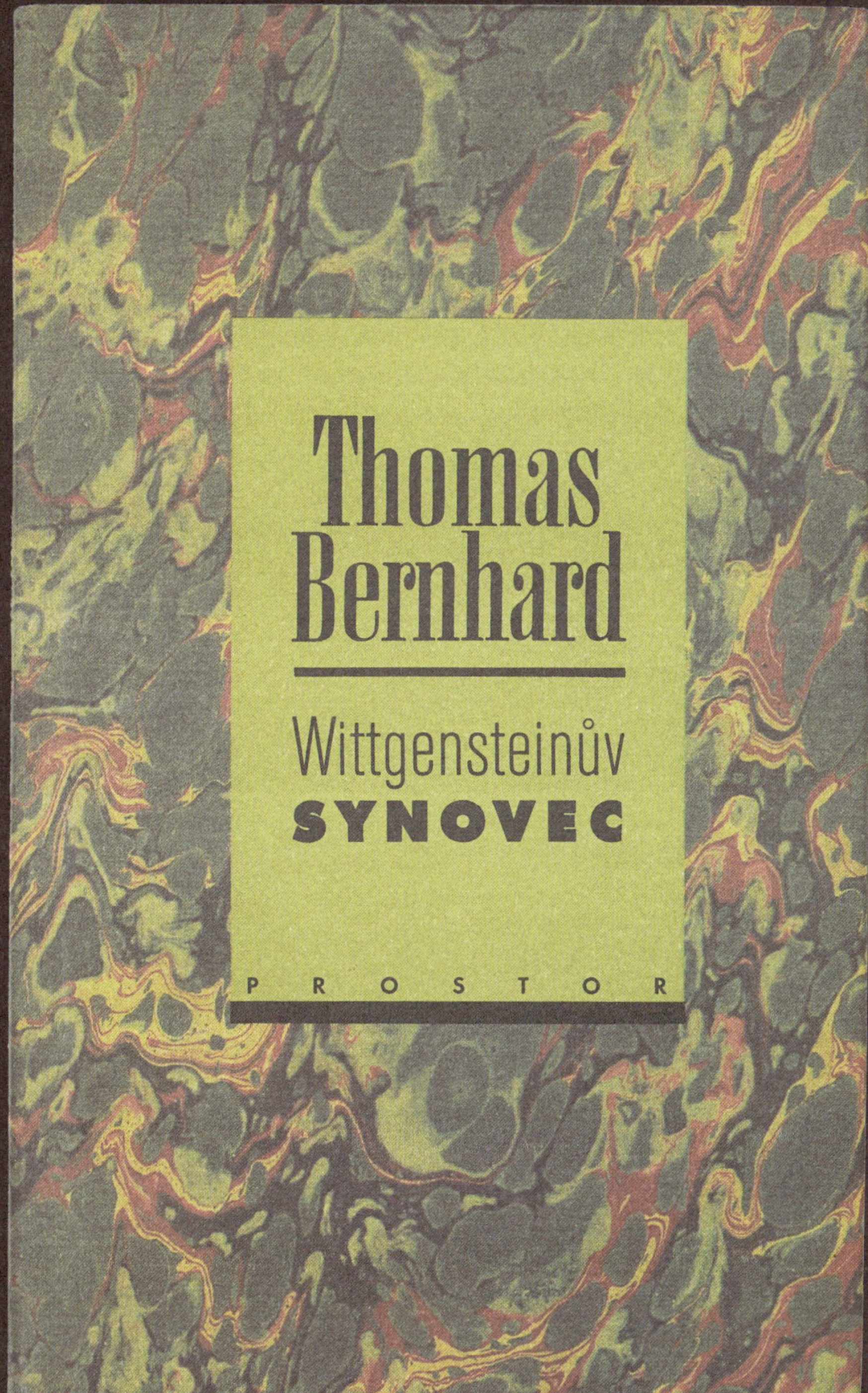

Thomas Bernhard
Wittgensteinův SYNOVEC
PROSTOR

07    Rostislav Švácha, *Od moderny k funkcionalismu*
      (From Modernism to Functionalism), 1995
      150 × 210 mm

The book was written at a time when five-color offset presses
with the possibility of using spot color were not yet available
in our printers. So, this book about architecture was printed
entirely in CMYK and we used to go with Honza Malý and our
youngest son, Honzik, to the printing house in Malešice in the
mornings to monitor the progress and results of the printing.
Fortunately, when the printer saw how invested I was, he paid
due attention to the work. In this case, it was a matter of making sure that the underlying gray, which could not be used as
a spot color, would come out the same everywhere. I chose this
graphic solution in order to link typesetting, pen drawings,
black-and-white and color photographs and to enclose everything, with reference to the content of the book, in a unified
whole, giving the impression of a stone block.

The book, however, despite the impression of simplicity it
gives, took a long time to create. Honza alone spent more than
four years photographing architecture because he often waited
for the right light. When he missed it, he kept going back until
the building had the lighting that suited him. Occasionally
he also got something wrong when developing slides. But the
resulting photographs were beautiful, and they were supple-
mented by Rostislav Švácha with original design sketches
and building plans from the archives. Honza made black-and-
white contacts of everything, which Švácha and I arranged
exactly according to his text in the book. With these materials
I created a whole laminated model of the book. I first bought
unlined thin school notebooks, cut them to the exact format of
the book, pasted the typesetting (it wasn't photo typesetting,
but monotype, so I got the outlines on paper strips) and the
contacts or enlargements of the architectural photographs.
This created a fairly thick mock-up with a high spine, which
was then used by the printer to break the typesetting, mount

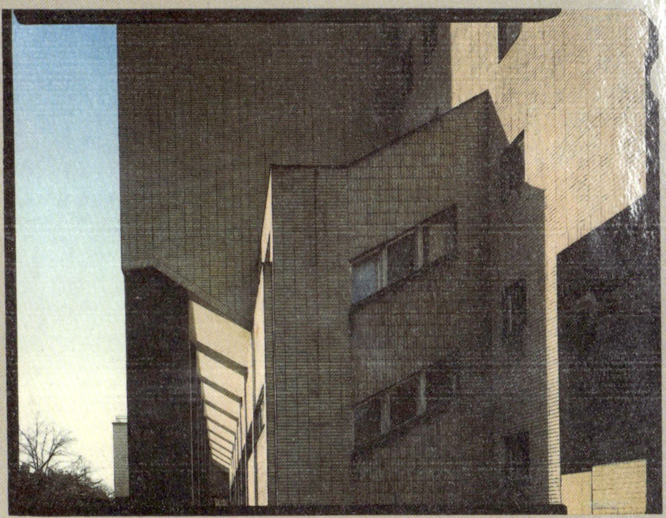



From Modernism to Functionalism

the whole book for reproduction, and illuminate the offset
plates. Honza enlarged the photographs, which appear in the
book as double-page spreads, on so-called document paper,
a special, amazingly thin photographic material supplied by
Foma in rolls, which allowed keeping the spine of the scrapbook
paper, although I put so much material inside. The document
paper was ideal for creating such a mock-up.

I carefully calculated the typesetting according to the manuscript so that the photographs would be exactly where the
architecture depicted in them is mentioned in the text. It was
necessary to decide well in advance on the font size and line
spacing, as it only went into the typesetting once. It was impossible to ask for the typesetting to be done twice.

So, first I drew a pencil sketch on all the pages and marked
where the typesetting of each chapter would roughly end. Then,
when I got the column outlines from the typesetter and cut
them, I could verify that I had calculated the rate correctly.
Fortunately, I had the experience of being in a graphic design
high school where the typesetting was always calculated this
way, and that's how I prepared all the books I edited before the
computer age. You had to think at the beginning exactly what
you wanted, and have a visual idea of the whole book, not just
how many pages it would be and how high the spine would be.

After a while, we got to proofreading. Where rivers arose in the
typesetting, I threw out or substituted one word in agreement
with Švácha, knowing that it would fit in and the typesetting
would be calmer. It was a bit of a pain, but if you want to do
something properly, you have to immerse yourself in it …

 On Books

From Modernism to Functionalism

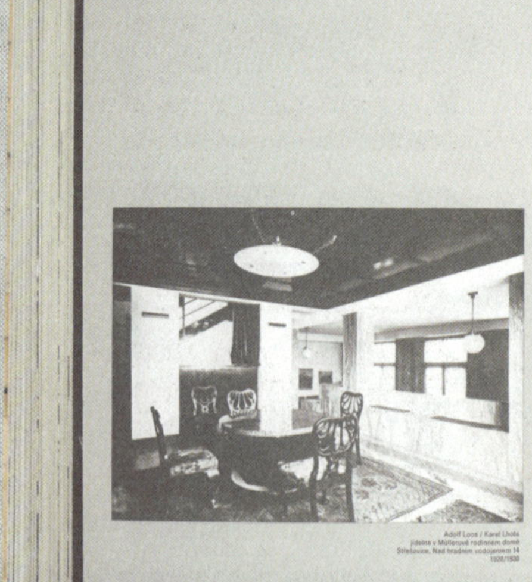
Adolf Loos / Karel Lhota
jídelna v Müllerově rodinném domě
Střešovice, Nad hradním vodojemem 14
1928/1930

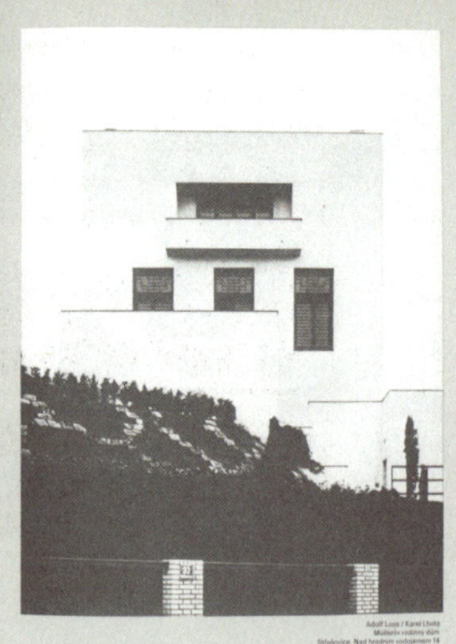
Adolf Loos / Karel Lhota
Müllerův rodinný dům
Střešovice, Nad hradním vodojemem 14
1928/1930

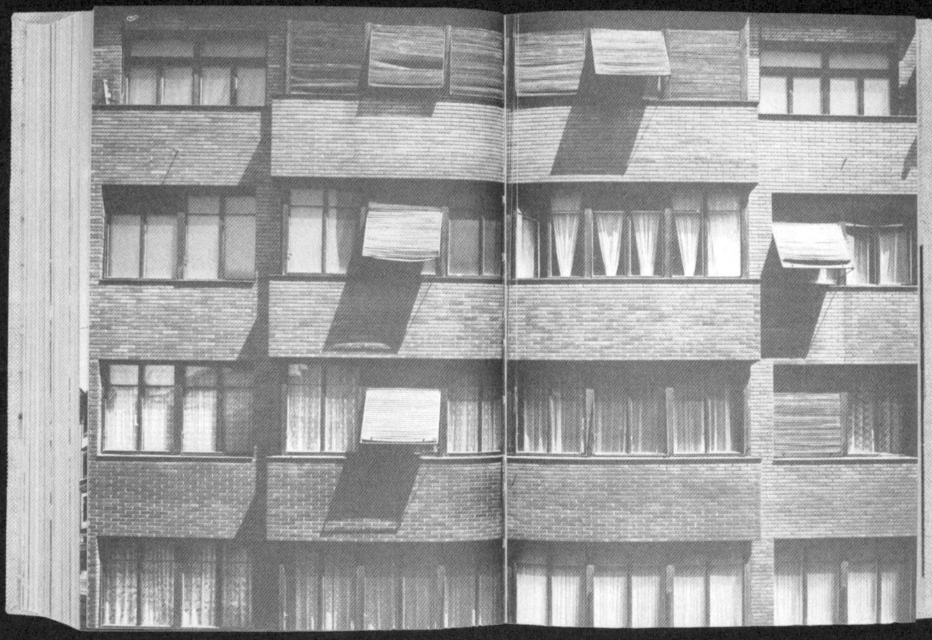

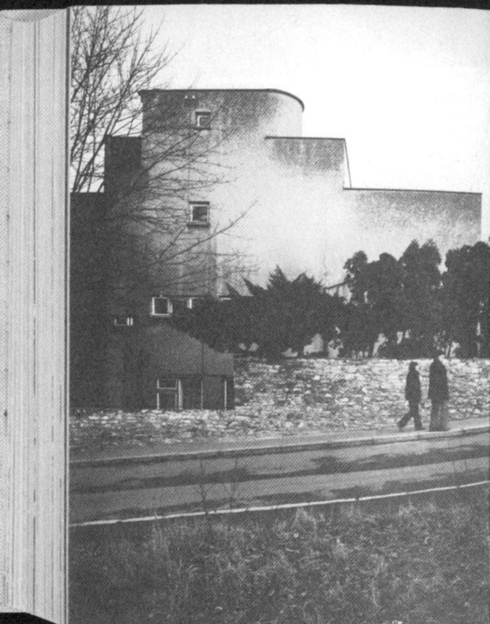

cionálního funkcionalismu jedinou alternativou. Ve svém pozoruhodném manifestu Nová architektura z roku 1939, který je zároveň manifestem jednoho z nejvýznamnějších emocionalistických výtvorů, *Skleněného paláce* na náměstí Svobody z let 1936—1937 od Richarda Podzemného, Josef Chochol sice Honzíkovu metodu zprvu přijímá; vzápětí však vykresluje představu nové architektury, která *osciluje* mezi věcností daných technických možností a individualitou architektovy tvůrčí síly a která v tomto procesu může v rukou *architekta-umělce* vykvést až do *sublimních květů lyrické básně.* [245]

Ohniskem teorií funkcionalistického emocionalismu se ve třicátých letech stal zejména Spolek výtvarných umělců Mánes, sdružující — vedle Josefa Gočára, Pavla Janáka, Otakara Novotného, Josefa Kalouse, Kamila Roškota, Josefa Štěpánka a některých jiných starších příslušníků spolku — zejména řadu bývalých členů Devětsilu, jehož aktivita uhasla kolem roku 1930, a s nimi pak mnohé Gočárovy, Janákovy a Novotného žáky z pražských architektonických učilišť. S někdejším programem Devětsilu mělo zaměření architektonické sekce Mánesa mnoho společných znaků. Především si však obě tyto organizace dobře rozuměly ve svých sympatiích k Le Corbusierovi, jehož dílo se od pokročilejších dvacátých let stávalo jakýmsi bojovným symbolem architektury nerezignující na umělecké cíle. Spolu s tím také Mánes od Devětsilu přejímal corbusierovskou koncepci svitivého tvaru a jeho plastické krásy.

Téměř vždy šlo o revokaci Le Corbusierova stylu, jak se rozvíjel ještě ve dvacátých letech: bílé objemy jsou sice rozkládány pásovými okny, ponechávají si však svou plastickou plnost. Jedním z nejzdařilejších a nejvýmluvnějších výtvorů tohoto pražského novopurismu je mohutná vila U Ladronky (1938—1939) PAVLA SMETANY, jejíž výrazovou zásobu, oplývající citacemi z Le Corbusierovy vily v Garches (1926—1927), začal Smetana shromažďovat už o dvě léta dříve v poněkud méně přesvědčivém rodinném domě ve Střešovické ulici (1936, společně s Karlem Stráníkem). Rodinné domy v Perucké (1931) a Na Podkovce (1935—1936), kterými se KAREL STRÁNÍK představuje jako samostatný projektant, prozrazují obdobné výtvarné přesvědčení, což s ohledem na Stráníkův pobyt v Le Corbusierově ateliéru (1925) ani nepřekvapuje. Příklad Le Corbusierových vil v Garches a Poissy jistě vyzařuje i z prvních pražských realizací LADISLAVA ŽÁKA. Z umělců stojících mimo vlastní okruh Mánesa mají příbuznou stylovou orientaci například některé práce JAROSLAVA ČERMÁKA; architektův vlastní rodinný dům ve Velvarské ulici (1937—1938), jehož svitivý novopuristický kubus korunuje nízká stanová střecha, a kostel sv. Jana Nepomuckého v Nepomucké ulici (od 1938), pojatý jako krajně jednoduchá, a tím i krajně riskantní kompozice krabicovité lodi a vysoké štíhlé věže. Výrazová účinnost stroze geometrického bílého tvaru upoutává také tvůrčí zájem velmi nadané architektské dvojice manželů OSKARA a ELLY OEHLEROVÝCH, jejichž rodinné domy V Nových Bohnicích (1935) a především Na bateriích (1931—1932) suverénně obstojí i ve srovnání s nejlepšími zahraničními výtvory tohoto typu a orien-

Pavel Smetana
rodinný dům
Břevnov, U Ladronky 31
1938/1939

411

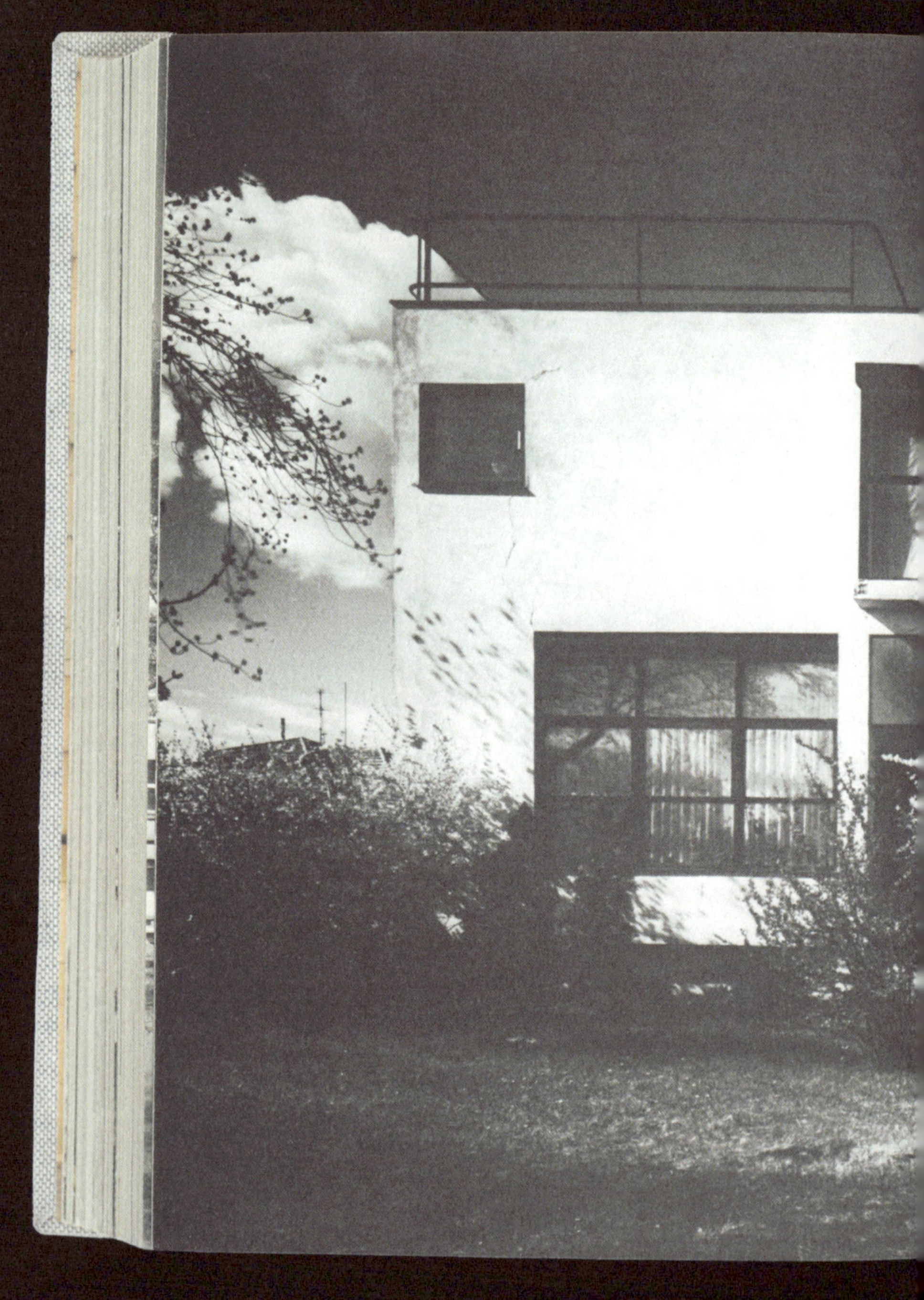



On Books

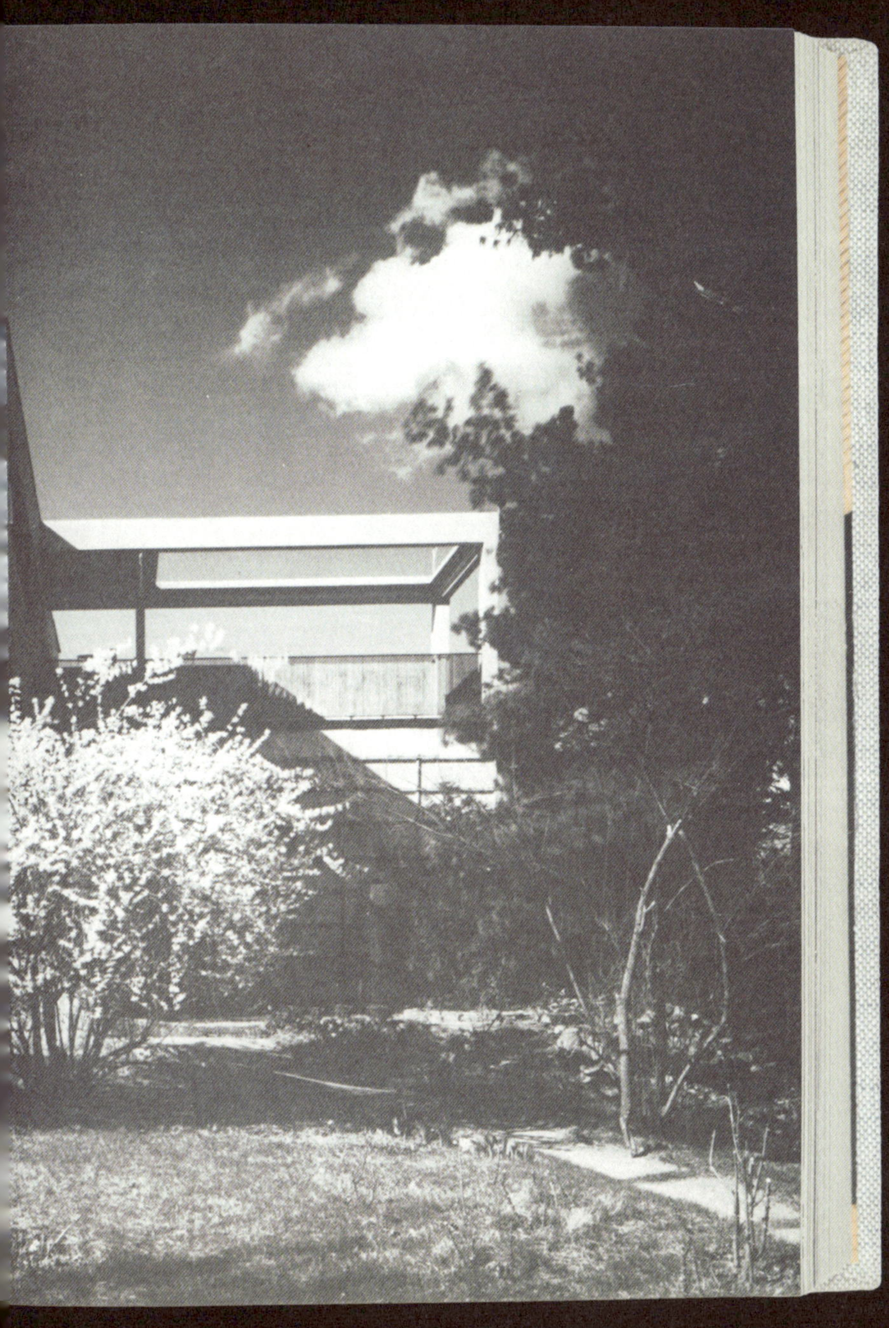

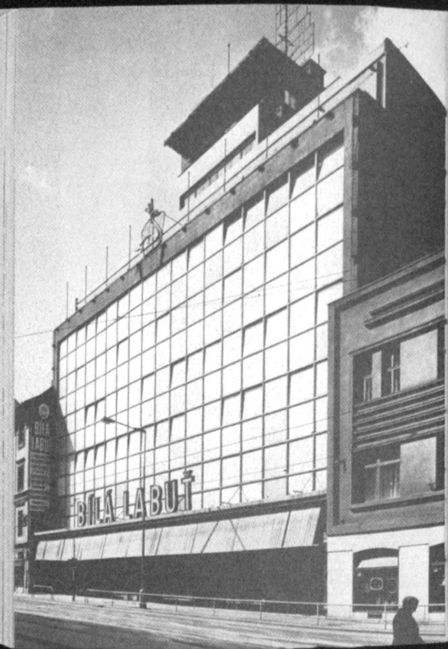



Josef Kittrich / Josef Hrubý
obchodní dům Bílá labuť
Nové Město, Na poříčí 23
1937/1939

počalo přibývat teprve po roce 1935. Polem vědeckofunkcionalistické aktivity se proto spíše stalo teoretické rozvíjení „socialistických" forem bydlení — od pásmových *socgorodů* skupiny PAS přes *kolektivní domy* až k *nejmenšímu bytu* — nebo sociologické analýzy architektury a bydlení za kapitalismu a socialismu, jak se jimi tehdy zabývali Karel Teige, Jiří Kroha i jiní členové architektonické sekce Levé fronty, jejímž nejvýznamnějším kolektivním činem v tomto směru byla příprava Výstavy proletářského bydlení v roce 1931.

Neméně důležitým bodem vědeckofunkcionalistického programu však přirozeně byla vlastní koncepce architektury jako vědy. Ta se pro všechnu ostatní aktivitu tohoto proudu stala metodickou, ne-li filozofickou základnou. Také zde již měli vědečtí funkcionalisté na co navázat, ať už máme na mysli radikální „konstruktivistickou" teorii Karla Teigeho, jejíž zdánlivě ryze marxistický charakter byl pro architekty krizové doby stále přitažlivější, anebo umírněnější, ale někdy také příliš utilitaristické formulace Oldřicha Starého či Vladimíra Ježka. Jak víme, od funkcionalistické architektury Teige požadoval, aby její forma přesně opisovala příslušnou funkci; aby byla přísně racionalistická a odsubjektivizovaná, zkrátka aby se stala úplně vědeckou disciplínou. Taková architektura bude zároveň *levá*. Proti ní pak Karel Teige staví architekturu, která se funkcionalisticky a moderně jen tváří, ale ve skutečnosti *zkšeftařila a sešupačela*, a vyjadřuje tak zájmy pravice — architekturu, která nerezignovala na svůj umělecký ráz. Ještě otevřeněji se k tomuto prapodivnému sociologizování přihlásil ve stati Architektura a společnost Jaromír Krejcar. Na prahu třicátých let tento tvůrce rozeznává v české architektuře *1. stanovisko kapitalistické*, odvozené od Le Corbusierova purismu, a *2. stanovisko socialistické*, které se opírá hlavně o práci sovětských konstruktivistů.[334]

Bylo-li přesvědčení architekta, který se ve své tvorbě pokoušel poctivě vyrovnat se spletí dobových problémů, jednoznačně vědecké, jeho role byla poměrně snadná. Avšak pokud nechtěl úplně pustit ze zřetele umělecké stránky svého díla, a byl zároveň zasažen uvedenými Teigovými nebo Krejcarovými teoriemi, ocital se před obtížnou, téměř neřešitelnou volbou. Má tvořit umělecky, to jest subjektivně, to jest zpátečnicky, anebo tvořit vědecky, to jest objektivně, to jest na straně pokrokových sil? Syntézu těchto protikladů vědeckofunkcionalističtí teoretikové alespoň na počátku třicátých let nepřipouštěli, pro ně existovalo jen buď—anebo, podobně jako nebylo možné smírné řešit třídní rozpory. Snad právě proto mluví Vít Obrtel o porušené harmonii a možnost utvořit skutečně harmonickou architekturu přisuzuje až příštímu společenskému řádu.

Avšak jakkoli se zdála být stroze neosobní a vědecká koncepce funkcionalistické architektury na počátku třicátých let jedinou pokrokovou alternativou, setkáváme se ještě před polovinou desetiletí v teorii i praxi vědeckého funkcionalismu s pokusy oslabit jeho ortodoxii. Je už nesnadné zjistit, čím byl vlastně tento obrat podnícen. Svou úlohu tu jistě sehrály varovné hlasy ze Sovětského svazu, kde se velkorysé realizace vědeckofunkcionalistické architektury z rozličných důvodů neosvědčily, po-



---

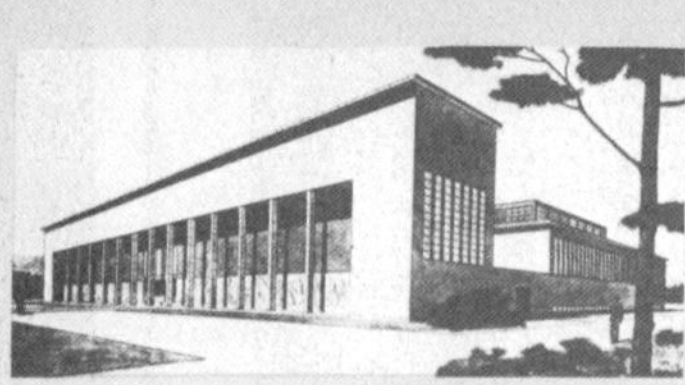

Josef Gočár
III. projekt Státní galerie
na Letné
1939/1940

Adolf Benš
soutěžní projekt
městské galerie na Klárově
1937

mu, vkládá pět monolitických sarkofágů, jejichž sestava vytváří — jak to vtipně vystihnul historik architektury Vladimír Šlapeta — *podivuhodnou iluzi slavnostní královské jízdy*.[271] Na ruzyňském letišti se podle Roškotových plánů v letech 1934—1935 staví dvojdomek ředitelů, 1934—1936 dvojdomek vrátných. Robustní symetrické objemy těchto domů, s příznačným motivem obdélného okna přetaženého přes nároží, jakoby znázorňovaly Stefanovu pozdější definici klasicismu jako rozumově probudované a citlivě odvážené formy. Poslední umělcovou realizaci, jejíž projekt vypracoval se svými spolužáky z Kotěrovy školy JANEM ZÁZVORKOU a JOSEFEM KALOUSEM, je budova ministerstva vnitra na třídě Obránců míru (1935—1939). K Letné se stavba obrací fasádou členěnou klasicistickými lizénami, k třídě Obránců míru pak masivní průčelní kulisou, s jejíž bílou keramickou plochou kontrastuje stínný výklenek označující hlavní vchod.

Dílo jiného předního *mánesáka*, FRANTIŠKA M. ČERNÉHO, má v tomto období širší spektrum stylových odstínů, od „běžného" emocionálního funkcionalismu až po jeho novoklasicistické vyústění. Řadu svých vynikajících prací třicátých let Černý navrhnul za pomoci Kamila Ossendorfa, Richarda Podzemného, Bohumila Holého a Stivo Vacka: klasicizující ráz z nich má hlavně druhý projekt motolské nemocnice (1936—1937). Z Černého samostatných výtvorů vyniká rodinný dům Na Kodymce (1938), jehož stereotomní bílé kubusy, rozložené pásovými okny, i asymetrická sestava jakoby se nijak nevymykaly ze slohové normy *internacionálního* funkcionalismu. V Architektuře ČSR 1939 a ve Volných směrech 1938—1940 však umělec publikoval fotografie, na nichž je průčelí jeho vily vkresleno do „apriorní" kompoziční sítě, vyvozené (podle vzoru Le Corbusiera) ze zlatého řezu, tedy z jakéhosi „věčného", „obecně platného" pravidla. Symetrická kompozice administrativní budovy motolské vozovny v Plzeňské třídě (do 1939) vzdáleně připomíná Roškotovy domky v Ruzyni.

Černého vrcholným dílem třicátých let, na jehož podobě se podílel ještě další Gočárův žák, JOSEF GRUS, mimo jiné projektant tří symetricky komponovaných vil v Matějské ulici (mezi 1938—1940), je soutěžní projekt dostavby Staroměstské radnice z roku 1938. S poněkud nereálnými nároky vypisovatele soutěže na kubaturu nových úředních a zasedacích místností, jež se všechny měly vejít mezi Sprengerovo novogotické křídlo a Dienzenhoferův kostel sv. Mikuláše, se autoři vyrovnali tak, že směrem k Husovu pomníku vysunuli do Staroměstského náměstí nový příčný trakt. Podle jejich názoru by toto řešení vrátilo Staroměstskému náměstí *intimitu uzavřeného prostoru* (1937—1938),[272] tedy kvalitu zcela protikladnou funkcionalistickému směřování za prostorem volným, otevřeným. Jednu z nejvýznamnějších paralel tohoto nového prostorového cítění, plynoucího zřejmě z emocionalistického zájmu o formu, která spíše než volným prostorem může být představována jeho věčným ohraničením, lze v rovině solitérní architektonické tvorby nalézt v adaptaci dvorany Zemské banky Na příkopě (1937, 1939—1941), jejíž tvůrce, příslušník Mánesa KAREL STRÁNÍK, jí pojal jako uzavřenou antickou celu obepjatou ve výšce re-

Kamil Roškot
dvojdomek vrátných
Ruzyň, K letišti 533
1934/1935

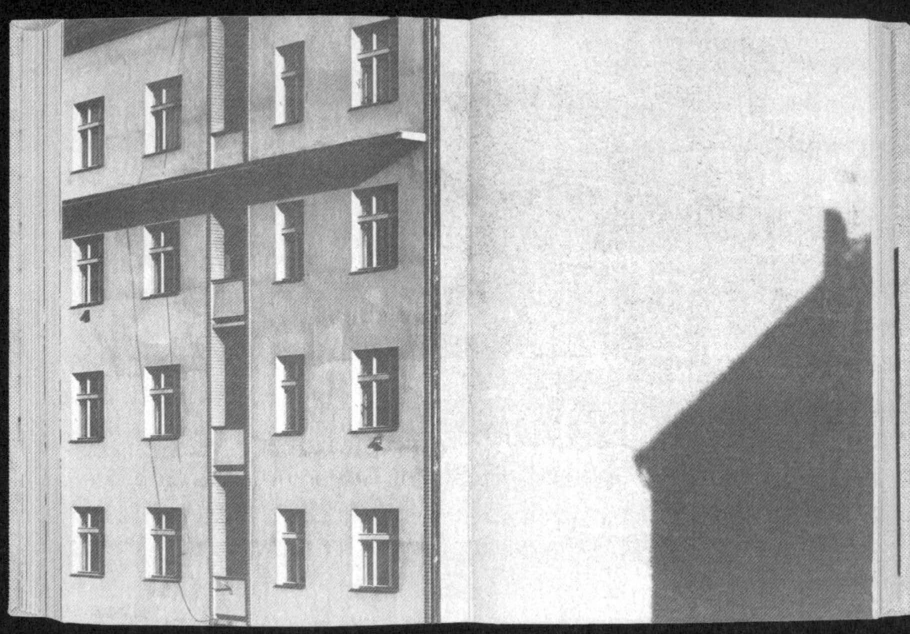

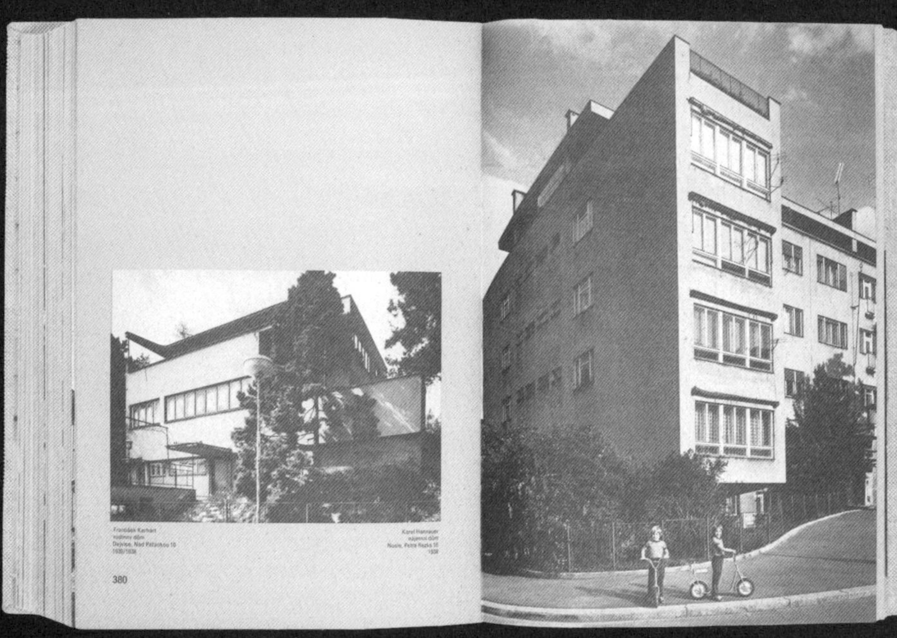
František Kerhart
rodinný dům
Dejvice, Nad Paťankou 10
1938/1939
Karel Hannauer
nájemní dům
Nusle, Petra Rezka 16
1938
380

I could typeset the book *Tachles, Lustig* by myself, but it was preceded by some absolutely rough times when I was learning on the computer.

With this book, I would like to mention a moment that I personally consider one of the most important for the work. I was having dinner with Karel Hvížďala on our holiday in Crete and the topic of this book, which was currently in the process of being written, came up. With my gaze fixed on the sunset over the sea, I imagined an all-yellow book in my head. I never backed down from that first image. Later, I persuaded the publisher to approve the yellow satin paper that I had carefully chosen. Our paper mill in Větřní used to produce colored satins, but OSPAP [a wholesaler of office and graphics supplies] could only offer me a more expensive, but very high-quality yellow satin. In the end, this expensive German paper was used in the book, but I argued that it was a thin book, so it would not ruin the publishing house financially. Also very important for the whole concept of the book were the authentic black-and-white double-sided photographs—portraits of Arnošt Lustig[1]—that my son Jan Malý took during the filming of the interview. The book was later reprinted and expanded by about sixty pages, with a black version of the cover, but the yellow paper remained.

The book, including the cover, is typeset in Helvetica, as I liked its clean shapes.

---

1    Arnošt Lustig (1926–2011) was a prominent Czech Jewish writer whose work focused on Holocaust themes. Born in Prague, he survived the concentration camps of Terezín, Auschwitz, and Buchenwald during World War II. In 1945, he escaped from a death transport to Dachau and participated in the Prague Uprising. After the war, he studied journalism and worked as an editor. Following the 1968 Warsaw Pact invasion, he emigrated to Israel and later the United States, where he taught at American University in Washington, DC. His most famous works include *A Prayer for Katerina Horovitzova*, *Dita Saxová*, and *Lovely Green Eyes*. In 2008, he received the Franz Kafka Prize for his contributions to world literature.

Karel Hvížďala

# Tachles, Lustig

Rozhovor

Mladá fronta

jsem věděl, když si je vezmu, stvrdím tím jeho smrt. Strýček E
umíral ve strašných bolestech, a aby to urychlil, vypotácel se z
rodky a skočil na dráty. V těch drátech bylo 10 000 voltů.
smůlu, v ten den bylo zrovna sucho a jen se popálil. Druhý
pršelo, o sebevraždu se pokusil podruhý. Protože byl mokrý, z
ho to.

**A vzal sis ty jeho boty?**

Ne, nevzal. Ty skončily nejprve u polského medika, který ho
třoval. Ale nakonec jsme mu je vzali, a tak jsem v Buchenwaldu
šel i k botám. Ty boty měly vůbec zvláštní osud. Z Buchenwaldu
spolu s Jirkou Justicem, dodnes žije v Českém Brodě a je to
vadnej kluk, převáželi v otevřených nákladních vagónech do
chau, už šest dní jsme nejedli. Pili jsme jen to, co napršelo. K
nás se jim nevyplatilo, chtěli nás stejně zastřelit, jenže to nec
udělat v blízkosti městečka, aby nebudili pohoršení a taky aby
vznikla epidemie. Proto nás vezli prakticky z Lipska až k Mnic
do Dachau, kde měli krematorium. Naštěstí vedle jel jiný vlak
pou a mně se podařilo jednu zase ukrást. A protože Jirka Justi
můj kamarád, půlku jsem mu dal. Tu svou půlku jsem okar
snědl, ale on si svůj díl rozdělil na dvě čtvrtky a snědl jenom je
Já měl ale stále hlad a povídám: Dám ti moje boty, když mi d
čtvrtku řípy. On na výměnu přistoupil, já snědl i tu jeho čtv
a pak se to semlelo.

**Co se semlelo?**

Napadl nás americký letec, hloubkař. Rozstřílel u Kraslic lokomo
my z vlaku vyskákali a prchali jsme strání nahoru. Nedávno jse
tom vrchu byl, dnes je zarostlý klestím. Tenkrát byl holý, byli

22

dobře vidět a esesáci, byli to Rumuni, po nás stříleli. Měli jsme štěstí, protože jsme byli první a ti, co vyskákali po nás, vytvořili živou zeď, která nás chránila. Strefovali se do těch bližších. Utíkali jsme a ten můj kamarád najednou začal kulhat. On totiž z jedné boty, kterou jsem původně nosil já, vylezl hřebík a bodal ho do paty, ale on mi to neřekl, protože měl zřejmě strach, že bych ho v lese mohl opustit. Takhle si to vykládám dneska. Tehdy mi nic neřekl. Taky asi nechtěl zpomalit. Šli jsme za sluncem, ale slunce nás vypeklo: večer jsme přišli tam, odkud jsme ráno vyšli. Navíc jsem si ze školy pamatoval, že strom obrůstá mechem na severní straně, ale je to blbost, jak se ukázalo. Do Prahy jsme se dostali za pár dní vlakem a jako dnes si pamatuji, že tam prodávali bez lístků pečenou vepřovou krev s bramborem. To bylo moje první jídlo v Praze.

**To jsi tedy do Prahy dorazil bez bot, jen s nohama ovázanýma hadry? To bys byl moc nápadný, ne?**

Ne, Jirka Justic mi dal své rozbité boty. A brzy jsme dostali peníze a koupil jsem si nový boty. Rodina Justiců měla schované peníze v Českém Brodu u lidí, o nichž si mysleli, že jsou slušní. Původně byli, ale mezitím se z nich stali fašisté a potřebovali alibi, a proto nám peníze hned dali. Neměli jsme se špatně. Praha mi taky připadala jako bohatý a téměř mírový město. V květnu 1945 už se zvláště mladí lidé Němců moc nebáli a pohrdali jimi. Psychologicky to bylo výborný.

**A kdy to bylo?**

Myslím si, že jsme utekli 13. dubna 1945 a do Prahy jsme dorazili asi za týden. Od té doby věřím na třináctku. Pamatuji se i na první jízdu tramvají. Jeli v ní kluci starý jako my a měli na sobě dresy

Už z pouhé slušnosti máme sklon přizpůsobovat naše věty myšlení těch, k nimž mluvíme. K upřímnosti je třeba odvahy. Ta Lustigovi nikdy nechyběla, ale jak čas pokračuje, zdá se mi, že ještě vyrostla. S tou otevřeností se spojuje vášeň vidět svět zdola, v konkrétních setkáních, v konkrétních konfliktech a detailech, což není vůbec běžné v naší době zglajchšaltovaného myšlení, kdy veškeré soudy jsou hotovy předem a paměť ztrácí právo si pamatovat. Arnošte a Karle, přijměte můj dík za ten nádherný, bohatý text.

Váš

Milan Kundera

ISBN 978-80-204-2354-2

On Books

# Selected Works

# School work

| 1963 | *Žalostné a plačtivé rozmlouvání jedné ztracené duše s tělem svým* (A Lost Soul's Sad and Tearful Conversation with His Body) | 100 × 135 mm | |
|---|---|---|---|
| 1963 | Walt Whitman, *Opěvuji elektrické tělo* (I Sing the Body Electric) | 90 × 140 mm | |

## František Muzika Studio at UMPRUM

| 1966 | Milan Nápravník, *Básně, návěstí a pohyby 1958–1960* (Poems, Announcements, and Movements 1958–1960) | 145 × 190 mm | |
|---|---|---|---|
| 1967 | F. X. Šalda, *Kniha jako umělecké dílo* (The Book as a Work of Art) | 145 × 190 mm | |
| 1967 | *Gleb Gorbovskij, Intelekt v kůži jelení* (Intellect in Deer Skin) | 210 × 295 mm | |



Selected Works

| 1968 | Édouard Jaguer, *Dějiště stávky* (The Scene of the Strike) | 210 × 295 mm | |
| 1968 | Jan Tomeš, *Staré zahrady* (Old Gardens, diploma thesis) | 210 × 295 mm | |

## Film posters

| 1976 | Tři mušketýři (Three Musketeers) | 420 × 594 mm | |
| 1976 | Hrabě Monte Christo (The Count of Monte Cristo) | 420 × 594 mm | |
| 1976 | Dny všední a dny sváteční (Ordinary Days and Festive Days) | 420 × 594 mm | |
| 1976 | Lord z Barmbecku (Lord of Barmbeck) | 420 × 594 mm | |

| 1977 | Harry a Tonto (Harry and Tonto) | 420 × 594 mm | |
| 1977 | Den kobylek (The Day of the Locust) | 420 × 594 mm | |
| 1977 | Ta, která přežila (The Survivor) | 420 × 594 mm | |
| 1977 | Dokonalý plán (The Internecine Plan) | 420 × 594 mm | |
| 1978 | Nechci nic slyšet (I Don't Want to Hear Anything) | 420 × 594 mm | |
| 1978 | Budiž blahoslavena (Blessed Be) | 420 × 594 mm | |
| 1978 | Divoká kachna (The Wild Duck) | 420 × 594 mm | |



Selected Works

# Posters for exhibitions

| 1976 | *České malířství 20. Století* (Czech Painting of the 20th Century) | 594 × 841 mm | |
|---|---|---|---|
| 1985 | *Devětsil: česká výtvarná avantgarda dvacátých let* (Devětsil: Czech 1920s artistic avant-garde) | 420 × 594 mm | |
| 1985 | *TYPO& – Výstava užité grafiky a typografie* (Exhibition of applied graphics and typography) | 594 × 841 mm | |

# Book series

| 1974 | České básně (Czech Poems), Československý spisovatel Publishing House<br><br>From the series: Ilja Bart, *Kde* (Where); Eva Bernardinová, *Strom z ráje* (The Tree from Paradise); Petr Skarlant, *Hebká kůže* (Soft Skin) | 120 × 195 mm | |
|---|---|---|---|

| 1981 | Klub přátel poezie (The Poetry Friends Club), Československý spisovatel Publishing House<br><br>From the series: William Blake, *Napíšu básně kytkám na listy* (I will write poems on the leaves of flowers); Pierre-Marcel Adéma, *Guillaume Apollinaire* | 120 × 185 mm | 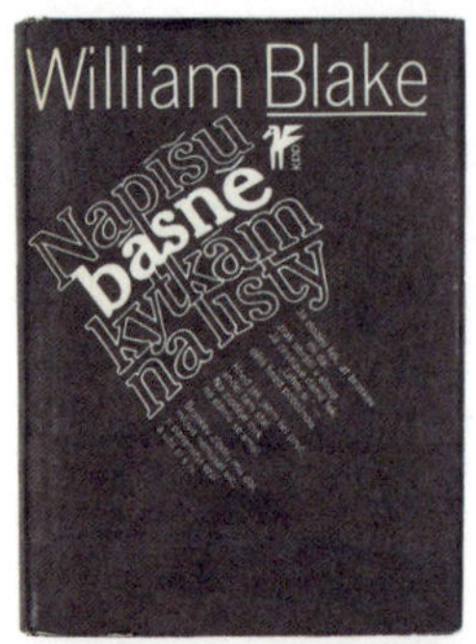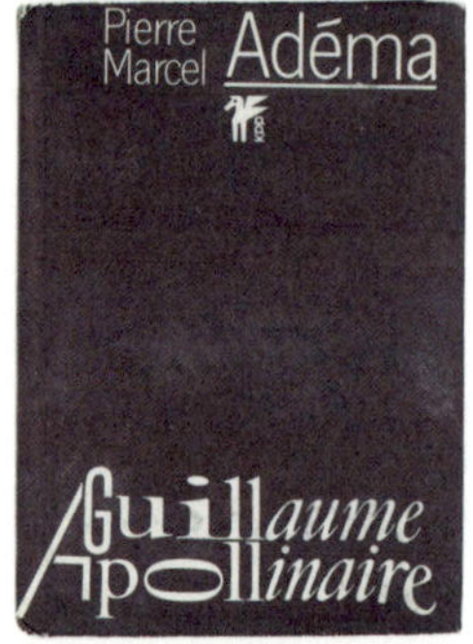 |
| 1980 | Máj (May), Mladá Fronta Publishing House<br><br>From the series: Joseph Joffo, *Z Paříže do Paříže* (From Paris to Paris); Arčil Sulakauri, *Zázračné šaty* (The Miraculous Dress); Jean Anglade, *Mramorová deska* (The Marble Slab) | 135 × 205 mm | 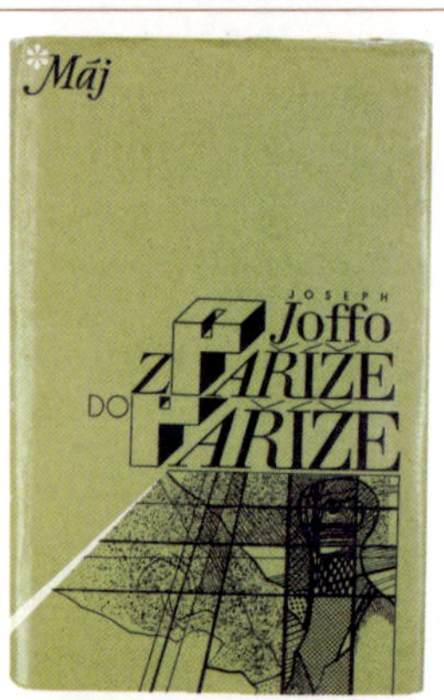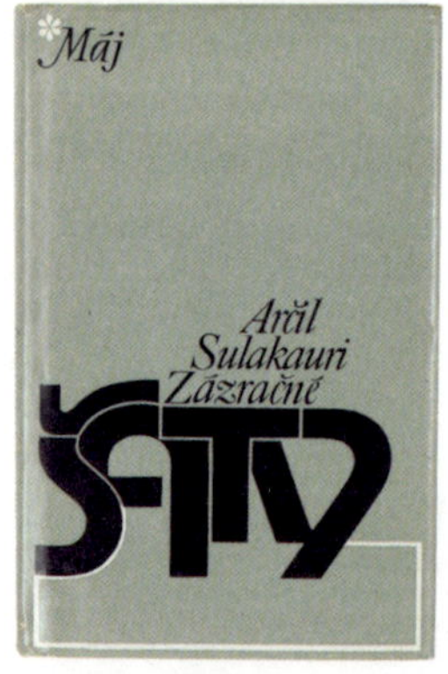 |



Selected Works

| 1981 | Reflexe (Reflections),<br>Vyšehrad Publishing House | 135 × 205 mm | 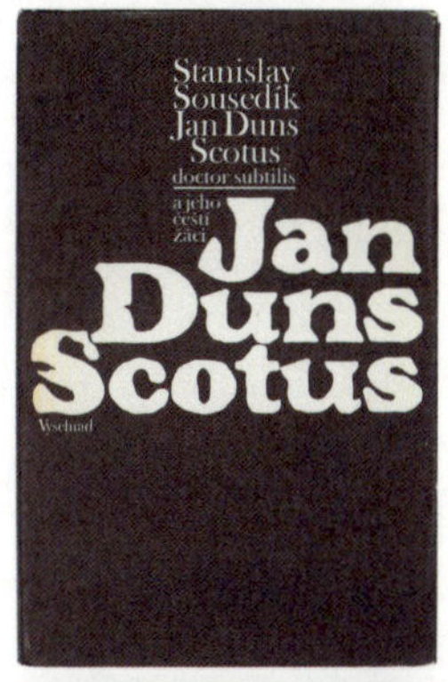 |
|---|---|---|---|

1981 · Reflexe (Reflections), Vyšehrad Publishing House · 135 × 205 mm

From the series: Anicius Manlius Torquatus Severinus Boëthius, *Boëthius – Poslední Říman* (Boëthius – The Last Roman); Stanislav Sousedík, *Valerian Magni*; Jan P. Kučera, Jiří Rak, *Bohuslav Balbín a jeho místo v české kultuře* (Bohuslav Balbín and His Place in Czech Culture); Blaise Pascal, *Svět Blaise Pascala* (The World of Blaise Pascal); Erasmus Rotterdamský, kolektiv autorů, *Živá tvář Erasma Rotterdamského* (The Living Face of Erasmus of Rotterdam); Stanislav Sousedík, *Jan Duns Scotus*

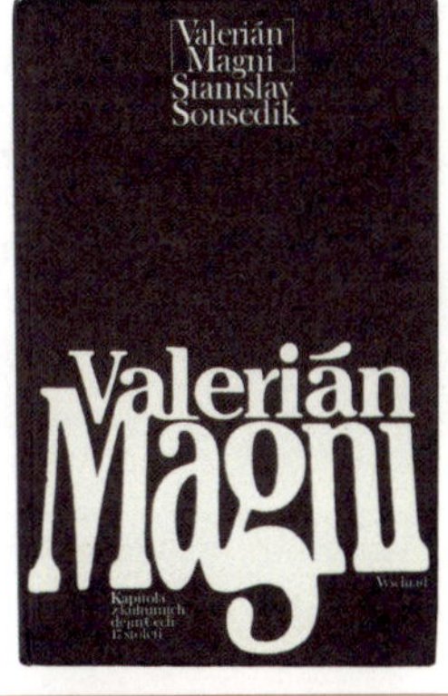

---

1980 · Střed (Center), Prostor Publishing House · 120 × 195 mm

From the series: Milada Součková, *Sešity Josefíny Rykrové* (The Notebooks of Josefína Rykrová); Peter Handke, *Tři pokusy* (Three Attempts); Thomas Bernhard, *Staří mistři* (Old Masters); Thomas Bernhard, *Wittgensteinův synovec* (Wittgenstein's Nephew); Vladimir Arsenijević, *V podpalubí* (Under the Deck)

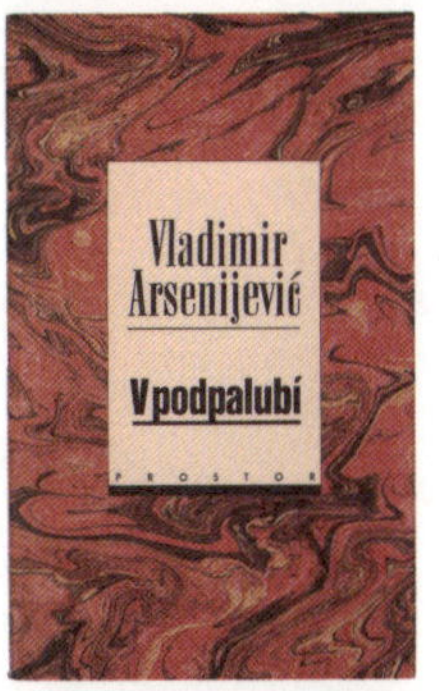

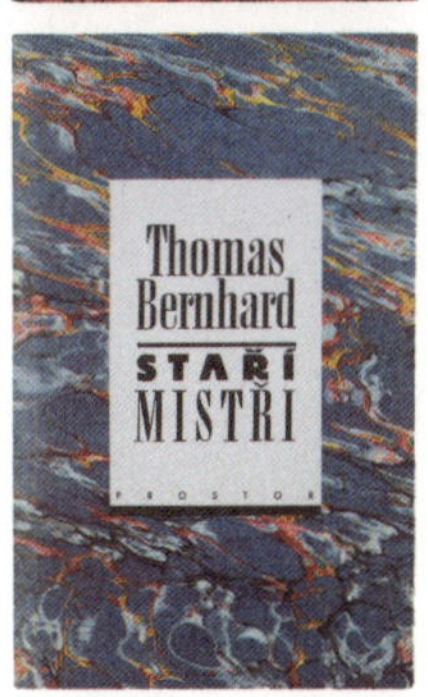

# Books about architecture

| 1985 | Rostislav Švácha, *Od moderny k funkcionalismu* (From Modernism to Functionalism) | 150 × 210 mm | |
| 2000 | Rostislav Švácha, *Lomené, hranaté a obloukové tvary, Česká kubistická architektura, 1911–1923* (The Pyramid, the Prism & the Arc: Czech Cubist Architecture 1911–1923) | 230 × 315 mm | |

# Books for children

| 1986 | Jacques Prévert, *Pohádky pro nehodné děti* (Tales for Naughty Children) | 297 × 210 mm | |
| 1987 | Josef Brukner, *Ostrov, kde rostou housle* (The Island Where Violins Grow) | 125 × 190 mm | |

| 1989 | Michail Jevgrafovič Saltykov-Ščedrin, *Historie města Hloupětína* (The History of the City of Fools) | 210 × 295 mm | |
| 2000 | La Fontaine, *Bajky* (Fables) | 210 × 295 mm | |
| 2005 | Hans Christian Andersen, *Pohádky* (Fairy Tales) | 215 × 300 mm | |
| 2005 | Alexandre Dumas, *Tři mušketýři* (Three Musketeers) | 215 × 300 mm | |
| 2006 | Pohádky bratří Grimmů (Grimms' Fairy Tales) | 210 × 295 mm | |

## Books of poetry

| 1990 | Pavel Šrut, *Kolej Yesterday* (Dormitory Yesterday) | 125 × 160 mm | |
| 1991 | Jiří Teper, *Milovaný obraz* (Beloved Image) | 125 × 180 mm | |
| 1991 | Naděžda Plíšková, *Plíšková podle abecedy* (Plíšková by Alphabet) | 125 × 185 mm | |

## Exhibition catalogues and books on art

| 1976 | Ludmila Karlíková, *České malířství 20. století* (Czech Painting of the 20th Century) | 210 × 100 mm | |

| 1985 | Rostislav Švácha, Rudolf Matys, *Vít Obrtel/Projekty a texty* (Vít Obrtel/Projects and Texts) | 145 × 145 mm | |
| 1986 | František Šmejkal, Rostislav Švácha, Jan Rous, *Devětsil: česká výtvarná avantgarda dvacátých let* (Devětsil: Czech Artistic Avant-garde of the 1920s) | 205 × 290 mm | |
| 1987 | Karel Srp, *Tvrdošíjní a hosté, 2. část* (Tvrdošíjní and Guests, Part 2) | 210 × 300 mm | |
| 1988 | František Šmejkal, *Skupina Ra* (The Ra Group) | 205 × 290 mm | |
| 1991 | Michal Bregant, Karel Srp, Antonín Dufek, Lenka Bydžovská, Aleš Zach, *Aventinská mansarda: Otakar Štorch-Marien a výtvarné umění* (The Attic at Aventinum: Otakar Štorch-Marien and Visual Art) | 210 × 300 mm | |



Selected Works

| 1985 | Jan Kotík: *Reprodukce/Reproduktion 1939-1991* (Jan Kotík: Reproduction 1939-1991) | 290 × 210 mm | |
| 1986 | Karel Fabel, *Typo&: Výstava užité grafiky a typografie* (Typo&: Exhibition of Applied Graphics and Typography) | 210 × 295 mm | Štyrský Toyen artificialismus 1926 1931 |
| 1994 | Josef Koudelka, *Černý trojúhelník* (The Black Triangle) | 295 × 230 mm | |
| 1994 | Karel Srp, *Karel Teige, 1900-1951* (Karel Teige, 1900-1951) | 210 × 300 mm | typo koláže dekalky foto & film nejmenší byt obrazové básně grafika kresby karel teige 1900-1951 |
| 1996 | Eva Uchalová, *Česká móda 1918-1939: Elegance první republiky* (Czech Fashion 1918-1939: The Elegance of the First Republic) | 215 × 305 mm | Česká móda 1918 elegance první republiky 1939 |

| 1996 | Karel Srp, *Český surrealismus 1929-1953* (Czech Surrealism 1929-1953) | 240 × 320 mm | |
| 1997 | Ivan Lutterer, Jan Malý, Jiří Poláček, *Český člověk* (The Czech Person) | 210 × 295 mm | |

## Books created in collaboration with Karla Hvížďala

| 2000 | Karel Hvížďala, *Výslech revolucionářů 89* (Interrogation of the Revolutionaries of '89) | 155 × 230 mm | |
| 2010 | Karel Hvížďala, *Havel, Landovský, Suchý* (Havel, Landovský, Suchý) | 140 × 200 mm | |



Selected Works

| 2011 | Karel Hvížďala, *Tachles, Lustig* (Tachles, Lustig) | 125 × 190 mm | |
| 2011 | Václav Havel, *Motomorfózy* (Metamorphoses) | 140 × 185 mm | |

## Periodicals

| 1990 | *Přítomnost* | 297 × 430 mm | |
| 1993 | *Historické listy* (Historical letters) | 210 × 297 mm | |

| 1995 | *Osobnosti osvobozeného divadla* (Personalities of Liberated Theater) | 40 × 50 mm | 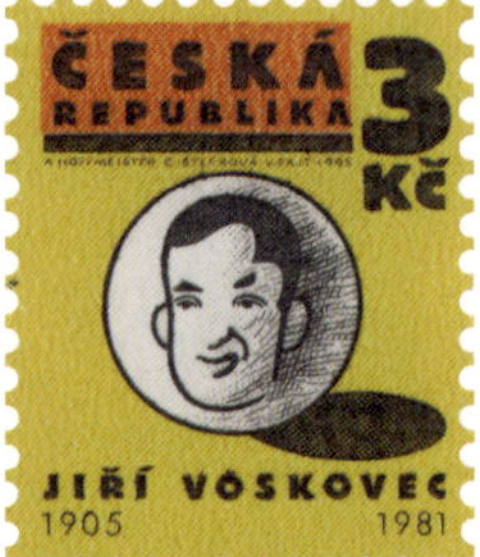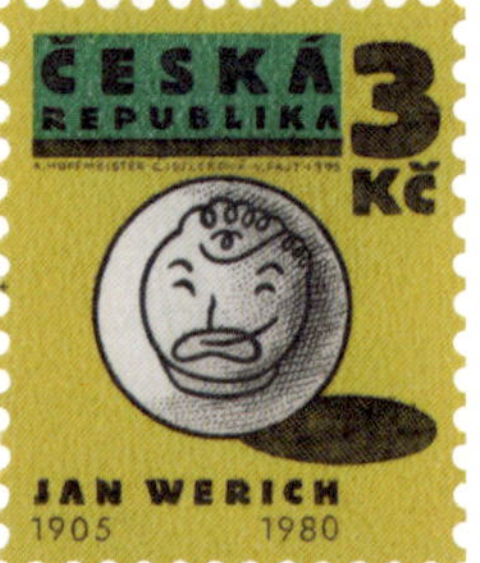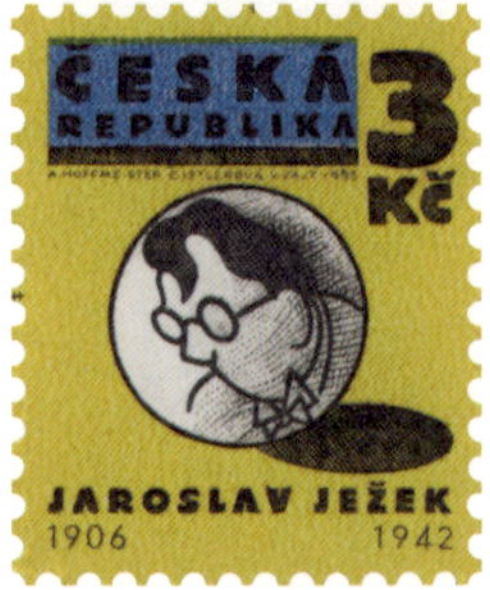 |
|---|---|---|---|



Selected Works

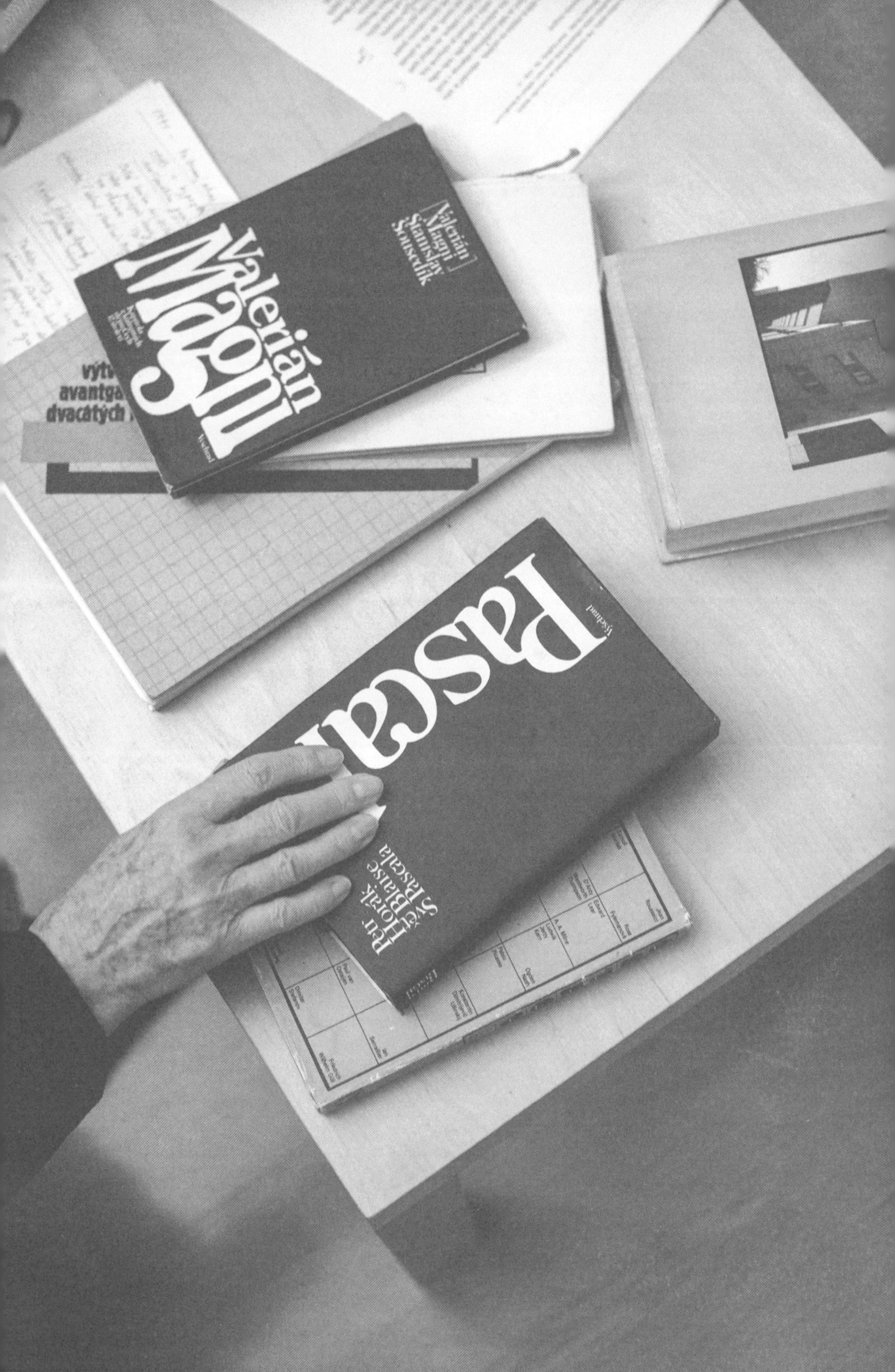

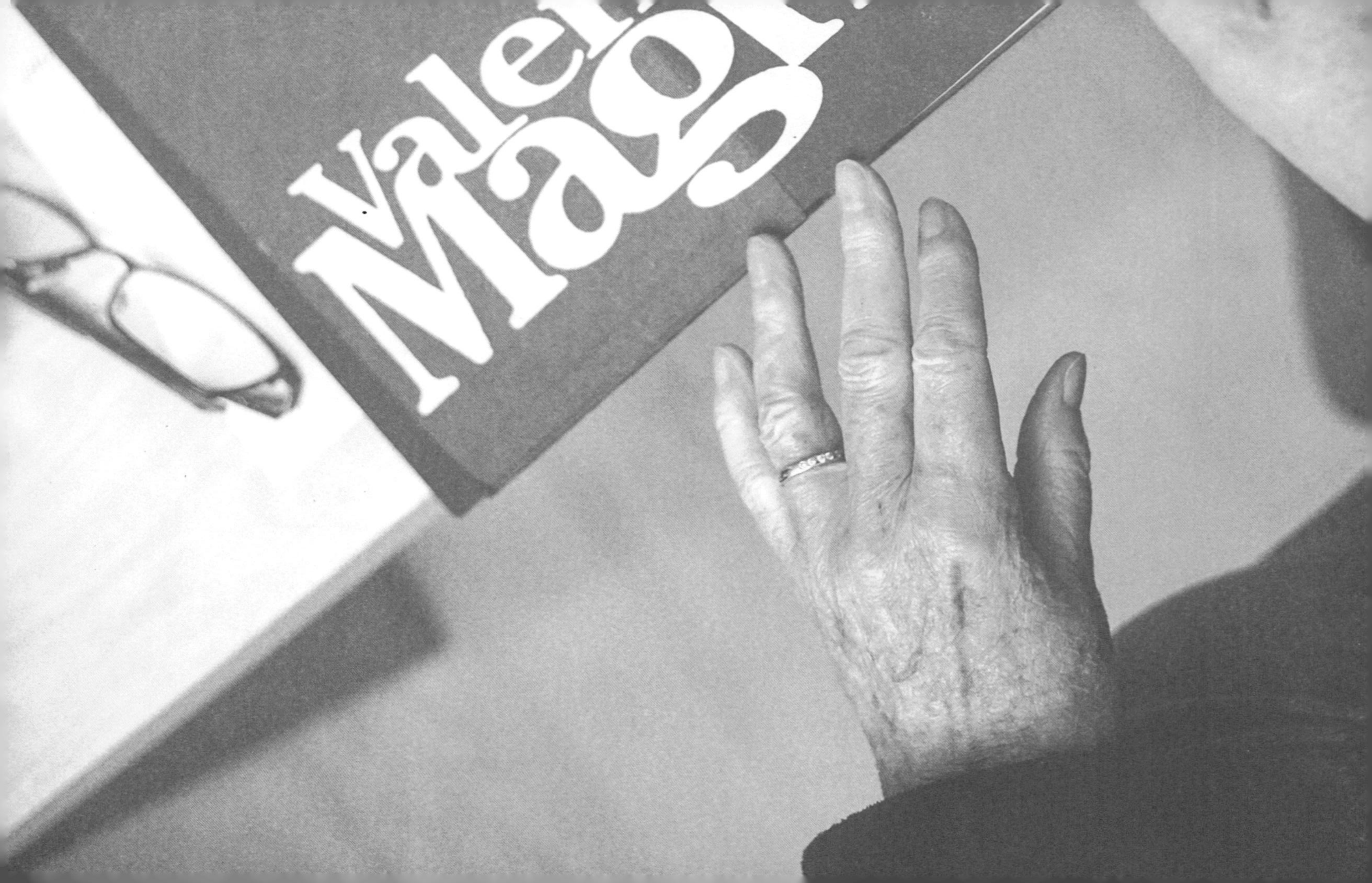
Vale
Mag

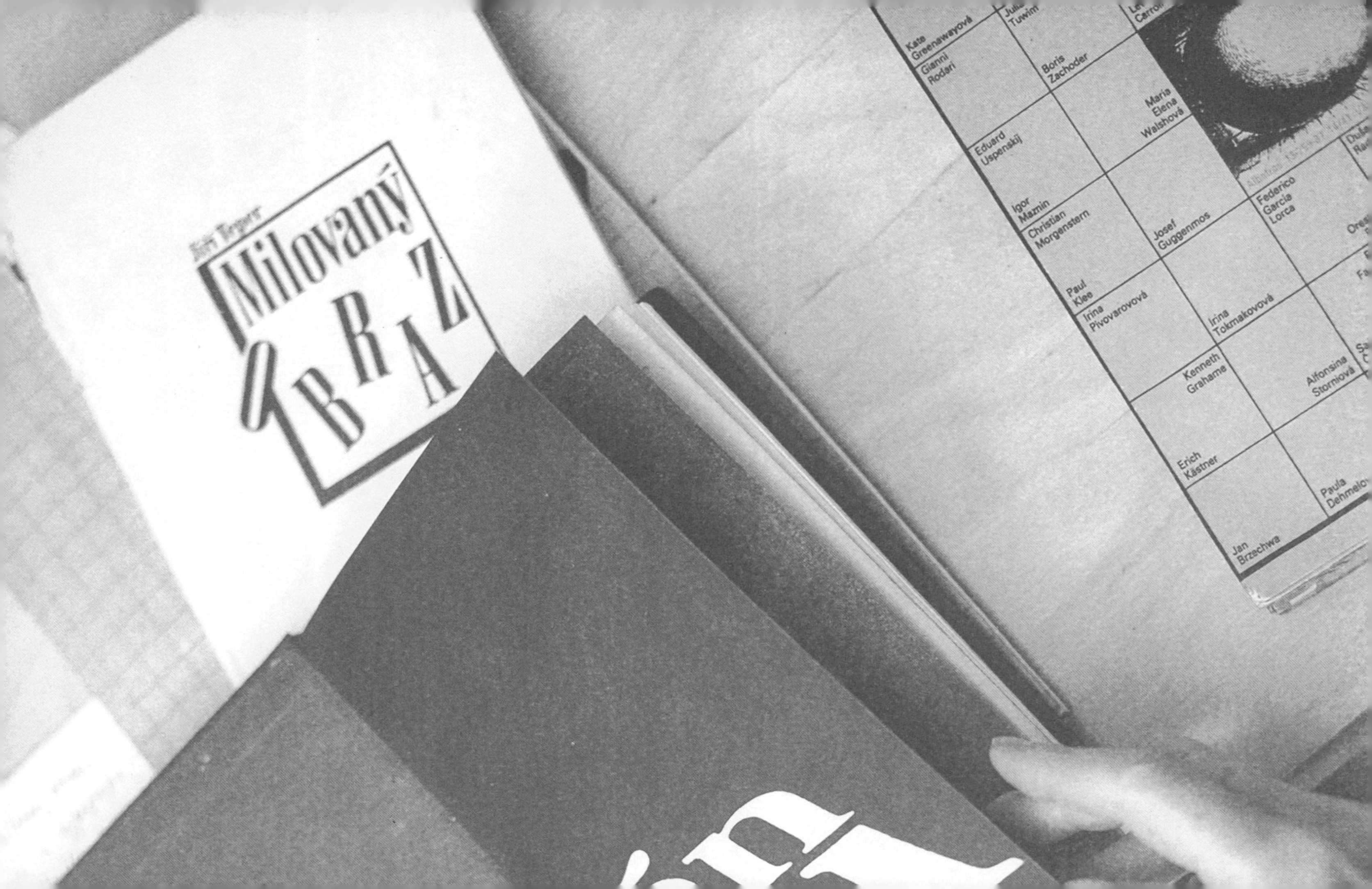

Jiří Teper
Milovaný
OBRAZ
Kate Greenawayová
Gianni Rodari
Eduard Uspenskij
Igor Mazmin
Christian Morgenstern
Paul Klee
Irina Pivovarovová
Julian Tuwim
Boris Zachoder
Maria Elena Walshová
Josef Guggenmos
Irina Tokmakovová
Kenneth Grahame
Erich Kästner
Jan Brzechwa
Lewis Carroll
Federico García Lorca
Alfonsina Storniová
Paula Dehmelová

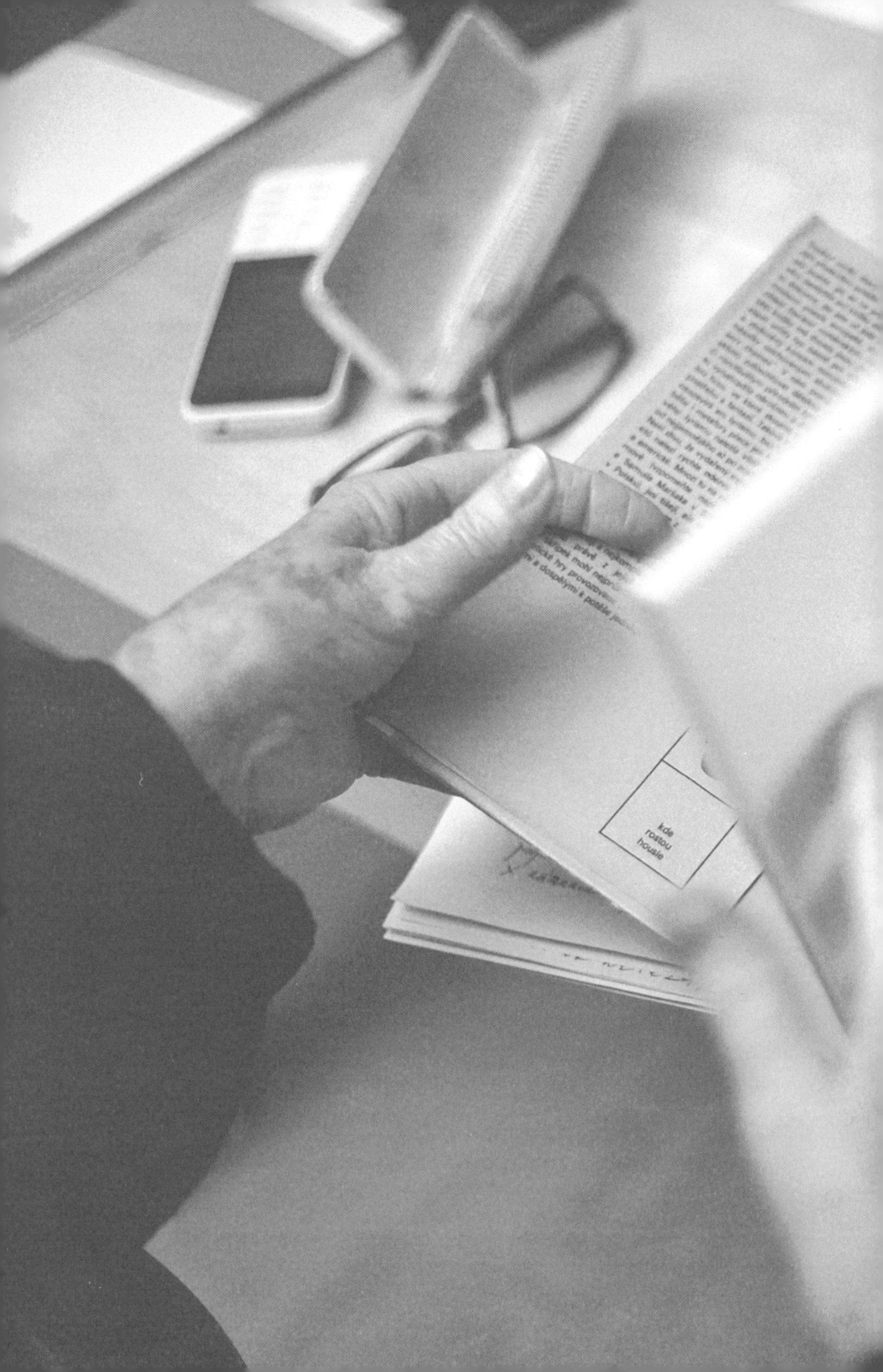
kde
rostou
housle

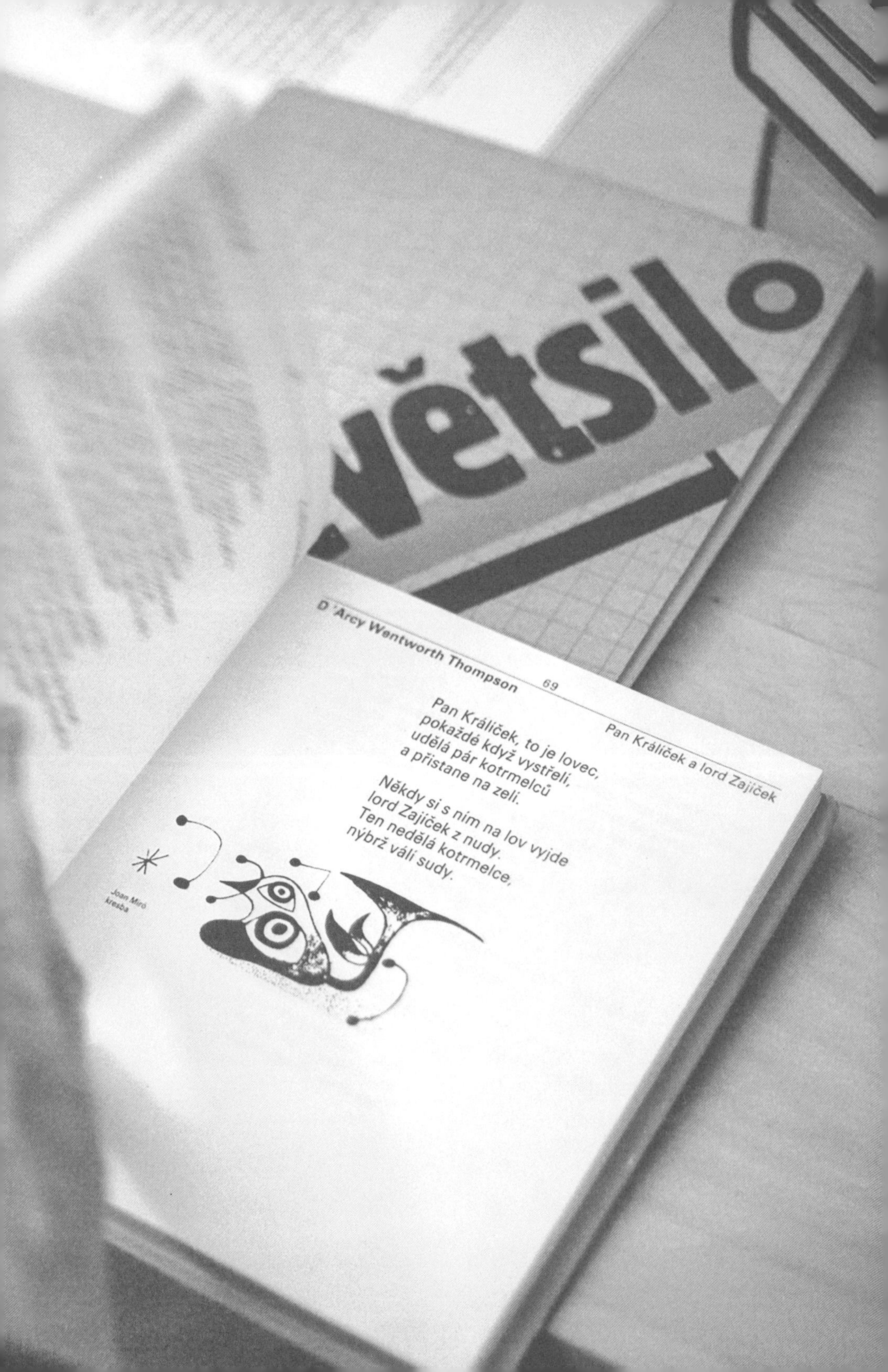
většilo
D´Arcy Wentworth Thompson
69
Pan Králíček a lord Zajíček
Pan Králíček, to je lovec,
pokaždé když vystřelí,
udělá pár kotrmelců
a přistane na zeli.

Někdy si s ním na lov vyjde
lord Zajíček z nudy.
Ten nedělá kotrmelce,
nýbrž válí sudy.
Joan Miró
kresba

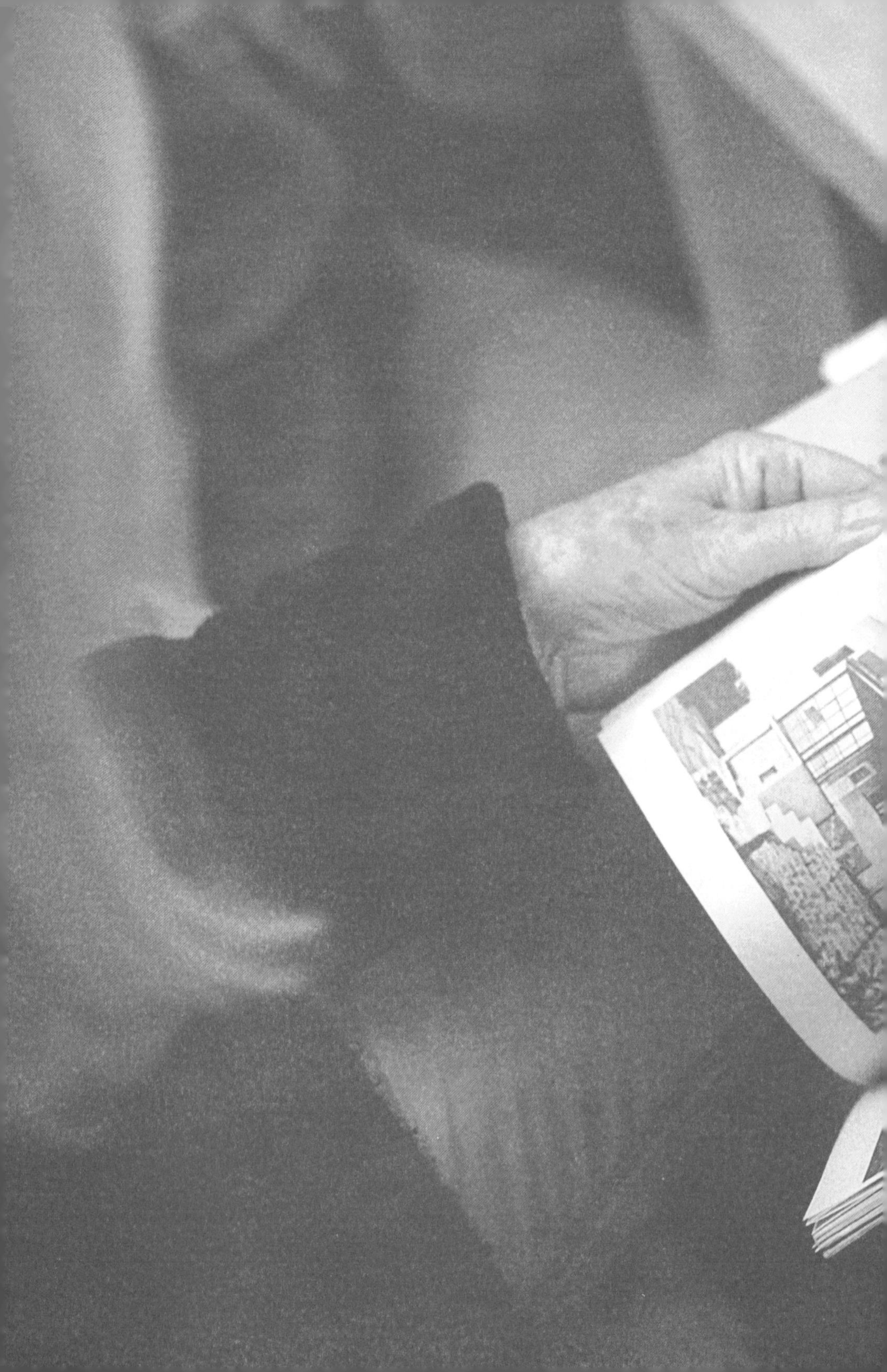

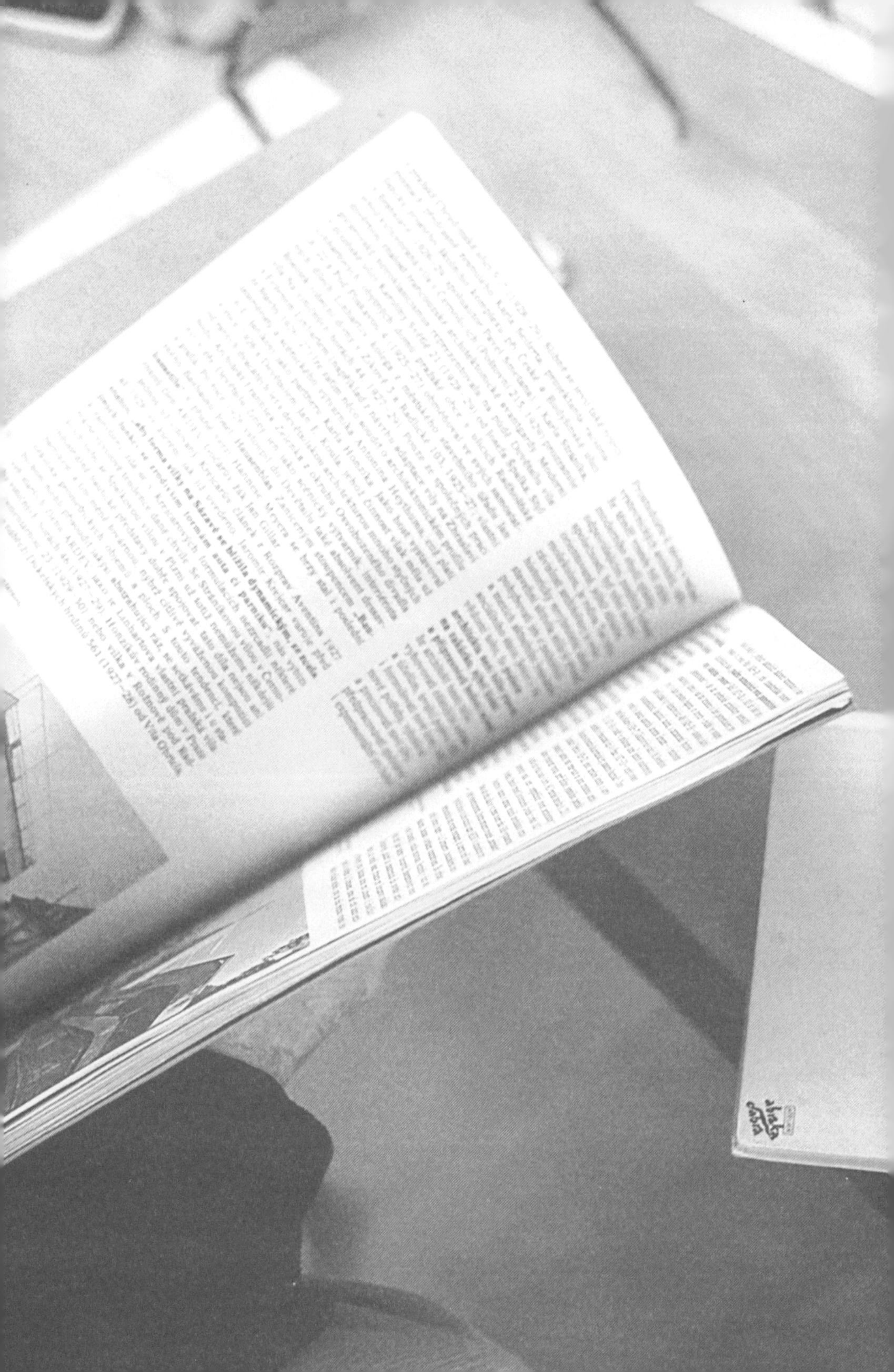

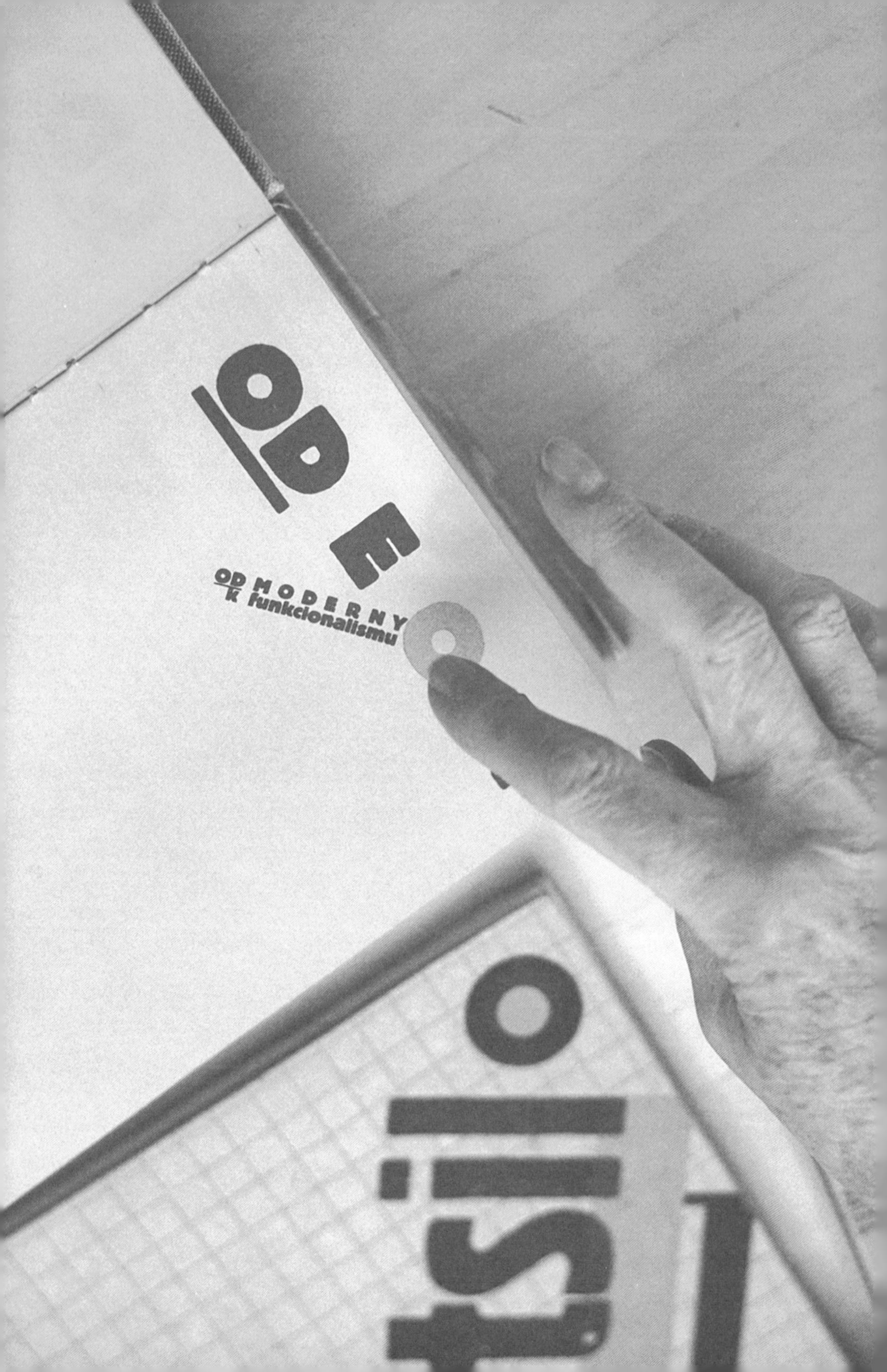
OD E
OD MODERNY
k funkcionalismu

# A Book As
# a Woman's Life

## Zuzana Lednická

Did you work at home?
"Always at home. There was no other way with kids."

—Clara Istlerová interviewed by Anežka Minaříková


You hold in your hands a surprisingly small and inconspicuous book whose relatable format makes it feel more like a pocket novel than a scholarly monograph, as one would expect from a book dedicated to the important Czech typographer Clara Istlerová, a woman who managed to establish herself in a field that during her career belonged exclusively to men. However, it is precisely this modesty and the lightness of the feminine approach, so characteristic of Istlerová, that is reflected in the visual form of this book.

After all, if there is a place to find a difference between women's and men's creative work, it is precisely in the approach to the work itself. For women, it often involves lifelong multitasking, naturally switching and balancing between family, personal creativity, and an endless array of small tasks. In my own life, during brief breaks while preparing dinner, I send requests to the printer or work out the concept of an upcoming book project in my head. There are countless examples of such work past and present. I remember, for example, the diaries of the photographer Eva Fuková, in which she described how she took pictures just for herself while pushing a stroller, or Libuše Niklová's testing of inflatable toys on her own children during a family weekend. The challenging and complex position of a housewife and creator, on the other hand, brings a much needed (and often missing in men) perspective, a certain lightness of approach that prevents an excess of ego and sense of self-importance. The downplaying of oneself and one's work was Clara Istlerová's hallmark.

This natural flow of life, where everything is linked and interacts with everything else, eventually became the basis of this

     A Book As a Woman's Life

monograph through a free-flowing conversation between two women. The result is a very frank and subjective text in which Clara sometimes speaks openly about very intimate matters that are usually excluded from specialist monographs. Photographs of friends, family, children, and favorite dachshunds are interspersed with calligraphy, book covers, or posters produced at the time, creating often surprising connections. While the book does look at Istlerová's work through a scholarly lens in Jan Rous's text, such an assessment is ultimately not its focus. Rather, the recording of an ordinary human and the work-related, and often unexpected, connections that had a profound influence on Istlerová's work are. The result is a far more vivid and authentic measurement of a life, one that focuses not only on the work of this gifted designer, but also on what was and is happening simultaneously around her, which is so characteristic of a woman's understanding of life.

Zuzana Lednická

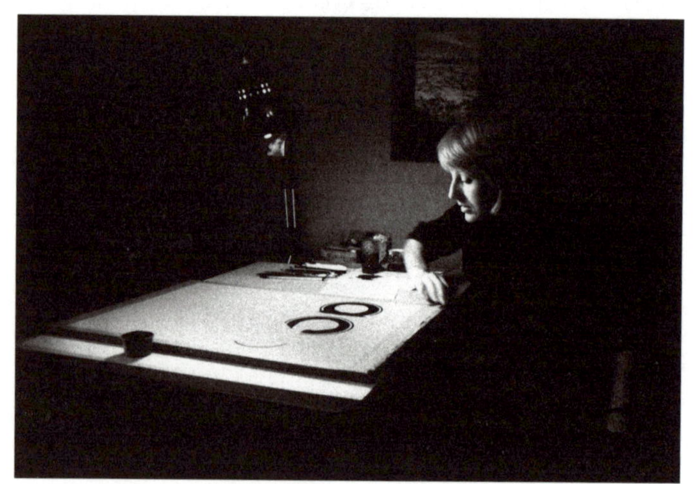

Clara Istlerová at work, 1976

        Biography

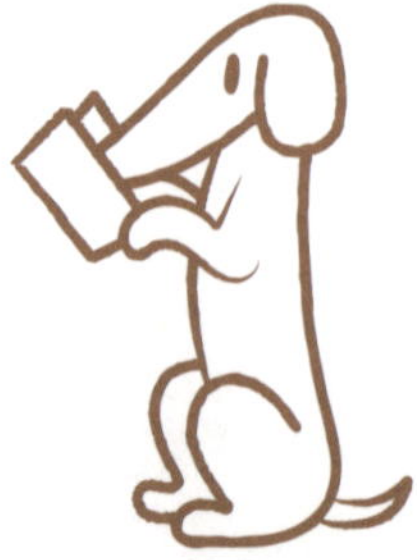

December 11, 1944
Born in Prague

1959–63        Attends the Secondary Industrial School
               of Graphic Arts in Prague

1963–69        Attends the Academy of Arts, Architecture
               and Design in Prague, in the studio of František
               Muzika, specializing in book graphics and
               poster design

1970–71        Postgraduate studies
               London Central School of Art and Design
               Studies abroad in France, the Netherlands,
               and the United States

1971–74        Teaches at the Secondary Industrial School
               of Graphic Arts in Prague

1974           Daughter Marie is born

1975           Son Matěj is born

1982–90        Exhibits in exhibitions as part of the group
               TYPO&

1983           Son Jan is born

1996           Becomes a member of TypoDesignClub

1969–2005      Recipient of numerous awards in the Most
               Beautiful Czechoslovak and Czech Books
               competition, including: *Czech Poetry Series*
               (Československý spisovatel) *From Modernism
               to Functionalism* (Odeon)

1983           Wins the Vyšehrad Publishing House Award
               (for the Reflexe series)

Clara Istlerová

| 1984 | Presented with the Ministry of Culture prize at the Brno Biennial (for her annual reports for B.I.G. agency) |
|---|---|
| 1988 | Wins the Premio Grafico Award at Fiera di Bologna |
| 1989 | Wins a bronze medal at the International Book Art Exhibition – Leipzig |
| 1990 | Wins a silver medal at the Brno Biennial |
| 1994 | Receives the World's Most Beautiful Book Award at the International Book Fair Frankfurt am Main (for Jiří Teper's *Milovaný obraz* [Beloved Image], published by Atelier Abrakadabra) |
| 1998 | Wins the TypoDesignClub Prize (for *Lomené, hranaté a obloukové tvary – česká kubistická architektura* [Broken, Angular, and Curved Forms – Czech Cubist Architecture], published by Gallery) |
| 2009 | Wins the Academia Publishing House Award (for *Cesta života – judaismus* [The Path of Life – Judaism], by Rabbi Karol Sidon) |

 Biography

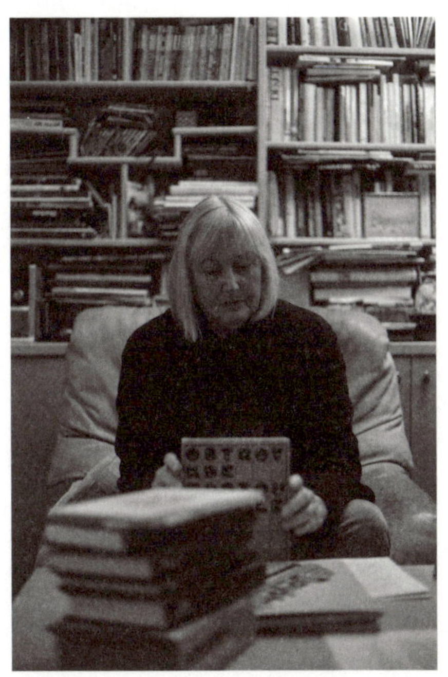

Clara Istlerová, 2020

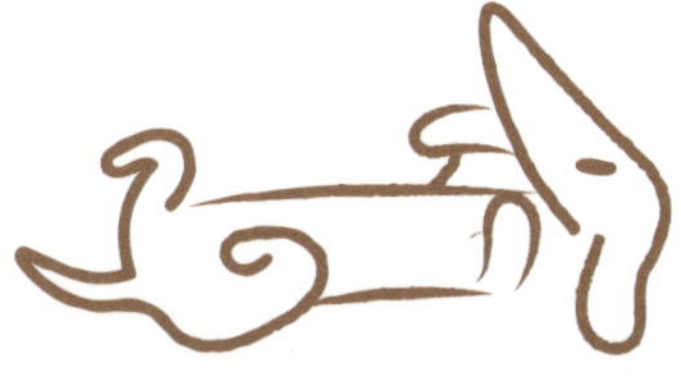

*Clara Istlerová: A Life Among Letters*

Published by
Inventory Press
2305 Hyperion Ave
Los Angeles, CA 90027
www.inventorypress.com

© 2025 Inventory Press, Los Angeles,
and the authors

All images courtesy Clara Istlerová

Editing
Anežka Minaříková
Jaroslav Tvrdoň

Design
Anežka Minaříková
Marek Nedelka

Copyediting and Proofreading
Eugenia Bell

Translation
Nathan Fields

Reproduction of Clara Istlerová's Works
Filip Beránek

Photo Reportage
Filip Beránek

Printed and bound in Czechia by
Tiskárna Protisk, s.r.o.

Typefaces
Quadrant Text by Matter of Sorts
Logic Mono by MCKL

Special thanks to Fedrigoni Czech
Republic for generously providing
Arena Bulk and Arena Smooth.



This publication has been made possible
by the Graham Foundation for Advanced
Studies in the Fine Arts, and Ministry of
Culture of the Czech Republic.

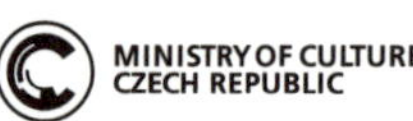


Founded in 1956, the Graham Foundation
fosters the development and exchange
of diverse and challenging ideas about
architecture and its role in the arts,
culture, and society.

Published in English by arrangement
with the Academy of Arts, Architecture
and Design in Prague.

Originally published as *Clara Istlerová,
práce a život* in Czech © 2020.

ISBN: 978-1-941753-80-4
LCCN: 2024945385

Distributed by:
ARTBOOK | D.A.P.
75 Broad St, Suite 630
New York, NY 10004
www.artbook.com

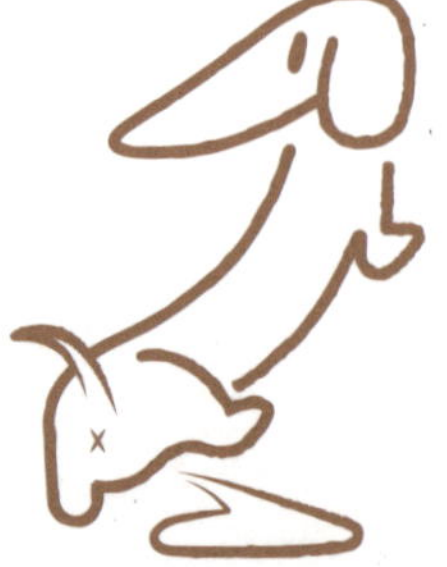